Teaching Writing

Essays from the
Bay Area Writing Project

Series Editor:
GERALD CAMP

BOYNTON/COOK PUBLISHERS, INC.

*Published in Association with the
University of California, Berkeley*

For information address Boynton/Cook Publishers, Inc. 206 Claremont Avenue, Montclair, NJ 07042

Printed in the United States of America

Library of Congress Cataloging in Publication Data
  Main entry under title:

Teaching writing.

    Bibliography: p.
    1. English language—Composition and exercises—Study and teaching—California—Addresses, essays, lectures. 2. English language—Rhetoric—Study and teaching—California—Addresses, essays, lectures.
I. Camp, Gerald. II. Bay Area Writing Project.
PE1405.U6T4 1983   808'.042'07073   82-22808
ISBN 0-86709-081-2

Preface

What we now know about the teaching of writing comes to us not only from the world of research but also from the world of the classroom. Both sources of knowledge are equally important.

Since 1973 the Bay Area Writing Project has been tapping the expertise of scores of outstanding teachers who teach in classrooms from kindergarten through university in the nine counties surrounding San Francisco Bay. The Bay Area Writing Project and the ninety-three site National Writing Project that evolved out of the BAWP experience have succeeded because they put a premium on teacher knowledge of what *is* working. They celebrate teaching.

The BAWP staff development model includes these key assumptions:

- that while most teachers in the schools have never been adequately trained as teachers of writing, there are, nevertheless, teachers at all levels—elementary school through university—who out of necessity have learned how to teach students to write and have, through trial and error and in the privacy and isolation of their own classrooms, developed effective approaches to the teaching of writing;

- that these successful teachers can be identified, brought together through campus Summer Institutes, and trained to teach other teachers of writing in project-sponsored workshops conducted in the school districts throughout the school year;

- that the best teacher of teachers is another teacher—teachers believable as consultants because their ideas and the specific teaching strategies they demonstrate have been developed with real students in real classrooms;

- that teachers of writing must write themselves; that they need to experience regularly what they are asking of their students; that they need to discover and understand the process of writing they are teaching through their own writing; and that they need to write during inservice workshops, testing new ideas, new approaches, as if—for the moment—they were their own students;

- that real change in classroom practice happens over time; that effective staff development programs are on-going and systematic—programs that make it possible for teachers to come together regularly to test, try out, and evaluate the best practices of other teachers;

- that effective programs improve student writing should involve teachers from all grade levels and teachers from all content areas; that the idea of writing as a way of learning is an idea that teachers across the curriculum and across grade levels find compelling.

The essays in this collection are an extension of the BAWP assumptions. Not all teachers are able to participate in a Writing Project staff-development workshop, and no workshop series can cover all of the expertise of all of the outstanding teachers who have been trained in the Summer Institutes. For these reasons, beginning in 1978, BAWP has asked a number of its Teacher/Consultants to put some of their ideas into writing. These essays were then published as a series of Bay Area Writing Project Curriculum Monographs.

This volume represents a selection of those essays which we feel will be most useful to other teachers throughout the country. Each was written by a classroom teacher; each is based on the experience of that teacher working with his or her students. Many contain samples of writing done by students in response to the writing tasks described.

We offer the ideas in these essays as suggestions only. They have been effective in specific classrooms with specific teachers working with their students. But for other teachers to adapt these ideas without making them their own would be as unproductive as to teach by rote from a textbook. Teachers are still the best source of knowledge about what will work in individual classrooms. It is our hope that these essays will stimulate teachers to continue the process of learning how to teach students to write.

JAMES GRAY, Director
Bay Area Writing Project
School of Education
University of California, Berkeley

Contents

Preamble

What We Already Know About Composition and What We Need to Know

Josephine Miles
Professor of English Emeritus, University of California, Berkeley

The term *we* here means us literally, students and teachers of English composition, not just an editorial figment but a lot of practiced people. At least, my proposals aim toward such a meaning.

First, we know that good writing, like good thinking and feeling, can't be taught "once and for all." It's not a simple skill like swimming: indeed even a swimmer can be coached to get better and better. Thinking is one of our most complex abilities, and writing is an evidence of it. So students need help with writing at many stages, from third grade to eighth, to tenth, to college and beyond, and from subject to subject. Whenever a new stage of thought and a new subject-matter come along, the accumulated abilities of the student need conscious and thoroughgoing adapting to the new material and maturity. Therefore, the concept of "remedial" work is misdirected: the teacher who sends a student back to brush up on technical details is trivializing his own serious job of helping the young writer adapt his present active skill and latent knowledge to important new demands.

The latency of much knowledge is rich and easily to be called on. In conducting an experimental study of student writing abilities during the 1950's we found that a majority of junior and senior students in fifteen departments at Berkeley could improve from one paper to another by a whole grade merely by one half-hour of reminders by their readers and instructors, these in turn having been reminded by readers from the English Department about the essentials of composition. Even so-called technical problems, like spelling, decreased measurably when larger compositional problems decreased—that is, when the students were called upon seriously to use what they knew. If such a program of reminders could be used systematically throughout the students' careers, working at all stages and in all departments of knowledge, aided when necessary by support from English department advisors, that invigorating sense could be fostered of building on what we know we know.

What do we know good composition is? Shucking away the varieties in such terms as *descriptive, narrative,* and *expository* or *creative, scien-*

1

tific, and *historical,* at what kernel do we arrive? At the combination, suggested by the term *composition* itself, the putting together of two processes, the selection and the arrangement of the materials for consideration; to choose and to put into order; or to have in mind an order from which then to choose. The processes of this combination may be relatively spontaneous and unconscious, organic or fused, as some say, but in learning them, we need to distinguish and practice their interrelations for the sake of understanding and future use. Some orderings are relatively more sequential, like narrative; some more subordinating, like argument; some more substantiating and qualifying, like science and description; or, in other terms, some more presentative, like drama and film; some more analytical, like debate; some more involved in close sound pattern, like poetry—with cross-currents for all of these. *Genre* is indeed a vital stabilizing force for recognition of intent.

But whatever the kind and purpose, the guiding idea focuses and asserts itself in language toward its effect, from writer to reader. The step-by-step response of the reader is guided by what the writer tells him and establishes expectations at each point. As we know, the medium serves the message, because it combines the *what* and the *how* of expression and communication. Therefore, it would seem wise to teach at every level the possibility of many sorts of combination—not just stories in grammar school, descriptions and journalism in high school, and exposition and poetry in college, but how each of these can supplement the other or can be chosen by a student at any level. The principles of composition will hold for all and can be strengthened by the perceptions and practice of their varying forms.

So what do we know about the principles of composition? A putting together of parts to make a whole implies a recognition of parts and of wholes. Parts from which to select; wholes towards which to arrange. Or wholes intuitively felt, parts more analytically recognized. The lack of clarity in our sense of the working of language has been one of our greatest difficulties; but now we know from the clarifications of linguists how the parts of our language function. The predicate says what is being said, asserts or questions or commands a relation, verifiable in terms of time: "The boy is a good scout now; but was he then?" The subject: noun or pronoun, phrase or clause, about which the predicate speaks. The adjunctives: adjectives and adverbs and determiners, which qualify both subjects and predicates—"good," "now," "then." The connectives: prepositions and conjunctions, linking predicates, substantives, or adjuncts—*is* "and" *was, boy* "and" *boy, good* "and" *better*—or linking more complex units of phrases and clauses to function as words—"in those days" or "when he was younger" as a substitute for "then." As structuralists point out, not only do various forms have varying functions, but also various functions can take varying forms, so that selection and arrangement may the better interact.

When we know these simple forms of grammar, we know that logic and rhetoric follow in their emphasis on the predicate as the organizing force because of its statment-making, its verifiability. The noun "boy," the adjuctive "good," the connective "when" may have powerful associations of denoting and connoting, of image, metaphor, symbol, but still can tell us nothing precise unless given a context by their predicate statement. So when we come to composing, we need the predicate to do the organizing: the steps of our composition are the steps to be taken by the whole statement, not merely by some of its materials or qualities. So we have learned, I trust, not to talk about "defining the topic" or "cutting down the material" to make composition more wieldy; it's not the size of the cities but the trip the predicate takes between them that controls the arrangements. Any writer can take full responsibility for any selection of subject—death, taxes, New York, small town, my cat, your lion, Argentine oil—so long as he knows what he wants to relate it to, to get said about it, and thus the steps, the stages, of the saying.

There are just a few basic relations in these steps: to a larger or smaller class, to comparable or contrasting items, to alternatives, to consequences. "New York has become a trade center for the world"—this will be a tracing essay for "has become." "New York used to frighten me, but it doesn't any more"—this will be a contrastive essay for "used to," "doesn't." "New York need to be rebuilt"—this will be an essay arguing, giving evidence, for "needs to be." Or the meaning may be given structure in other forms, "in other words." In all these, temporal contrast may still apply—we may transform the active verb "frighten" to an adjective ("The old frightening New York is gone") or to a subject ("My fright in New York is gone"). The alternatives for selection are many and are a part of style, as style is a habit of writing toward certain ends. Any student at any age can be made aware of his habits and his purposes and of how to choose and bring them together.

We know, or should if we have read the many histories of prose style in the past few years, that various grammatical alternatives have been emphasized by different authors and by different traditions in literary history so that we cannot wish to say that one is absolutely better than another but rather hope that the range will be available to all. It's not that one part of speech or function is weak; rather it is that any one of them may be overstressed or ineffectively used. Elizabethans were powerful arguers, subordinators, and connectors; Augustans by a fascinating shift of interests began that change toward greater adjective and phrase modification, which would culminate in the scientific prose of Darwin and Huxley, as well as in the serial poetries of Whitman and Dylan Thomas. Some moderns like Joyce and Lawrence, meanwhile, have returned to the curt predicative styles of some Elizabethans, eschewing not only adjectives but connectives also, creating the fragmentary juxtaposed effects of much present-day prose.

Who are we to condemn adjectival prose or the verb *to be* or strings of phrases or short sentences, or passives or abstractions or generalizations, when these are the life-blood of one style or another? Rather, we may talk about their suitability to certain purposes, the choices that may be made from among them by students aware of the possibilities of choice. Any student may master any style if he knows what he is doing and practices enough. Practice in reading, in paraphrasing, in making précis of styles of the past as well as the present, will make him aware of what he wants not to do as well as of what he wants to do, and that is a big step.

Those of us who emphasize spontaneity, fluency, the naturalness of situation, as in journal-keeping and letter-writing and creative invention of all kinds, need not fear this other cognitive kind of knowledge in what we know about language and composition. What we know about the whole human being tells us that intuition and cognition are complementary, support each other. Intuition invested in learning brings it to life; learning invested in intuition gives it strength to work with new materials to simplify complexities. The student adrift on a sea of language is an object of pity we need not allow; his language, understood, is, rather, his transportation and his farthest shore, his chance to make mistakes and survive them. Free flow of expression allows for one sort of success and error, careful practice and repetitive analysis for another; gradually, the two blend to support each other so that one can learn from the error to increase the success.

It has been also the idea of many leaders of the past that the special function of education is the development of rationality. As California Superintendent of Schools Wilson Riles says, all life is education, and all life, especially in early years the life of home and community, prepares us for skills and sympathies, for careers and values. But reasoning can be especially taught by schoolroom practice and needs to be, because every new stage of learning requires the study of a new stage of reasoning in increased complexity.

Rational thought considers ratios, that is, proportions, the connections made in composition, what is important in relation to what else. It deals with choices, priorities in making decisions, not only immediate but future ones as hypotheses. The logic of rational reasoning, the way it works as we have seen by the basic methods of adding or comparing or arguing, in putting ideas together, requires both positives and negatives to be considered in time and space. Addition and subtraction work by "and" and "then"; their negative, "but" and "then not." Multiplication and division, "on the one hand," "on the other," "either...or," "neither...nor." The possibilities or causes and consequences of these work by "if," "therefore," "though," "yet." All .work on the ratio or relation of one idea or proposition to another, whether in sequence, alternation, or supposition, so that we need not be stuck with mere immediate cue-responses but can extend our wishes into time and space and try to figure out how they fit.

The heart of the matter, the student's own life, his own home, his own community may require the rationality of a primary and secondary education, of reading, writing, arithmetic, a workable skill. A wider reaching out, for those who desire it, may include the rationality of a community order: social work, politics, tradesmanship, teaching, professing. The farthest reaching out, the peripheries or boundaries of education farthest from the center, are those of university research study, most hypothetical, most like the outposts of a frontier, where possibilities are contemplated both for protection and advancement. It is farthest from home and even from community, and it is the least part of the standard culture, except as it may predict by forethought what will happen as new changes occur.

At each of these stages, from central home to widening community to peripheral frontier, the processes of rationality, of changing priorities, need to be reapplied to newly complex materials and problems. So education never stops, working either wider and wider or deeper and deeper. Nobody can do everything. Nobody can make all his choices work. But he can learn how to make the choices, and composition of ideas is one good way to learn.

I hope we agree that an educated life makes deeper and more complex mistakes, not just fewer, and education in reading and writing can give superb opportunities for making errors not fatal. So we learn. So we teach by the encouragement of thought-about-experience: not about "summer-vacation"-experience, which is beyond our reach, but about the kinds of thought relevant to the kinds of writing available to our direct scrutiny. Why do sequences of narrative often begin effectively in the middle? Why is a strong debater one who allows most strongly for all the evidence on the other side? Why is negative evidence, that which is not to be found to support a proposal, as necessary as what is?

Some realists complain that the development of an idea is not a real form, not in demand except by college classes. Rather, it is the realist unit I know, giving practice in what is most asked of citizens every day, choice-making and the adding of reasons for choice, generalizing and giving evidence pro and con for the generalization. "We should wait till Saturday to visit the Joneses." There's a potential composition. "Why don't people like cabbage?" "Which school would be better for Jim?" "Shall I keep this radio?" "Shall I work in politics?" "If that's fire we hear, what shall we do?"—these are the practical everyday processes by which people live, the *ifs,* the alternatives, the accumulations of experience which lead to plans and conclusions, important and real. Of course, they are not usually written down in essay form. But the essays give the helpful, formal written practice to make them work. And there are enough actual demands for reports too, in all sorts of work, to make the form practical— the report formed, as it needs to be, on the basis of purpose and perspective. If we can think easily of generalizable propositions, say, quickly, "The days grow shorter," then the how and the when will follow to support the idea rather than to outline the substantive; and more serious ideas will grow more easily: "There is a better way to live this life," as the writer is freed from the materialism of subject matter.

Often, as Moffett, Macrorie, Christensen, Berthoff, and others have said, the student needs to be aware of his main responsibility toward the reader, to establish an expectation and then to fulfill it. Often he's not aware of expectation, of the stance or voice or ethos of rhetoric, of the explications of true dialogue, of the suspensive qualities of language-structures; he doesn't recognize his own power because he has been working hit or miss. He doesn't see his audience in friend or class or teacher or general reader. He doesn't recognize the consistency and power of his own dialect and its relation to standard dialect. He doesn't recognize the relation of writing to art as controlled limited experience. He doesn't recognize the power in the very limits of thought and language—that thought works in certain basic ways.

Such awareness is naturally so common, so enjoyed, that it provides the basis for jokes, the humor working in the slip from one expectation to another, for any grammatical form we can think of. Do we confuse singular and mass? "I'm worried that my hair is getting thin. But who wants fat hair?" Or abstract and concrete? "She has curves in places most people don't even have places." Or the power of the predicate in "Why does Uncle Sam wear red, white, and blue suspenders?" We know that the *wear* is the crucial term. With such humor, who needs confusion?

We know that composition is an art and that in addition to principles of logical and rhetorical relation, principles of aesthetic judgment function. So we are able to talk about effective forms: parallel structures for example, theme and variation, negative contrast, cumulative series, balances and other values of art, as in painting and music also. And so we support intuition and knowledge with strong sense impression, the very body of thought, and with practice in running these scales, drawing these lines and colorations.

We know enough about students, language, art, reading, and writing in English to make the study of composition in English a sustaining and steadily accruing and culminating practice, supportive of subject matters other than literature as well as of literature and supportive of the maturing of the student's confidence and sense of responsibility.

What don't we know, so that we don't bring students to a stage of confident maturity in English at age 11 or 18 or 30, ready to go on to a new stage? We don't know how to follow our own principles, to compose not our own field merely but our own purposes. We don't communicate with each other, and therefore repeat or forget certain partial necessary steps at every level. We forget the powerful latency of knowledge, of competence, in bilingual students and can build much more than we do upon strengths, progressively rather than remedially.

We forget the powerful relation of grammar to logic and rhetoric and to the principles of art, so we let the debris of grammar confuse our own striking modes of predication in English. And, without security in our own principles, we cover papers with corrections of detail which in fact would follow easily from a clearly purposive voice in the writing of a paper. Instead of *awk, sp, ref, ww,* and such other non-parallel examples of our principle of parallelism, we need chiefly the responsive critical statement: "The main idea of this paper is...," "the main steps of its development are...," "how then does paragraph 4 fit in, and what transitional connective terms would be helpful?" Teachers in Subject A, the special pre-college course in written English at Berkeley, have found that the use of a few basic connective terms of agreement and reference will indicate the student's degree of mastery over the arrangement of his motives. So diagnostic tests become a special kind of helpfully sharable communication.

There's a nucleus of teaching to be much further developed, a nucleus involving the teacher of composition in departments of literature, the teacher of composition in other subject matters, the apprentice teacher who attends the classes, reads many of the papers, and confers with many of the students, under direct and daily guidance, the young graduate who goes out to teach in college, high school, or grade school, and his colleagues and students there in their roles of associates and apprentices in the teaching of English. At every level, teacher and associate and apprentice and novice, all need to participate in a plan of learning, of agreement on a few basic principles of composition.

We need to know what we believe to be a good composition in the English language, so that we may know what are the values of judgment at every stage. And we need to know what are the main effective and cumulative ways of teaching such composition to students, apprentices, teachers, and associates, so we may work in the strength of our knowledge and help each student to recognize and work in the strength of his or hers.

1. The Writing Process

Sequences in Writing, K-13

SEQUENCES OF INSTRUCTION, K-3

Gail Siegel
Reed School, Tiburon

From Speech to Writing

"How do you spell 'oranges' without the 'o'?" a child asked me.

"What?" I said.

He repeated the question. I remained baffled. Finally he showed me his paper and I realized that he knew how to spell the 'o'. It was the 'ranges' of 'oranges' that he was struggling with.

For me, the anecdote illustrates an important lesson. Young children must learn the delicate synchronization of mental and motor skills required for writing. But the most difficult task is translating ideas into words. The child above knew what he needed from me, but not how to express his need to me.

I find it useful to view young writers as passing through a series of developmental stages:

1. Transcribing Stage
2. Re-copying Stage
3. Sentences/Whole Phrases Stage
4. Independent Stage

The stages aren't rigid; they have soft edges. Some children pass from stage two straight to stage four. For others, stages three and four happen simultaneously. In a kindergarten, first, second, or third grade class, I expect to find some children at every stage, depending on their individual maturation and writing experience.

I also find it useful to consider the developmental stages as coinciding with the student's progression from fluency (ease and confidence with language) to coherence (making formal and grammatical sense) to correctness (punctuation, paragraphing, etc.).

Transcribing Stage

Pre-writers need to have their spoken language transformed into writing by an adult. The children tell a teacher, aide, or parent volunteer what they want to say, and the adult transcribes the children's words into writing.

The sequence is as follows:

1) Child talks, adult writes, child illustrates; or 2) child illustrates, child talks, adult writes.

Children at this stage want to illustrate what has been written for them. Transcribed speech, or a pre-writer's "writing," usually involves simple sentences, while the pictures may be quite detailed. Pictures illustrate the feelings and details not expressed in the language.

For instance, one six-year-old dictated: "I feel bad because my Mommy and Daddy went away." Her picture shows a lone child standing in the open doorway of her home. The parents are leaving, holding their packed suitcases. The little girl in the picture has big tears rolling down her cheeks. Her face is obviously forlorn as the parents wave good-bye. The reader feels the emotion and impact from the picture, not from the transcribed writing. There is a narrative quality to a child's illustration.

In a primary classroom, particularly kindergarten or first grade, it helps to have several adults or older children available during the writing worktime to take dictation. Young children often have short attention spans and need someone to listen to them when they have ideas. Although children are not actually writing during this phase, they are developing foundations upon which writing will later build.

The following are further examples of transcribed speech of five and six year olds:

Today we painted boxes for the Halloween play.

At art we made a map of Ross and we put our houses on it.

My Dragon—he lives in the sea. He is green and he likes to drink water. He cracked out of an egg. He likes to eat grass. He flies. When he flies he swoops down and catches birds and eats them. Sometimes he goes in the water and eats fish.

My magic machine makes bubble gum and it crushes up rocks. They're not wrapped yet. Then they're wrapped and then they're picked up and then they're put in the box. It doesn't have a special flavor.

If these children are asked, they may be able to give more detail, but normally there is little "meat on the bones" at this stage. They tell stories about real or imagined events in short, simple sentences.

Re-Copying Stage

It is not long before children move into stage two and become re-copiers. This usually happens some time during the first semester of first grade. During the new phase, children still dictate, but they are able to re-copy what an adult writes. They can read, know the alphabet, and can hold a pencil. They feel an enormous sense of accomplishment when they can write on their own. They begin to view themselves as writers.

For children at this stage, the physical task is arduous. Holding a pencil, using an eraser, thinking of words and actually writing can be overwhelming to children. I frequently have them cross out each word they copy to help them keep track of where they are.

"Re-copy" writing has many similarities to the language of children in the transcribing stage. It is generally first person experiential or fantasy writing. Usually it is declarative and lacks detail, color, and substance.

A sample of class journal entries, as told to the teacher and then re-copied by the children:

> Robbie said in science that our heart is like our motor and the food is the gas.
>
> My Grandmother came to the play. I think she likes it a lot.
>
> Our Christmas banners are hanging all around the room and they are so pretty and green and sparkle and we can do more.
>
> We all learned our parts for the Christmas play and Mrs. Safford was happy. The boys do not want to be wearing tights.

Again the illustrations (and children's sound effects and verbalization during drawing) have the action and detail that the writing lacks. These children are given plenty of time and experience with telling and re-copying. Their writing is read aloud, displayed, published, and enjoyed. Gradually they gain the tools and confidence to pass on to stage three.

Sentence/Whole Phrases Stage

Children at this stage of development know what they want to say and are able to write down some of their thoughts independently. They are eager to write for themselves and are learning to be comfortable with words and thoughts, and consequently less dependent on adult help. Adults are available for help with phrases or whole sentences as the child needs them. For instance a child at this stage may ask the teacher to write "once upon a time," but that same child will then finish the sentence independently. Their writing sounds much like their speech and has characteristics of the first two stages of writing:

> I wonder how the raining got up in the sky so it could fall. I like rainy days because my Mom sometimes gives me hot cocoa.
>
> Yesterday I made a pre school for my brother we sang and played it was fun we have candy cans the end.
>
> last night is was raining so hard that our lights went out I had to get our hoemkeper I went out in the rain I went in my bare feet.

These children have the confidence to write even though they are making errors in spelling and grammar. What matters to them now is that they can write. Correctness and neatness can be considered after the initial writing is on paper. More importantly, fluency is now developing. Stage three writers are exploring how the language works and can translate their ideas onto paper. The task of transforming mental images and language into written words becomes less burdensome. Like new walkers, they slowly forget the awkward mechanics and get from one point to another with less conscious effort. The more frequently these children write, the easier it becomes for them to write. They begin to add flavor, color, detail, action, and characters to their writing.

Independent Stage

At some point during the sentence/phrase level, children begin to rely on themselves almost completely and may only ask an adult to supply an occasional word for their writing. As they become independent writers, many children gain fluency and begin to work for greater coherence. Young writers working to become coherent are concentrating on making sense and building structure and sequence into the writing. They may not be conscious of this process, but the writing shows evidence. During this period writers need to be able to hear their work and to have an opportunity to re-draft the pieces of writing. Of course these young independent writers may still struggle with either fluency or coherence:

> I like books because I like reading what most like the pictures what I like are the *"Where's Wallace?"* and *Curious George* and *Spiders,* and *Miss Nelson is missing* and *a Great Day for Up* and *Here Comes the Strike Out.*
>
> —Seven Year Old

This child is having difficulty with fluency. The thoughts are flowing so quickly in his head that it is impossible to get all of the necessary words on paper. As the student has the opportunity to share his writing, he will notice gaps, or the teacher or writing group will point them out.

Another example, this time of a child working on coherence:

> Last night I had a dream. That a big fercious monster came and took me to a planet called Pluto. And then he took me to see the king. The kings said you are on the plant Pluto. Do you have any sweters I said. No he said. I better go home and get my sweter. O.k. he said Zoink take her back to get her sweter so Zoink went back to my house and I got my warmest sweter on and went back to Pluto and saw the king. He said you a going to help us do experiment were going to turn the statue of liberty into a flying diamond so we can go back to pluto.
>
> —Eight Year Old

The author has little difficulty with fluency, although there are some minor omissions. She needs some work on sequence and structure, so that her story is clear and has purpose. She will have a chance to read her dream aloud to the class and then, after some peer and teacher response, she can make any changes she feels are necessary to complete this story.

Although both of these children are fairly independent writers, they need to hear their writing read orally so that they develop an ear for the sound of the language. Eventually they will learn to correct omissions and add missing thoughts as they experience this group sharing.

Sequential Teaching Strategies for Writing

I find it helpful to view the steps I use in teaching writing as a sequence. These are not ironclad rules; rather they are processes which encourage and facilitate writing. This is the sequence: oral language, pre-writing, group writing, individual writing, sharing/re-thinking. I use these strategies for children at any of the stages of writing development, whether they are transcribing or independent writers.

Oral Language

For many writers, particularly young children, the initial touching of pencil to paper seems like crossing the Himalayas. Constant pencil sharpening, playing with the eraser, getting the right paper, and other delaying tactics seem necessary. I have found that oral language experience prior to writing is of primary importance. Once children have a fund of vocabulary, it is much easier for them to begin writing.

The oral language part of writing involves developing a bank of key words which can be used in the children's writing. A young writer needs these words to draw from, just as a builder needs bricks.

If my class is going to write about "Fall," we brainstorm for several days. Children suggest words or short phrases such as "leaves turning colors," "crisp," "horseback riding on trails," "scrunching leaves on my way home," "crunchy apples in my lunch," "walnuts," "Halloween," and so on. These words are recorded on the board or on butcher paper and displayed for several days as additional words come to mind. The wealth of vocabulary that the children already know is tapped before the act of writing. When the actual writing takes place, many of the necessary words and phrases have already been "rehearsed."

Pre-Writing

Pre-writing is all of those experiences that the teacher plans for the class before they write. It may include reading aloud selections by other children or authors on the particular topic. As they listen to what someone else has written, children can consider the wide range of possibilities open to them. Films, experiments, cooking, art, or personal experience all provide illustrations from which young children may draw when they are ready to write. My class wrote easily about trees after we had taken tree walks, listened to tree poems, discussed familiar trees, and looked at tree bark in the microscope.

A tree is the best place for building a fort, because it is cozy. No one can find you there.

—Seven Year Old

A tree is nice because if something rolls down the hill, a tree can stop it.

—Six Year Old

Trees live almost anywhere, in streams, or lakes. Trees are important for food. We could not live without trees. They are good to live in or to use to build your house.

—Seven Year Old

I have found that writing facilitates the teaching of other subjects such as science and vice versa, an effective symbiosis. As part of a science unit, my class studied seeds and plants. The writing that took place prior to our study was non-descript, one-dimensional:

a seed is a small thing

seeds make plants

You put seeds in dirt and they grow

After our science study, the children's writing flowed more easily and was more vivid because the children had had numerous experiences with plants and seeds. Seeds had been soaked and cut; they had sprouted and were then planted. Logs were kept about these experiments. The children had become observers. Plant word lists were on the walls. Through writing, they were then able to explore what they had learned and experienced as well as what they thought:

A seed is part of our food chain to live. A seed is something that lives. We can eat seeds. Seeds grow and make plants. You have to have seeds to make a new plant.

—Seven Year Old

A seed can grow into a big bush in many months. A Seed can have a maroon coat that protects it. If you soak a seed in water overnight, it will get very wrinkled and the coat will be light. I have grown a bean plant and a corn plant from seeds.

—Seven Year Old

The children's experience is reflected in their writing. Exploring what they know, young writers may try a more poetic form:

If I was a seed...If I were a seed, I would be protected by my cover. My little red thing around me. When my cover turned wrinkly, I would be scared half to death.

—Eight Year Old

If I was a seed, I would stretch and grow my leaves. I would wish my owner would not be clumsy. I would want a nice owner who

would talk to me. If a farmer picked me and cooked me with my
other bean friends, that would be sad.

—Seven Year Old

When oral language and pre-writing are part of a writing lesson, the
final writing is like a well rehearsed play. The language and experiences
are part of the practicing.

Group Writing

For young writers, group writing is a helpful third step before (or in
conjunction with) individual writing. It helps them to try out their ideas
in a group before they write on their own. Both the pre-writers and writers
in a given class can participate and feel successful in group writing. An
adult or a child working with the group records the children's oral contri-
butions. Children have an opportunity to hear what other children think.
Group writing displayed in the classroom also becomes a reading experience for young children.

Describing a field trip, keeping a class journal, creating a class play, or
writing a letter to the principal are all possibilities for group writing; the
list is endless. Beginning writers can create a class poem in which each
child contributes one sentence, for example:

IF I WERE

If I were a snail I'd let you come in my shell and I will show you
my slime that I leave behind.

If I were a horse I would roam the country.

If I were a flea I would be somewhere nobody knows about.

If I were a great white shark I would let you ride me as long as
you want.

If I were a caterpiller I would crawl up your arm and make a
rainbow with my silk.

Individual Writing

The successful development of writing and other cognitive skills
requires that children have the opportunity to write about what they
know, what they experience, what they have learned, and what they
dream or fantasize about. They need to experience writing in many
different modes: directions, questions, reports, stories, haiku, poetry,
jingles, plays, tall tales, fables, and journals. Varied writing coupled with
daily writing practice allows the child to become comfortable with the
task itself, and consequently writing improves.

I teach spelling and language mechanics as independent subjects in my
classroom. But I find that frequent individual writing conferences are good
times to help individual students with usage and mechanical problems.
Writing habits are more readily learned this way than by filling in pages of
drill. For example, if children are using conversation in their writing, then

in our conferences (or as I circulate in the room) I will teach the use of quotation marks.

Exposure to many different kinds of writing is crucial to young writers' experience and development. As they hear how the language works, they realize the vast possibilities that exist for writing. They learn how sequence is used, what words work well, and what kinds of characters are interesting. I read to my class several times a day to further this exposure. On some days when they come in from recess I read humorous poems, and at the end of the day I usually read from a continuing chapter-type book.

Sharing/Re-Thinking

Young children love to share their writing aloud as soon as it is on paper. Regular writing-sharing sessions in both small and large groups allow children to hear their writing and to realize what may have been left out, or how much they assumed the reader already knew.

Group response is encouraged during these sessions and occurs in a structured way. For primary children, a set format will provide the necessary constructive response. I tell listeners to try to keep two questions in mind:

- Is the writing clear?
- What else do you want to know?

This type of response takes practice and has to be continually modeled by the teacher.

Following the response-sharing session (or teacher conference), the author can go back and re-formulate the piece of writing. Re-thinking and re-writing are periodic and necessary writing activities. My students don't re-write every piece of writing, but every month or so they choose a piece of writing to re-work, writing that is going to be read by other students or published in some way.

Writing is a satisfying if difficult task for young children. They gain confidence as they develop fluency. Their writing helps them clarify thoughts, ideas, and dreams. Children realize that writing is an important tool for self expression:

> We would be pretty dumb if we didn't know how to write. If we couldn't write we couldn't read. There would be no leters. You would not be able to read a book. It is fun to write. Writing is inportant because you can communicate without saying anything out loud.
>
> —Seven Year Old

SEQUENCES OF INSTRUCTION, INTERMEDIATE GRADES

Lynda Chittenden
Old Mill School, Mill Valley

During my first ten years of teaching at the upper elementary grades, a realistic structure for my own teaching of composition did not exist. The county courses of study were intimidating in their scope and detail. Perhaps of equal importance, they suggested a sequence and methods of instruction which simply didn't work for me in the classroom.

There were also "language arts" textbooks which were colorful, had a more realistic sequence, and even provided a script for the teacher to follow. But I didn't find them helpful either. The content never reflected what was actually happening in my classroom, and the script didn't help me deal with the variety of individual differences in pace, readiness, and achievement.

Then a "creative writing" school of thought became popular, based on the implication that children simply needed to *write* to be effective communicators. To "correct" their writing was to inhibit their creativity. So the students wrote and wrote. I read their stories, but was never able to answer my own question of "what next?" Their papers piled up, most students remained frustrated with writing, and I had a vague uneasiness that very little was being learned. With my uncertainty about what to do, I grew not to care very much about those stories and neither did the students. Consequently, I began to require less and less writing from the students, and naturally they were less and less receptive to any writing assignment from me.

But after working for two years with the Bay Area Writing Project, I have developed a sequence of instruction for the teaching of composition which is not only practical and useful, but which accurately reflects what children *can* do! I now feel able to answer the "what next" question for each student individually. My teaching sequence has two components, the first of which follows the development of the students as they struggle to master writing:

DEVELOPMENTAL SEQUENCE
FLUENCY ⟶ COHERENCE ⟶ CORRECTNESS

At the beginning of the school year, I find it important to look diagnostically at each child's writing and decide where he or she is along a line of writing development. This development begins with a student first achieving *fluency* in writing. From fluency, a student moves to working on *coherence* in writing. Once a student has achieved reasonable coherence in his writing, we then begin to work together on *correctness*.

I define *fluency* in writing as a child's ability to put initial thoughts on paper without struggling. A student who has not achieved fluency can be easily spotted in the act of writing even before I've seen his paper. He probably fidgets, is easily distracted, keeps asking questions about what he's supposed to be doing, and needs constant reassurance that what he's doing is okay. His writing has many omissions, rare punctuation, little supporting detail, and often jumps in content from one thing to another. The many omissions make it difficult to tell what his "sentence sense" is (i.e. how able he is both to recognize and write a complete sentence).

I define *coherence* as that stage at which the student's writing generally makes sense. While writing, that student will appear purposeful and will need only the spelling of certain words and other help in "mechanics." If that student has had experience in writing/response groups, she will often want to read what she's written so far to another child. She will want to know if she's making sense, or will want to talk about the language choices she's making. A piece of writing from a student at this stage generally does make sense, is written in complete sentences even though they may not be punctuated, and includes some supporting detail. It is rarely paragraphed, but it follows a coherent line of thought.

It is with small groups of students at this stage, students who are in the midst of revising pieces of their own writing for "publication," that I teach the mechanics of punctuation, spelling, and usage. I have found that it is only in this context that instruction in mechanics makes any sense to students and where any transfer of learning takes place.

I define *correctness* as that stage at which the student writes fluently and coherently most of the time and is usually correct in the mechanics of spelling, punctuation, and usage.

At the beginning of this last school year, I discussed with my fourth and fifth grade students this continuum of writing development. I then told them that I needed a piece of writing that I could use to diagnose their development. I said that we would write in class the next day and that they should come prepared with something to write about. We brainstormed to suggest some possibilities (e.g. a fictional story, a piece about themselves telling me things they wanted me to know, a detailed review or "opinion" of a book or T.V. show, or of course, "My Summer Vacation"). Letting them know ahead of time what would be expected enabled them to "rehearse" (practice ahead of time) what they would write about and how they would organize and write it. We also discussed the concept of "rehearsal" and how it could be an aid to writing.

The next day only three students came with nothing to write about. The rest of the class started writing while I talked further with these three. It took only a brief discussion (which I think functioned primarily to reassure them of my seriousness) and they began writing. I set neither a minimum word limit nor a time limit. I merely said, "Write until you're finished."

Here are some typical examples of intermediate students whose September writing is fairly fluent, but still not fully coherent. Most students at this level of writing, when given a multitude of forms from which to choose, will choose to write "stories"—to them, writing is story-telling.

One 10 years ago there where 2 men, Joe & Alan. Alan had 2 kids a wife and lived in a small house. Joe lived in a small house to but had no wife or kids. They both worked at the sandville minds and got about 2$ an hour. They where on assignment when Joe found a cave. They went it it, went to the end & came out. But when they came out it was a different place. Below them was a big cannon, Joe had a rope and said he would climb down it. So they did, but not as they expected. Because when Alan 10 feet off the ground the rope snaped. Sudenly Alan spoted a bright light. So they went to it. It was a passage to the sandville dessert, so they new they must be close to the town. Finely they got home. They have nevwr told this story to any of there freinds up to this day.

—Eleven Year Old Boy

It was the month of Oberon when professor Johnson and dr. Reide where going to drill through the center of the Earth. it was the month of Junoe of the year 657n. They hade a big stycillick that was a machine with a big drill on one end and a treds to whip out the tracks. they were reaching the ceter now wehn the power ran out. And then out of no where radiation. then the door busted open. "oh no ants" said dr. Reide. "the ants are intelligent" said professor Johnson. The ants took them to their King. their King was a humun. the King was nice and granted then freedom.

—Nine Year Old Boy

These boys have a sense of what a complete sentence is and have a fairly good, if inconsistently applied, grasp of punctuation. They also have a sense of the narrative: both pieces have clear beginnings and endings. The primary writing goal for these boys is to write a lot, focusing on including all necessary words and more supporting detail. They also obviously need to work on the pronunciation and spelling of basic words. For the next months, every writing assignment done by these students is evaluated in terms of success in meeting these specific goals. That evaluation is continually done by themselves, their peers, and me.

Once students have some understanding of that linear development of writing and have achieved a fair measure of fluency, I encourage them to take "language risks" in their writing. Through reading, being read to, and listening to each other's work, their language awareness is growing. They begin to realize that they have choices of different vocabulary, phrasing, and styles. They hear new ways of putting words together and begin to try to use them. Therefore, at the *coherence* level, a variety of individual problems appear.

Here is a student who begins by trying to include detail, but has difficulty with *how* it's done:

CAMP!!

There I was ridding on the bus to camp wait what is that in a distant field there? it was a deer it was leaping through the brush it was gorgeous! Finaly we arived it was about nine oclock we met our counselors...

—Ten Year Old Girl

By working in small response groups, reading her work aloud, and listening to others read their efforts at coherently including detail in writing, this girl was later able to revise her piece:

CAMP!!

There I was ridding on the bus to camp. "Wait what is that in a distant field," I thought, I looked closer. A deer was leaping through the brush it was gorgeous! We drove out of sight, of it. Well it was nice wile it lasted. It was boring the rest of the time. Seeing farm after farm is not fun. Finaly, it got dark it wasn't as boring then because I couldn't see anything out side. Finally we arived it was about nine oclock we met our counselors...

This student writes fairly coherently, but has difficulty with organization:

KENYA

In Kenya our main bace was Nairobi which is the main city in Kenya. We stayed in the Hilton Hotel. A man from a tour agence drove us to game parks where we stayed in the lodges and went out in the evening and at about 6:30 in the morning. The main tribe in Kinya are the Massi. The wemen ware big round neck lecklesses and the men carry spears and sheleds. The animals we saw mostly of were zebra, willderbeast, buffalow and hippos and so much more. We saw 4 loin mothers and about 9 cubs eating a willderbeast! We also saw a male loin which is very rare!! We past over the equator and my dad said if you pass it in an airplane the toilet will flush the wrong way. We saw the massi men dance. They jump into the air super high! The men wear a strip of cloth and lots of juillrey. The wemen wear a peice of cloth made into a sort of dress. The Massi are sort of tall but not as tall as people say they are. They only drink cattle blood and milk and...

—Ten Year Old Girl

Reading this piece aloud to others, she easily heard this sequencing problem and stated that in a revision she would keep all the animal information together and then tell all about the "Massi."

Here is a student who writes quite coherently. She includes some detail and her story has no organizational problems. Her difficulty is another one typical of a student at this level:

THE ELF VILLAGE

Once there was a group of elves. They lived in a little town with
no name. They lived very happily. Until, one day the village caught
on fire! yells and screems cold be heard miles around. Everyone
got away. Nobody was hurt. The mayor said, "Let's find another
place." Everyone agread and went off to get ready. They came
back ready to leave. So off they went. They was many places. But
they would have to be cleared. They went on. Sudenly they heard
a growl. It was the dragon. Everyone ran and hid. The dragon got
a little boy. Then he went on. They came out and went on. Only
very slowly, they were sad about the little boy. But then someone
saw just the right place. it had places for homes and a little stream
and paches of grass. They all rushed to it. They all started to
build. And lived happily ever after.

—Nine Year Old Girl

Her sentences, although technically complete, are simple and immature. Her goal now becomes writing "meaty" sentences. Through weekly
spelling sentence and sentence-combining exercises, a class list of "Words
Which Help Us Write More Interesting Sentences" evolves (i.e. *which,
who, although, after, while, when).* Children then begin to share with each
other their successful "meaty" and "interesting" sentences, and growth in
sentence complexity occurs. Teaching the grammatical terms is unnecessary.

Often students who have previously written at the coherence level start
taking language risks and reach for "better" language. Sometimes this
reaching is done at the expense of coherence.

THE DREADED SIAMESE

The dreaded Siamese was perched up in a tree looking down on
a mouse hill. when a gigantic avocado came rolling in and when
it was rolling out it knocked over the tree that the cat was sitting
int, it fell like a pitcher pouring milk...

—Ten Year Old Girl

This girl was praised for her language and humor, but reminded that
her primary goal was that a piece makes sense, and that sentences should
be punctuated. A few weeks later, this same girl wrote a scary Halloween
story:

TO KILL THE LIVING DEAD

Over the hill, under the wind, through the dark forest and
down, down, down beneath the door of the dead.
     At midnight in the door of the dead everything was calm until
the peek of night the edge of death came. The dead were alive.
     The priest of a town called Edenburge went on a long journey

through the woods to kill the living dead because if he didn't they would kill him. He walked for days to find them, but they were nowhere in sight.

The sun went down quickly, and the moon came up. Night fell before him.

He didn't know what was happening, terror penetrated through his skin, the cry of terror spoke out, "Go back, go back." he stepped back a few steppes not realizing that a few more steppes back might lead to the door of the dead.

With a sudden movement he pulled out his bow and arrow and shot strate up in the midnight darkness, thinking that that's where the voice came from...

She received a great deal of sincere praise from her peers for this story and "terror penetrated through the skin" of many subsequent sentences written in the classroom.

Sometimes a student's writing is technically both coherent and correct, and yet he takes no language risks at all. Getting this type of student to begin to risk is often more difficult than dealing with the results of risking:

I went up the Sacramento River in an ℂ which stands for International One Design Class. It is a sailboat that is built to race. It is thirtythree feet long and it has a six foot beam. They don't have very much living room but they have enough room for two people to sleep in the cabin.

My dad and I went up the Sacramento River to Steam Boat Slough. We stayed there for a week. There were a lot of beaches and there were a lot of people on the beaches.

After a while we went back and we had a nice sail back.

—Ten Year Old Boy

This type of student is helped by being exposed to some of the language risks others are taking. I ditto student work, I encourage formal and informal oral sharing of work, and I continue sentence structure and sentence-combining exercises. I try to create a classroom climate which encourages and rewards language "risking" and "reaching."

This year, in a class of twenty-seven fourth and fifth grade students, there was only one student at the *correctness* level of writing in September:

A TRIP TO EARTH

"Ouch, Crazy thrower!" mumbled Cathrine, "Sometimes I wish he had better aim than that!" Cathrine Davis was on the middle-aged baseball team. Today she was playing left field. Jake Collins was pitcher. The runner had just hit the ball into right field. Joe was playing right field. Joe missed the ball, but he recovered it quickly and threw it to the pitcher's mound, where Jake caught it. The player rounded second, and was on his way to third. "Quick, throw it here!" Cathrine had said. Jake threw the ball, and missed. The ball had hit Cathrine in the leg. Her leg killed, but she still went up to Jake, and kicked him in the behind. "You jerk!" she said, "Someday, I'm going to get revenge on you!" She stomped up to bat. Jake rubbed his behind. Then he said, "Just throw the ball." Right then a U.F.O. appeared in the sky...

—Ten Year Old Girl

This girl subsequently has had great difficulty revising any of her work. A "final draft" for her is usually nothing more than a completely new "rough draft" of a similar story. A timid perfectionist, she has needed a great deal of hand-holding to get her to trust her instincts enough to know that if she senses a part of her piece is incomplete or unclear, it can be "fixed-up" rather than scrapped. Otherwise, for her, revision merely means starting over and still being frustrated with the finished product.

In addition to the developmental sequence students go through as they master writing (fluency → coherence → correctness), I have found it most helpful to look at each writing task as having its own sequence. This sequence can be labeled many ways, but every writing assignment should begin with a few or many *pre-writing* activities. Then, the actual *writing* is followed by some kind of *post-writing* activity.

Pre-Writing

Any child, no matter how skilled, rarely finds success in writing if he is asked to sit down and write without having had any time to prepare for that particular assignment. Field trips, art activities, individual and group reading, and group literature activities are all important pre-writing experiences which expose students to new ideas. All of these experiences give children much to think about, and through "thinking" and daydreaming, they are exploring these ideas. Thinking goes along with talking: small and large group, formal and informal discussions—all focused talk is pre-writing experience which also helps children to explore and organize their ideas. The connection of pre-writing experiences to success in writing is one which intermediate-age students can easily understand. Once they see that connection, pre-writing activities become even more profitable for them.

Writing

Most pre-writing activities are "group" in nature. Each student must then take up pencil and commit his or her own words to paper. It is quite appropriate at this age that the writing be primarily a solitary activity, although it is also appropriate sometimes to share in the process of group writing. Whether writing alone or in a group, students will often need to read their work-in-progress to each other before completing their pieces.

Post-Writing

I define *post-writing* as everything from an oral sharing of a finished piece of writing to actually "publishing" the work in some form. Post-writing also includes occasional revising or reformulating a piece of writing. I find revision is both easier and makes more sense to students when accomplished through small writing groups where they read and respond to each other's work with the goal of improving the piece. A frequent practice of whole class "group response" helps students to respond to each other's writing, and it also helps build a "community of standards" for composition. The following steps in group response have worked for me in the classroom:

- First, the writer *reads* a brief piece he or she has selected to share.
- The group then tells the writer what they can see he or she *knows* because it is in the writing. (This response can be to the content: "I can really tell that she knows how boring it is to ride on a bus" or to a language goal: "She knows how to begin a story and get your interest.") Alternatively, the group could simply tell the writer what the *strengths* of the piece are.
- The group then *asks questions* of the writer, thus making it known what more they want to know or what part of the piece is unclear.
- The writer then *tells* the group what he or she would add, change, or correct in a revision.

Underlying the sequences of instruction which structure my classroom writing program are some basic assumptions about what is necessary in language learning:

- Students need to write a lot. My students are informed at the beginning of the school year that they will write every day. Thus, the question is never whether or not they'll have a writing assignment, but rather just what the nature of the daily writing task will be. The quantity of "group groans" will diminish considerably when students accept that they *will* write and need only know from you *what* they will write. Also a great deal of self-initiated writing begins and the rush to the "In Box" of completed work ends.
- Assignments are done by all the students. Daily journal writing, working on stories, writing brief responses to given topics, (i.e. "What are the dreams of one born blind?"), writing about their learning processes in learning logs, or working on informational "report" writing are tasks appropriate for all of the students.
- Evaluation of the student's work is done individually in terms of the writing goals which have been set for that student.
- Writing is not something done only during the "language arts" period of the day. Writing is a tool of learning and something I require of my students in every aspect of the curriculum.

- As teacher, I also need to write and share my writing process with my students.
- Practice and drill in spelling, handwriting, and punctuation are best done outside the classroom. Individually prescribed exercises and workbooks which deal primarily with drill and practice in mechanics make very appropriate homework assignments.

Whether one has a self-contained classroom or a departmentalized "English" class, I believe that writing can be used as the core of the curriculum. Using the organization I have described has greatly improved my teaching while also making it more rewarding.

SEQUENCES OF INSTRUCTION, 9-12

Jean Jensen
Las Lomas High School, Walnut Creek (retired)

The Evolution of a Writing Program

1966, a vintage year for English teachers: the Dartmouth Conference brought teachers from all over the world together to discuss the state of the profession and resulted in the publication of Dixon's *Growth Through English* in England in 1968. Roger Appleby and James Squire's *High School English Instruction Today* appeared, a report studying the English programs in 158 high schools in 45 states. The names of Hook, Diederich, Hogan, Loban, Christensen, Miles, Macrorie, Kozol, Holt—an endless list—were beginning to become familiar in some colleges and high schools. James Moffett's *A Student Centered Language Arts Curriculum, Grades K-13, A Handbook for Teachers* was published. Across the land teachers were asking for answers which research and reports on innovative classroom techniques could provide. And in Walnut Creek, California, after fifteen years of stumbling through the yellow, red, green, and blue volumes of *Building Better English,* the Las Lomas High School English department enthusiastically if blindly began the development of a curriculum based on the growth cycle of the students in our classes.

To teach effectively we knew we must continue being learners. We wrote class assignments with our students in all classes, sharing our papers with them. We visited one another's classes, observing strategies, discussing results. We shared lesson planning sessions as well as miscellaneous dittos. Some of us read prodigiously and shared what we read at department meetings. We argued, questioned, reported at brunch, at lunch, during preparation periods, after school. We retired our grammar books to dingy corners in the backs of closets and prepared our own style sheet—a condensed collection of information about punctuation, spelling, and usage.

Las Lomas's writing program, having undergone its initial birth trauma, began to grow. We had acted on our firm belief that for too long publishers of grammar texts had dictated the English writing curriculum from New York to California, from Texas to North Dakota.

Planning Our Courses

In 1970 we separated the writing program from the literature program because we believed that writing about literature is significantly different from other writing tasks. In 1971 we bought Ken Macrorie's *Telling Writing* for our Advanced Composition classes. And in the spring of '72 our Faculty Council voted to use our style sheet for all students in every department.

It was not until late 1975, eight years after the publication of James Moffett's book and one year after the initiation of the Bay Area Writing Project, that we outlined in writing the Las Lomas Sequential Writing Program. Even then we felt that, although the freshman and sophomore programs developed logically, we were not satisfied with either of the two junior and senior courses. Practical Composition proved far from practical, and we questioned the breadth and scope of Advanced Composition. Back to the drawing board. Now we directed our efforts toward the juniors and seniors. We experimented, failed, tried again, and ultimately succeeded in developing a program which satisfied us, at least for a semester.

Writing From Experience

We agreed that all people write better when they enjoy writing, so we engaged our writing classes in activities providing experiences in the real world outside their classrooms. Our enthusiasm sometimes produced classroom experiences verging on the weird. However, they also produced writing which excited and pleased its audience—the students. In some classes students looked at the world as they lay prone on the classroom floor. Sitting in the warm sunshine, their backs against blossoming crab apple trees, they examined, thought about, and then wrote about blossoms, bees, trunks. They walked down to our creek and wrote about floating boxes, old bottles, rusty cans, abandoned shopping carts, sections of bedsprings, and minute creek creatures. They flew kites on the football field or sat high in the broadcasting booth and then wrote. They visited Kaiser Hospital across the street, or ventured into the Hickory Pit, a restaurant, walked over to Quail Court, a business complex, and observed Benny Bufano's mosaic statue of a hand. The papers they wrote as a result of these experiences became more than mere observations. They provided material for developed, controlled essays. Our department meetings were filled with a new excitement because our jobs had become, for the most part, exhilarating. Teaching English had itself become a trip.

From Experience to Idea

As we have worked in the program, we have realized that in order to justify any major curriculum change we must have a solid philosophy based on research. For this reason all members of the department have either read or listened to digests of Paul Diederich's *Measuring Growth in English,* Peter Elbow's *Writing Without Teachers,* Janet Emig's *The Composing Processes of Twelfth Graders,* Ken Macrorie's *Uptaught* and *A Vulnerable Teacher,* and James Moffett and Betty Wagner's *Student Centered Language Arts and Reading.*

As we read we discovered that many people agreed with us that spelling and punctuating are of secondary importance in the teaching of writing. Also research shows that naming parts of speech or diagramming sentences has absolutely no relation to success in writing. From James Moffett we learned that students do not write enough, nor do they write in enough different modes. Piaget appears to corroborate our experience that freshmen and sophomores do not write well if they are asked to produce expository writing because they are not mature enough to master "formal operations" or the ability to make conscious abstractions. Moffett also describes the ability to sustain abstract discourse as a late development in students. Our program allows students to progress from enriched experiences to a recording of what is happening to writing which generalizes and theorizes. In ten years, then, the program has expanded to include our growing knowledge, and we believe that we are finally providing a bridge between experiential writing and writing which is concerned with an end outside itself—informing, persuading, and instructing.

The Las Lomas Writing Program

The Setting

Las Lomas is a four-year high school of about 1200 students set in the middle of Walnut Creek, a suburban area under the shadow of the University of California at Berkeley and of San Francisco State University in San Francisco. However, Diablo Valley Community College, fifteen minutes away, provides the next educational experience for most of our students. These students come predominately from middle and upper class career-oriented white families, although each year we enroll more students from minority races. All ninth grade students plan to attend a four-year college, but by the time they reach twelfth grade the number has dwindled to sixty percent. Only fifty-one percent of any incoming freshman class will complete all four years at Las Lomas. In any given year, all but about fifty students are enrolled in one or more classes in English. We suspect that although we teach in a typical suburban school, the ideas which we use successfully will work with most students and for most teachers.

The Program

The English program at Las Lomas offers students semester courses only. Freshmen and sophomores must take writing one semester and literature the other. As juniors they enroll in one of the fairly traditional literature elective classes, although students who wish to take Advanced Placement English in their senior years may take Advanced Composition as juniors. All students must pass an upper division writing course to graduate. Seniors, therefore, choose between Advanced Composition, which is designed for students who plan to attend a four-year college or university, and Practical Composition, a course for those who plan to attend junior college or to get a job.

The entire Las Lomas program is based upon a model which sees writing as a process with three identifiable though overlapping stages: prewriting, composing, and editing. The chart below, developed by teachers in the St. Louis Area Writing Project when I worked with them in 1978, illustrates the variety of activities that can contribute to each stage of the process. Descriptions of these activities can be found in the works of the authors listed (see References). This model of the writing process is the basis for the writing course at each grade level. But different activities are used to help students develop prewriting, composing, and rewriting strategies at different age levels.

Establishing a Sequence of Activities, 9-12

Freshmen

Differences in the maturity of writers appear in the pre-writing stage as writers learn to identify an audience and to select an appropriate voice. Freshmen need to expand the number of forms they are able to choose from: letter, memoir, autobiographical sketch, journal, diary, monologue, or dialogue. Other differences emerge during composing and revising. Freshmen write description and narrative easily, especially when they write in the first person. As soon as they try to write exposition, however, they turn out sad, spineless, boring *Engfish* (a term used by Ken Macrorie to suggest the language students think teachers want.) Freshmen enjoy sentence combining, but have difficulty with the concepts of subordination and coordination. Freshmen are always in a hurry: they complete a paper, hand it in, and expect a grade two minutes later. They believe that to revise is to produce clean copy. They have difficulty seeing where they need help except, perhaps, in spelling. They know when they like a paper, but they seldom know why. Sometimes a very good freshman writer can identify sentence fragments or run-ons, particularly after having finished many O'Hare or Strong sentence combining exercises. Freshmen need to do much "talking about" before they begin to write.

Sophomores

As sophomores students become acquainted with cumulative sentences, the type of sentence Francis Christensen identified as the basic building block of modern prose. They work on modification, coordination, and subordination and quickly become able to write more mature sentences. Because students have shed most of their writing inhibitions by the end of

MODEL OF THE TEACHING AND WRITING PROCESS

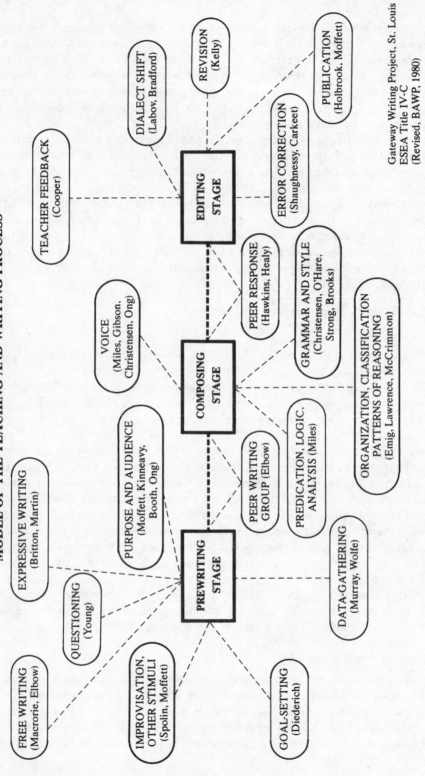

FREE WRITING
(Macrorie, Elbow)

QUESTIONING
(Young)

EXPRESSIVE WRITING
(Britton, Martin)

IMPROVISATION,
OTHER STIMULI
(Spolin, Moffett)

GOAL-SETTING
(Diederich)

PURPOSE AND AUDIENCE
(Moffett, Kinneavy,
Booth, Ong)

PEER WRITING
GROUP (Elbow)

PREDICATION, LOGIC,
ANALYSIS (Miles)

DATA-GATHERING
(Murray, Wolfe)

VOICE
(Miles, Gibson,
Christensen, Ong)

ORGANIZATION, CLASSIFICATION
PATTERNS OF REASONING
(Emig, Lawrence, McCrimmon)

GRAMMAR AND STYLE
(Christensen, O'Hare,
Strong, Brooks)

PEER RESPONSE
(Hawkins, Healy)

TEACHER FEEDBACK
(Cooper)

DIALECT SHIFT
(Labov, Bradford)

REVISION
(Kelly)

ERROR CORRECTION
(Shaughnessy, Carkeet)

PUBLICATION
(Holbrook, Moffett)

PREWRITING STAGE

COMPOSING STAGE

EDITING STAGE

Gateway Writing Project, St. Louis
ESEA Title IV-C
(Revised, BAWP, 1980)

their freshman year, we feel that published examples will no longer intimidate them. We want them to be aware that published writers use the same techniques they are experimenting with, so we ask them to read such autobiographical authors as Joan Baez, Gordon Parks, and Maya Angelou. As they struggle with autobiographical fragments of their own, students look carefully at the way these writers use language.

Juniors and Seniors

When we began teaching Practical Composition, the course consisted of a complete review of freshman and sophomore writing followed by nine weeks of such assignments as writing resumés, filling out applications, and writing letters of various kinds. The course had little appeal, and it became clear that changes were needed. We began by inviting members of the business community to speak to the class. One of our speakers, a woman from the State Department of Employment, told our students how important writing could be in preparing to enter the job market. "You must write a great deal in order to find out who you are and what you want to make of your lives," she told them. "When you are almost written out, then learn to do the practical things." Her comment suggested new possibilities for this class. Students now write assignments such as a personality sketch of a person who has made a strong impact on them. They use techniques practiced in previous years to observe, interview, and write. They write papers which answer questions like, What satisfies you? What do you dislike? What skills do you have? How can you prove you have them?

During the second nine weeks students read Studs Terkel's *Working* and write summaries of three jobs. They listen to and question managers of condominiums, used-car salesmen, or gas-station operators, describing their jobs and writing short summary opinion papers. They also tape a job interview and meet with the teacher individually to critique it. As a result of these changes, Practical Composition has become one of the more popular classes.

Advanced Composition has also changed since its beginning. Because of the improved uniformity and general excellence of the teaching in the ninth and tenth grades, we are able to cover in nine weeks what previously had taken eighteen. The saturation report, previously the final paper, is now the midterm assignment. Students now progress through additional expository assignments which culminate in a synthesis paper using all of the writing techniques covered in the course. Ken Macrorie's *Telling Writing* provides specific techniques to make student papers clear and forceful: selection and ordering of detail, creating tension through the use of oppositions, telling facts, dialogue, tightening, sharpening, repetition. These students see the usefulness of the expository essay and are able to select the appropriate techniques for their purposes.

Establishing an Atmosphere of Trust and Respect

All English classes spend their first weeks establishing a warm and friendly classroom. Freshmen play a variety of values clarification games. As a group they interview the teacher and then individually interview each other to help them get acquainted. In some classes students engage in oral activities like identifying themselves with specific flowers, food, animals, cities, television shows, or sports cars. These oral games help both teacher and students begin to see the class members as individuals. Other classes do a number of free word association writings which they read aloud.

Tenth-grade classes spend time talking about experiences: the earliest they remember, embarrassing moments, times they were really afraid. In some classes teachers find students are more comfortable "making up" stories which they can share.

In junior and senior classes, students introduce themselves by writing limericks using their own names. Teachers may ask them to write a list of three things about themselves they are willing to share with the class and three things they will share only with the teacher. Everyone reads his or her "public" list and the discussion centers on the makeup of the class and its likes and dislikes. Generally the first composing assignment is "Bring an object which you will never want to part with. Write a paper in which you describe this object and tell why it is important to you." The personalities of the students are clearly on display during the week the class participates in this activity. Certainly by the end students feel comfortable with both the class and the teacher. The teachers encourage a group feeling by actively participating in all of these activities themselves.

Making Assignments

As a department we have agreed on several procedures to follow in making assignments. First, the teacher never makes a new assignment until the last one has been graded, commented upon, and returned. We rarely ask students to write a single paragraph unless we are doing finger exercises. Instead the typical assignment will begin "Write a paper..." Students learn that audience and purpose determine the length of a paper and that changes of place, person, subject, time, and sometimes tone dictate divisions into paragraphs.

We never mark all errors on a paper because we believe students seldom learn from this practice and indeed sometimes become so inhibited they cannot write at all. Instead we write comments in the margins and a long note at the end suggesting revisions, responding to ideas presented in the paper, and listing perhaps one or two types of errors the student needs to work on.

Each teacher is free to experiment as she or he pleases, but generally the class spends time between long assignments working on shorter, in-class assignments including sentence combining, coordination, and subordination. Freshmen and sophomores also do improvisations as a prewriting activity. Some days are devoted to workshop-type classes.

Most of the teachers in our department believe in writing their own papers to assignments they give their students. Students need to know that we really think writing is important, and seeing us struggle with the same writing they're doing helps us convince them.

We do not use outside readers to help with our paper load. Readers tend only to "correct" papers, and in our program, this is not enough. We read all papers ourselves.

Editing Groups

This year we introduced the use of editing groups in all classes, whereas previously we had only used them in Advanced Composition. Each group consists of five to seven students who remain together for the whole semester. At one time the teacher selected the members of the group, and in some classes it still seems wise to do so. In most classes, however, we allow students to group themselves because self-selected groups seem to work more efficiently than the teacher-chosen groups.

At the beginning of the year we encourage a discussion among students about the value of playing an active role in this group. Students must discover that unless everyone contributes his ears, his voice, and his paper, the group cannot function properly. We have them identify traits of a "blocker," a "mover," a "monopolizer," a "facilitator."

Editing groups meet the day the first rough draft of an assignment is due. The teacher distributes check sheets applicable to the specific assignment containing questions like:

Can you hear the voice of the writer?

What is his main idea?

Is it explicit or implicit?

Which is better for this paper?

Does the paper begin and end well?

Is the writer aware of his audience?

Are the tone and diction appropriate?

In addition to questions, the sheet will contain a check-list of problems the teacher believes may arise: mis-use of passive voice, weak verbs, too many adverbs, lack of subject-verb agreement, dangling participles, run-ons, fragments, problems which have appeared in student work and have been discussed in class. The list grows longer as the class does more and more writing. We tend to emphasize different editing skills for each paper.

The students in each group may choose either to read the papers aloud or silently or both. They discover that sometimes the voice of the reader changes their perceptions of the paper. Comments are supportive and specific. Freshmen students say, "That's a neat paper, I like it because the same thing happened to me and that was exactly how I felt." Freshmen learn to talk about special sentences or words they like. They learn to recognize words or sentences which are misplaced so that the meaning is not clear. They become able to hear a good beginning or a satisfactory conclusion. Seniors move to, "Aren't you shifting tense? Maybe you should throw out the first two pages and begin with the third." Sometimes when a student reads a revised and polished paper in class, someone will say, "You did what we suggested. Wow, what a difference!"

Freshmen work less well in groups unless the group task is carefully structured. They work well with check sheets which are turned in at the end of the period.

Public and Private Papers

Students who are very unsure of themselves as writers are often hesitant about exposing their writing to the whole class. For this reason we categorize papers as either "public" or "private." Public papers are those the student writes for a public audience; private papers may be read by an audience of one—generally the teacher. Either the student or the teacher may decide a paper is private. Frequently in the beginning students will label even the most neutral papers "private." Soon, however, with the teacher's encouragement, students begin to see the value of sharing papers in the writer's voice and become more willing to read their papers to the class. Because of the importance of response from other students as well as from the teacher, this aspect of our program is crucial. It is only when the student realizes that her problems are shared by others, when she sees the teacher struggling too, and hears the teacher's paper read aloud, that she discovers the challenge and excitement of learning to write well.

Revision

By the time a student is a senior, he has been reading his papers either to an editing group or to the class for three years and should be fully aware of the meaning of revision. Unlike the freshman, for whom revision means clean copy, the senior realizes that much thought goes into selecting the proper word, focusing so that his audience will follow his ideas, deleting and adding when necessary. The ability to revise well depends upon how well the student has retained information covered in his earlier English classes. We try now to give him the professional writer's vocabulary so that he has the correct names for concepts he has been mastering since ninth grade.

We do little whole class teaching about any grammatical problem unless the mistake appears frequently in students' papers. We have found that when we teach a grammatical or usage concept before its time, the next papers tend to include that particular error more frequently than previous papers have.

All students are encouraged to revise and resubmit papers until they are satisfied with them.

Sample Assignments

Below are examples of some of the specific assignments we have used successfully. I have included samples of student writing done in response to each assignment.

Sensory

We repeat our assignments adding more complex requirements during the four-year period. The first sensory assignment for freshmen pairs them and sends them to various locations in the school: the library, the faculty room, the commons, the auto shop, the attendance office, the nurse's office, the activity director's office. On their return to class they discuss what they've seen, and write a single short paper as a group.

> As kids straggle in, they line up for lunch. At one end is the hall where students noisily push and shout giggling and laughing. At the other end is the cash register where students pay for their lunches which usually consist of pizza, salad, milk, and French bread. They take their trays to the sunshine and lawn or to the commons where they sit with their friends. Some sit alone at tables in the commons; some outside on long wooden benches; some sit on the grass. They divide themselves into loners, jocks, stoners, rah rahs, and then there are 'the others.' Perhaps these are the most interesting. Some of them just read. Some of them just sit and never look up. The bell rings finally and all leave; the commons and the lawn are deserted, strewn with brown bags filled with garbage or with candy wrappers. Everywhere it is very quiet.

At the senior level, students again go to specific places on campus, but instructions now are to report back with sentences using the techniques they have learned in sentence combining exercises. Since all students forget, their writings are horrifying, amazing, and sometimes delightful. We ditto all of them and use them for discussion and review.

> The spindly legged freshmen meander lazily out in the command of their mechanical half lunged teacher. They arrive at the tennis courts where the teacher hoarsely barks instructions to the comatose students as they hit tennis balls to each other. With their warped and loosely strung menace rackets. The sagging nets are useless; games are all that is seen in a hailstorm of tennis balls over a sea of green asphalt. Finally, the period ends with a shrill whistle from the decrepit teacher. Unenthused students stumble towards the locker room and the court is abandoned.

Certainly this writing lends itself to all kinds of discussion—sentence fragments, passive voice, word choice, even the use of the semi-colon.

Because we will have from five to ten similar paragraphs it is possible to review a great deal rapidly.

Memories

The freshman can write memories, but his are incomplete and often immature. He cannot stay easily with one subject because he has not yet understood the value of brainstorming to expand or enrich a single idea. He has not yet learned how to focus his writing.

A Memory

The warmth of the sun beaming down woke me. I climbed out of the warm sleeping bag onto the still dew wet earth. I gazed over the river. It was thirty feet wide now from the rain last week. The Christle clear water molded around the smooth rock. It traveled at a pace twice as fast as I walked, making shoots, dips and whorls flinging water into the air. The opposite bank had boulders larger than I that have been etched by the constantly running water. Beyond the land stretched up into an enormous mountain. The left side of the mountain was bright green with small trees and grass. A few large gray rocks columned up to make sheer cliffs. The right side was an ugly black burn left over from the fire last year. I could see no vegetation. I decided to take a dip in the cold clear water. The sides of the river were shallow and here the water slowed because of the rocks. I stepped off a rock and into the cold ankle deep. The icy water sent a chill up my legs. I stepped on a rock, slipped off, stumbled back and then fell in totally submerging myself in water which felt as cold as death. I jumped up and tried to run out, but I fell on the rocks. I discovered two kinds of rocks: slippery and hard. I slipped on the slippery ones and fell on the hard ones.

—Ninth Grade Boy

The senior has learned to focus; his memories are specially selected to fit his purpose and his form.

Orland is a small town not far from Chico. It has a main street four blocks long, two dime stores, a hardware store or two, a Big Joe's Supermarket, and a small J. C. Penny's. For action all the girls sit around and get fat while all the guys watch the alfalfa grow. Orland has two kinds of weather, cold and wet or hot and dry. A summer in Oreland is a sauna without the steam. And Oreland in the summer is heaven. Oreland is where my grandfather's farm is.

—Twelfth Grade Boy

Clustering

A technique we learned from Professor Gabriele Rico of San Jose State University, clustering works well in any class. Students are instructed to write a key word, usually supplied by the teacher, on the center of a piece of paper. Then, letting their minds flow freely, they write whatever associations occur to them, drawing lines to show the relationships between the words. Whenever they can see an idea fully enough to develop it with a beginning, middle, and end, they stop clustering and begin writing.

The cluster below began with the word *up.* The instructions were: "Cluster whatever comes into your mind. When you think you have enough ideas to write, do so. Be sure to come full circle."

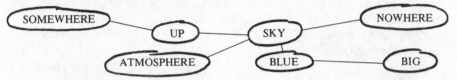

What is nowhere? Who knows? Not me! Everywhere (if there is a somewhere) has to be somewhere. If you're out in the middle of nowhere, you're somewhere. There is no such thing as nowhere because everywhere is somewhere.

Nobody has ever been to nowhere, so how does anyone know that there is a nowhere? We don't. But, why then, do we say, "Nowhere?"

I don't know why we say "Nowhere," or where nowhere is, but when I asked my mom if I could go to the movies this weekend, she said, "You're going nowhere this weekend." What can I say? I didn't want to go "nowhere" anyway.

—Ninth Grade Girl

Clustering works well both in literature and writing classes. Because it is spatial rather than linear, relationships not always apparent become visible surprises. It also provides a way of reviewing materials in other subjects. The center of a cluster may be a word, a name, a line of poetry, a quotation. Students learn easily how to make their writing come full circle. The sophomore paper below is a good example.

Autobiographical Fragment #2

I really hate the Walnut Creek Bart station. I can't stand to go there. I hate the way everyone sits around looking stupid, waiting for the shuttle bus. I hate the way people think they can operate the machines and end up having to call the attendant for help. Then they both hold up the line.

Finally you get inside. The train just got in and any minute I am going to be attacked by business men coming home from work. Here they come, swarms and swarms of unseeing mean faced men. As usual they push me all the way over to the other side where I don't want to go.

Now there is a giant flight of stairs, 29, 30, 31, 32,...top. The top is different. There are usually just two or three people up here at this time. Finally the lights flash above me...Concord...the train arrives. The doors open and swarms and swarms of business-men attack again. After I almost get squished by the closing doors, I step aboard. Everyone stares at me. The train starts and I fall backwards as a big jolt tells me I am on my way to Pleasant Hill. They are still staring when I pick myself up and find a place to sit.

After a bit we get to Concord. The doors open and I get pushed down stairs with the traffic. Now I am one of the people who knocks everyone over to the other side of the station and that's another story...

— Tenth Grade Girl

Here is a senior paper—longer—which begins and ends with both focus and a flare.

A cool, whispering breeze lapped at my face and hair as I sat at the top of the cliff, one hundred and forty feet above the ocean. I was alone, gazing across the flames which were engulfing the setting sun. Long streamers of orange and red and purple her-alded the setting of the sun on this particular evening. What had once been a brilliant ball of fire in the sky was soon a glowing ember, sinking in the vastness of the Pacific distorting as it did so. Like some mushroom cloud from a nuclear explosion in reverse, it grew smaller and smaller until it fell beneath the waves to light some distant land. I was calmed, hypnotized almost by this scene. Then—WHAM—a cold knife of panic stabbed. A paper, a saturation paper due in English.

"Don't they understand? Elk is not a place for writing. Never was, never will be. Elk is a place for hiking, fishing, seeing, talking, looking, and sometimes for reading, but never for writing.

. . . .

Even though the whole area was stripped of redwoods in the late eighteen hundreds when Elk's population numbered 1200, this second growth of trees seems primeval. The redwoods cover the steep sides of the creek canyon, cutting the sunlight to create a twighlight even at noon, and muffling all sounds. This atmo-sphere allows only for whispers. The road is slowly being destroyed, washed out, or overgrown with ferns and plants of the forest. The few manmade pieces from the past used to exploit this wilderness are being engulfed by the same growing wilderness. Unlike many places on this earth, Elk's natural forces are overtaking man's endeavors, and I'm glad.

Elk is not a place for writing. Elk is not even a place for reading about. Elk is a place for experiencing first hand.

—Twelfth Grade Boy

Free Writing

At one time we required every student to keep a journal. Because of the size of our classes we have replaced that requirement with a twenty-minute free writing done in class every third week. The papers below illustrate the variety of forms students choose.

The growth from freshman to senior appears in the following typical selections.

LIKES

These things I love to see:
    A sunset before the day turns dark
    Children laughing and teasing
    A blue and endless sky on a hot day
These things I love to hear:
    Loud music ringing in my ears
    A brook churkling as it continues its journey
    Birds chirping in the early morning
These things I love to feel:
    A cool breeze on a summer's night
    Hot sun against my back
    My kitten's fur brushing my bare leg
These things I love to taste:
    Ice cream spilling down my throat
    Hot chocolate on a winter night
    Snowflakes melting on my tongue
These things I love to smell:
    Steaks broiling in the oven
    Flowers in early spring
    The dew-wet morning air

—Ninth Grade Girl

Sophomores move from enumerating to choosing, arranging, and reflecting.

POEM

The wild horse
  fast, smooth
Running through
the open grassy fields
Hoofs slow down
  legs slower
    body
      slower
        stops

Still, calm,
standing like
a statue
gazing into nowhere.

    — Tenth Grade Girl

POEM

The bee
came
Swarming toward me.
I
held still
and
he
landed on
my
  arm;
slowly
the stinger
came
out
and
entered my
arm

    — Tenth Grade Girl

And I am proud to introduce S. K., world famous orchestra conductor. The cheers of my colleagues, the lights, the trumpets, the trombones, the drums all reached into my heart as I stepped forward receiving recognition at last. The harmonious sounds of the orchestra reached a climax as I accepted the award I had so long labored for. I was smashed back into reality by the honk of a horn. A car passed.

I dodged a little closer to the curb, continuing to run and realizing I ought to get off this busy street. I turned onto a shady, lonely, and comfortable side road. Listening to the pitter patter of my feet on the cool asphalt as they slowly pick up the tempo, I return to my thoughts...

D. R. was piter pattering over the PA system and a special announcement caught my attention. "I would like to call for a moment of silence this morning dedicated to S.K. who died across the street at Kaiser a few moments ago..." Dead stillness around school, great sorrow. I felt like yelling to the whole school to tell them I was not dead, but I knew it was useless.

I reached the end of my road and continued along a path in a tired sort of way, conserving my energy to enable me to continue without stopping.

Smelling the smells of cows and of hills and watching my breath vaporize, I trudged over a small pass between two sleeping giants. I climbed the back of one and perched myself in its head. There were things I wanted them all to hear. I realized all at once that even if they did, they wouldn't have given a damm.

I was thankful for my existence, for my own world. And suddenly I realized that this is what makes running fun.

—Eleventh Grade Boy

JJ's great black body leaped through the bushes. The muscles of his legs flexing along his black coat as each paw returned to the ground and then pushed away again. His nose was tight to the ground sniffing the wet Sudan grass and he sounded like a vacuum in the middle of a thick shag rug. His tongue lolled out almost hitting the ground whenever he looked up. He was exhausted, but he never stops.

With a sudden burst of enthusiasm he began to travel faster, his tail wagging happily like a windmill. Narrowly missing JJ's crushing teeth, a large cock pheasant exploded from a bush sending feathers drifting to the earth. I pulled my shotgun to my shoulder and fired off two shots but the pheasant continued on up only hurried by the thundering of my gun. JJ turned his head from the flying bird, his expression showing his disgust at my poor marksmanship.

Thinking about that day now, I remember his proud head and keen brown eyes which looked up at me affectionately. I never wanted the day to end or my dog to stop being my dog. But even then the killer cell was working.

JJ died of cancer two months later.

—Twelfth Grade Boy

Interview

One of the most successful assignments we give is the interview assignment seniors write. As we have done with all complex assignments, we have developed prewriting activities to prepare students for the writing of the paper. First we ask them to arrange themselves in pairs, preferably with someone they do not know well. Each member of the pair then chooses a role to play. These characters must be as different from each other as possible: the hostess at the local bar and the Queen of England. For twenty minutes these "people" converse in writing. During this time only giggles disturb the quiet classroom. When the twenty minutes are up, students read their papers aloud. This activity teaches students how to ask and answer questions, requires them to review the use of quotation marks, and reminds them that they must select materials for their papers carefully. We then distribute the following dittoed assignment:

Select a person over forty to interview. He may be a friend, an acquaintance, a relative, a stranger. Select a time when you can talk uninterruptedly for at least half an hour—an hour or more is better. Make an appointment. Think about your questions before you meet. Try to think about questions which will allow you a glimpse into the many facets of this person's personality. Encourage him to elaborate. Ask questions which will elicit detailed answers. Listen carefully. You may use a tape recorder if the person does not feel trapped by it. Take careful notes if you do not use a recorder.

In your paper include a physical description of the person and of the setting. Try to establish and maintain a definite tone which will add a dimension to your paper. If possible, try to organize by idea rather than by time.

This assignment brings together several kinds of writing: dialogue, reporting, description, and always those telling facts. You must digest verbal as well as experiential data and include both in your paper. We want to see this person as he appears to you.

You are responsible for clever use of dialogue. Should you be unsure about how to punctuate, or how to introduce it into the body of your paper, be sure to check the dialogue in any published interview or in any piece of fiction.

After the assignment is handed out, we invite a member of the school staff to be interviewed by the class. We spend one period interviewing. Every member of the class must ask at least one question. We warn them to be wary of "yes" and "no" answers. We urge them to pick up on hints the person drops about himself. The next day everyone is to have a single multilevel sentence capturing the "essence" of our interviewee. These are all read and discussed.

Below is a sample of the papers that result from this interview assignment:

CHAZ

"On my first night of work in a hospital as an orderly and lab technician I was asked to take a body down to the morgue. I tried to transfer the body from a stretcher to a gurney, but it fell on the floor. I attempted to pick the body up, but it was like picking up a bag of mush. I rolled, dragged, and pushed the body across the floor and with a burst of energy stood it up in a corner, I put the body over my shoulder and eventually got it delivered to the morgue.

"I had another unpleasant experience with a corpse when a three hundred pound preacher died of syphilis. I was supposed to take the body down to the morgue and put it on a refrigerated slab. The gurney was a foot higher than the slab, and when I rolled the body off onto the slab the supports broke. The body and the slab both crashed down onto my feet. I spent three hours in that morgue with my feet trapped underneath that fat preachers body until an orderly finally discovered me," said Charlie T. as we sat in the backyard of his modest suburban home.

With the sun shining brightly, a breeze drifting through the trees, and leaves cluttering the lawn, he went on to add, "thats how I paid my way through college, working forty two hours a week at a hospital in Cincinnati.

In nineteen sixteen Charlie T. was born in a small town in northern Kentucky. He spent his early years working on his grandfather's farm and going to grade school where he met his future wife. Work on the farm was hard, but it supported the family along with the money from his father's trucking business.

"I was a poor dirt country boy just trying to earn a living," said Charlie. He still looked the part as he sat across the leaf covered table in muddy old work clothes picking the dirt off his hands. He had been working in his garden.

When Charlie was sixteen his uncle became interested in airplanes and Charlie spent a lot of time barnstorming with him. Charlie learned to fly and helped his uncle build a biplane which the design of was later bought by the Wakle Aircraft company.

"I learned to fly in a Curtis Robin biplane and flying was a lot easier in those days. All you needed to fly was a compass, a turn bank indicator and a road map."

At one point Charlie held a commercial pilots license, but he quit flying because it became too expensive.

When I asked him about the great depression and how it affected his life he replied, "It didn't. We didn't have any money, but we always had plenty to eat because we lived on a farm."

Charlie went to the University of Cincinnati and played semi-pro football for a team that was to later become the Cincinnati Bengals.

"I got ten bucks a game. I quit after one year because I was too small; they played too rough, and I was getting the hell beat out of me."

During college he became interested in research biology and ichthyology. He spent many a night fishing with a friend at a pond in a nearby cemetary. With the fish they caught, they were able to study the growth rates of the fish in the pond.

After college Charlie married his childhood sweetheart, Lois. He spent the years of world war two helping develop an anti-malaria agent. This synthetic drug helped prevent U.S. soldiers from getting malaria while in the South Pacific.

In nineteen fifty-eight Charlie and Lois moved from Cincinnati to California. Charlie got a job with _____ Laboratories as a research biologist. He helped develop the first fertility pill. I asked him more about his research work. His eyes began to glow and a smile reached his lips. I knew that I had touched upon a subject that he really wanted to talk about.

"Its all about being able to influence physiology. Creating a molecule that is built the same, but blocks the receptor sites within the body. Its basicly a "lock and key" theory and it was my job to help find the key, to help cause fertility in women."

He continued to talk about hormones, estrogen, testosterone, steroids, and non-steroidal substances. It was a little hard for me to follow, but he made it all sound so simple.

Today Charlie T., better known as Chaz to his friends, wears glasses, chain smokes, has a stocky build and is sixty two years old. He is the Director of Corporate Compliance at _____ Laboratories. His job is to see that the companie's plants apply to government regulations. Charlie has two daughters and two grandchildren whom he sees often. He dislikes his present job and hopes to retire by the end of the year. He wants to pick up some of his old hobbies which include fishing, hunting, boating, waterskiing, and gardening. His favorite hobby is fishing and he wants to do more of it once he retires.

After shaking Charlie T.'s hand and thanking him for his time, I left his green leafswept backyard and headed for my car. I realized what a contrast there was between the early years of his life and the present. He has come from being a poor dirt country boy to being and extreemly successful pharmacologist. He has built himself a successful career in the research area of pharmacology and has spent forty two years in the business. It seemed to me that he was now ready to relax and spend more time enjoying life. I think that Charlie is now planning on going back to being a country boy again and spending a lot of time fishing.

Conclusion

In the ten years since we have separated writing from literature, we have grown more dependent on each other as teachers and writers. We write assignments with other teachers who teach the same classes; we talk about our craft in department meetings; we admire the other members of the department as professionals. At the present time we look forward to a year in which we are to begin the development of a program for our literature classes which will mirror our writing program. We hope to evolve a focus for each literature class which is rational and increasingly complex. We will then design assignments that will provide students with opportunities to use the same writing techniques they use in composition classes. Meanwhile the composition program continues to grow and change as the world changes; and we change too, because as we read, discuss, reflect, we discover new ways to intrigue both ourselves and our students.

SEQUENCES OF INSTRUCTION, 13

TEACHING THE BASIC STUDENT

Jan Wall
Laney College, Oakland

When we all came to Laney College ten or twelve years ago, we came to an unusual situation. Laney was a large inner city college with a sixty percent minority student population. We all came within a five-year period. We were young; most of us were not long out of graduate school. The English faculty increased from two to twenty within a short period. The original two teachers were Shirley Nedham and Oliver Kellogg, who were surely the most progressive of all possible old guards.

Like most English teachers, we had been trained in Shakespeare and Hawthorne and Chaucer. No one had ever taught us how to teach composition, and certainly, no one had ever taught us to teach reading. But we were interested in teaching or we would not have come to a community college, and we were willing to work with the students now defined as "non-traditional." We were convinced that even though our students had serious educational problems, they were not fools. And, God help us, some of us were probably even asking ourselves what we could do for our country rather than what our country could do for us.

A tradition of complete non-interference grew up in the department. We could do any foolish thing we wanted in our classes, and no one would bother us, not the department, not the administration. Wally Homitz was president then, and he believed that traditional methods were failing with our students, so we should try new ones. "If they don't work, we'll change them." He practised his preaching, team-teaching hare-brained multi-media and touchy-feely courses that had huge drop-out rates.

And so did we all. Our students showed us what worked by sticking around, or what didn't work by leaving. We shared what worked with each other, and for the most part, listened to each other. When things went badly, we just didn't say much about it. As soon as possible we tried something else.

Homitz was an articulate and inspiring president. His short and somewhat tempestuous term left a permanent mark on the teachers at Laney. I am grateful for his brilliant if somewhat erratic leadership.

Our students were generous and patient with us while we learned. We wasted the time of many of them, and I'm sorry about that. I comfort

myself with the thought that I don't know of any other school where they
would have done better, and perhaps they wouldn't have done so well.

We understood early that most of our students were not traditional
students in the academic sense, but as Theodore Gross observed in the
Saturday Review, the parents of the next generation of academic students.
Unlike him and his colleagues at CUNY, we never considered the possibility that teaching them was not worth while.

The political climate of the area and the time added to the urgency of
our job. People talked of revolution all the time, inside and outside our
classes. The faculty went on strike. Someone pulled a knife on the president. One of our commencement speakers showed up in dark glasses, his
mortarboard at a rakish angle, so stoned that he couldn't come to the end
of a sentence, much less to the end of his speech. In spite of all this, we
doubted that any revolution would come. Our students wanted to make it,
to succeed in the good old traditional American ways, and I came to feel
that the decision had to be theirs. I decided that I would teach anything
that they wanted to know, and if I didn't know how, I'd try to find out.

We never reached agreement. About half the department still teaches
traditionally structured academic composition. About half of us use some
variation on the approach described here, with many individual adapta-
tions. I think this diversity has been a great strength. It gives our students
a choice, and maintains our freedom to go on changing as we feel the need.

Developmental Sequence in Composition

In composition classes, and in writing centers particularly, we often
assume that the sequence of development is sentence-paragraph-essay.
If the student can't write a successful essay, we have him write a paragraph.
If he can't manage that, we teach him the sentence. If he can't do that, we
teach the period, the comma, and maybe the semicolon, and this study is
a great weariness of the flesh. I don't believe that this imagined sequence
is real. These steps backward become lobster traps that open only one
way, so that we never work our way back to writing about important things.
The result is often what my colleague Marlene Griffith describes as
"fragmenting the skill and isolating the student."

We stumbled upon a developmental sequence in teaching remedial students at Laney which was already known to teachers of learning disabled
children. The developmental sequence in language use is listening-speak-
ing-reading-writing.

Reading remediation was the first priority. At first, this was less because
of any developmental theory than because of the extreme disability non-
readers suffer in our society. Not being able to read is almost as devastating
as not being able to walk. Not being able to write is less crippling. Now,
our experience confirms the finding that reading precedes writing, and
that remediation in writing will be limited unless remediation in reading
precedes or accompanies it.

Free Writing

The next sequence is that fluency in writing precedes form and correctness. Many of our students, intelligent adults with adequate reading skills, have simply never had the experience of transferring their perfectly good oral skills and ideas into writing.

A colleague wandered into a bookstore one day and happened to find a copy of Ken Macrorie's *Uptaught.* He began to experiment with free writing techniques in his classes and was soon button-holing us in the hall and making us listen to the remarkable essays he was getting from his students. We finally listened; and indeed, they were good, much better than the essays I was getting about the causes of the Viet Nam war and the pros and cons of smoking marijuana. (That's what passed for relevance in those days.)

Free writing enables the students to use the skills they already have in narration and description and persuasion to achieve fluency. Gradually, we learned from our students that fluency can and must be taught.

For the first two weeks of class, or longer if necessary, ten or fifteen minutes of each class are set aside for free writing:

> I'm going to give you ten minutes to write. Write whatever comes into your mind that you're willing to share with the people in the class. If you decide you don't want to share it, put a note at the top and I'll see that it's confidential. If nothing comes into your mind, write "Nothing comes into my mind," but keep the pencil moving. Try to cover a full page of paper in ten minutes.

From the beginning, these free writings produce interesting fragments. The fragments are used in class as examples of good writing: images, metaphors, descriptions, whatever turns up. Most of them will look like this:

> Today is a good day. I'm going to try to get a job today. I'm praying to God that I get one. I really need one. I'm tired of bumming off of my dad.
>
> Everything today so far is going good.
>
> I'm bored with my Psych. class. I'm learning a lot in every other class. I think I'll drop my class. Is all I need is a job and a car, and then I'll be the happiest person in the world.
>
> I'm hungry and tired. My hair is dirty. I need to take a shower. I want to go home and start on the job hunting. I feel it in my bones, I'm definitely going to get a job!

Once in a while, something like this will turn up:

> You told us we might mess the paper up a little, bend the corners and it might get smaller. I know the feeling of a big sheet of

paper, but all I've ever done is put paint on them. And for me to put the small end of this pencil to a sheet of note book paper is something I've not done many times. When you said something about ideas & words coming out of you like water from a faucet. The words come to mind of what would an artist do if paint was flowing from those faucets full force and he had twenty foot canvases stacked in front of him as I do these small sheet of 8½ × 11 green lined paper. When the paint starts to run and drip in to the shape and forms he want's how will he stop all the shapes from running in to each other? How will I know when I've read enough books, worked out enough paper for English class? What I really want to know is will I be able to stop the shapes from running together? And when will I know it's time?

As the good fragments turn up, they can be dittoed or put on transparencies. We discuss the fragments, asking, "What makes this sentence good?" "Why does this description work so well?"

At the same time, we study student models of good writing, fragments as well as some short pieces. The example above is by Tim Sutherland, and appears in Myrna Harrison's *On Our Own Terms,* a collection of student writing from Laney published with all the warts. These examples of brilliant fragments don't seem out of reach of the students, and the experiences described are familiar to them. I would suggest that each teacher collect his or her own student models, for it is important that the students be able to identify with the writers.

Using the models, we begin to work on what I call the *horribles.* These are the three or four most serious errors that make a paper look illiterate. They must vary from school to school, but at Laney, they are 1) lack of indication of paragraphs, 2) random use of capital letters, and 3) run-ons and comma splices. We practice editing the models to correct these errors, first as a group, then individually, moving to exercises from a handbook. I like *Grassroots* (Houghton Mifflin) because it is straightforwardly written and offers three levels of difficulty in the exercises: fill in the blanks, complete the sentences, then generate your own sentences.

We deal with these errors carefully and introduce them *one at a time.* No correction is made, nor are errors indicated on the class members' writing. Instead, we use models and exercises. If students begin spontaneously to correct their own errors, and some will, that's well and good. But the emphasis of teaching is still *fluency,* particularly in the free writings.

Now for two weeks students have been doing regular free writings. We collect and keep these in individual folders in the Writing Center. The instructor reads them all and writes *only* positive comments to identify strong or interesting passages. At the end of that time, we go through the free writings and select subjects for focused free writings.

Focused Free Writings

The next step is longer papers, two or three pages, in which we ask the student to write freely whatever comes to mind on the chosen subject. The subject should emerge from the free writings and should be mutually agreeable to the student and the instructor. We look for passages that are interesting, that seem to have some spontaneity and energy behind them. If we narrow it down too much, the student has to write about something that doesn't interest him or that is emotionally threatening. We give him at least three choices. We might say, "Tell me more about your older brother,"or "Did you get the job you were looking for? If you did, what's it like working there?" "You describe Puerto Rico very vividly. Can you describe a special place, or tell an incident that happened there?"

A word here on the subjects. Advanced students will spontaneously write in a variety of modes: description, analysis, exposition. But the usual developmental sequence for genuinely remedial students is more like this: description-narration-dialogue-argumentation. Our first aim is still fluency, and it's important to begin with the student's spontaneous modes. If we require her to write arguments or exposition, her fluency will suffer, as will her form and correctness. Look at this example of a student's fluent and competent use of narration:

"BIG TRIP"

It was April, 1970. I was in the hospital. I didn't want to be there, but my mother and doctor insisted. Lying in the bed, I thought of the horrible procedures one goes through having an operation. Of course it was my imagination, my mother told me, but I had a good one.

It was 9:55 a.m. The nurse came in to prepare me for this horrible journey of intoxicated sleep. She assured me that the anesthetic would be a pleasant one, and it would soon be over, as she gave me the shot of anesthetic in my right arm. Going down the hall, the nurse had realized that the local anesthetic was given to me in the wrong location, so she had to give me another one, which was in my hip. "Oh no, I'll never wake up," I said to myself.

In front of the operating room, I commenced to sleep. GREEN, BLUE, and YELLOW monsters were floating in my head. It was frightening. My eyes opened instantly, and my heart was pounding. The hallucinations felt like an L.S.D. trip.

By the time I was in the operating chair, it felt as though the anesthetic had worn off. The doctor came in a gave me a shot of novocaine. My head and throat felt swollen. It was as though someone had pumped helium into my head, and I would float out of the chair. My throat was dry. Hot flashes went through my body. I couldn't swallow. More hallucinations. I wanted my mother.

"I see you're ready," said the doctor. When I looked into his face, it was a big balloon face. He looked funny, but scary. I became frightened when he approached my throat with a pair of surgical scissors. I began choking. "DON'T COUGH," said the doctor. I was strangling with blood. I could hear the scissors ripping at my throat. It sounded like cutting of paper. Finally I could breathe when the doctor removed my tonsils.

Going back to my room, I saw my mother. The only thing I remember telling her was, "Mother, they didn't put me to sleep."

The End

Things go along more easily if we make sure students have gained fluency in description and narration before asking them to do more academic writing. Neglecting this sequence may result in a defeat which neither student nor teacher can afford.

We collected two or three focused free writings, allowing time in class to write at least one of them. They look something like this:

I wish I could get this dumb silly paper over with, I've been working on it for four days now, and I still can't bring myself to stick to one thing. What my teacher dosen't seem to realize is that it's pretty hard to just sit down and start writing a paper, tunning out everything. That maybe I didn't have time to eat breakfast before classes, or the last problem Mr. B____ "threw out" five minutes before the end of class has got me "spaced-out" and feeling more lost than I was when I first came in class. Or when I'm really getting started on my paper, really getting in deep into my thoughts, finally, finally I can think of an idea to start *a paragraph,* then comes your sister (who's in the same class as I am), who starts gapping about "how good that chinese rice was yesterday" and about "that cute guy" she met on her last spoon of egg noodles simmering in soy sauce (or something) completely wipping out all previous thought of my "great idea" for my paper. And all I could think of than then was is taking a big bowl of chinese rice, and smearing it all over that big three page paper she's just finishing.

But don't get me wrong though, really people I digs this class. When I first came into the Writing Center I knew it would be a new experience for me. I mean, the teacher and tutors are really concerned in developing our best points in English, and really helping students to gather their thoughts and putting them down on paper. To help students cut down on a paper that is really too long without explaining anything, or (as in my case) to help you lengthen a paper that is to short.

I don't know though. I've always had this problem. I could talk and talk and talk about a certain subject and have people begging me to shut up. But let a teacher ask me write a paper (A paper I don't think I've ever wrote a paper before "Thats a shame") But just let a teacher ask me to write a paper on my views on Freud's Theory of Psychoanylisis. I can't even write a paper on my views of "The Daily Adventures of Popeye the Sailor" something I watch daily. I mean I really freeze up. My mind turns completely off. But now I'm becoming a little more relaxed in the class. I can think a little more freely now because I know I'm not alone. There are lots of people in this class with writing problems somewhat similar if not the same as mine. And I no longer feel "shy" about trying to write a paper. If it dosen't look right to my tutor, he discusses it with me and tells me what he thinks would help my paper, and helps me think more into what I am trying to write about. Without just slapping a "C" or "D" grade and telling me to write something else. Something I've experienced in my earlier years of school.

Form: The First Draft

The next stage is a draft of the final essay. The student chooses the focused free writing he thinks is most promising, and the instructor reads it, asking very specific questions for development. "Describe your brother. What does he look like? How does he talk? Tell some more incidents involving him that show what he's like." "What color was the car? What did the upholstery look like? How did it sound when it was running?"

We want the student to do several things at this level:

1. Organize the essay.
2. Develop it, giving it details, description, and dialogue. One of the tutors says, "Make it 3D." To elicit this development, we must ask specifically for what we want. "Describe this." "Tell what he said then."
3. Take out the major errors. The student should indicate paragraphs, check use of capital letters, and eliminate run-ons and comma splices.

For many students, this is asking a lot at once. We give class time for writing this draft, expecting to work individually with people who are revising their focused free writing. As the semester goes on, they need less help.

The Sequence

We try to get a variety of writing from the students, something like this:

1. Description of a person
2. Description of a place
3. Incident

    4. Dialogue
    5. Case history (narration used as argument)

If the student spontaneously produces other kinds of writing—argument, exposition, or analysis—I certainly accept it instead of any of the above. But most remedial students produce narration and description. We don't rush them. For dialogue, Macrorie's chapter in *Telling Writing* is useful, as are student models. The case history is usually last and is a nudge in the direction of argumentation. Typical papers are narratives used in arguments: a thesis like "The marijuana laws are too severe" illustrated by a narrative describing the experience of an acquaintance who was thrown in prison for seven years for possession of a joint; "Social Security payments are not enough to enable elderly people to live with dignity" illustrated by the experiences of an acquaintance on Social Security.

The student brings five of his focused free writings up to this level. So far, the major emphasis has been fluency but now we introduce the idea of form, and begin to work a little on correction of major errors. When a draft is completed, it goes into the folder for further work at the end of the semester, when the focus shifts to correctness.

Grading

About this time (after Easter in the spring semester), we make the move from fluency and form to tightening and correcting. For the first time, I grade the papers. If things are going well, most drafts will be worth a C+.

"This is one of your five good papers for the semester," I say. "So far, it's a good C. If you want a higher grade, tighten it and correct the minor errors."

Final Revisions

We spend a week on tightening, using student papers which have been duplicated or put on transparencies. Work on grammar, punctuation, and spelling is largely individual, concentrating on a student's errors one or two at a time. Perhaps he has agreement problems or faulty tense endings. He works on those two problems in an exercise book. I point out where they occur in the paper, and he revises.

Some students with many errors and much determination may do yet another draft to remove misplaced commas and to correct spelling. Some students will be satisfied with the C. Generally, students do at least three versions of each paper: free writing, focused free writing, and revision. Many students do four drafts, and some do all five. As they develop as writers, the required number of revisions decreases. Here is a typical "fair copy."

    Taco Bell was the first and only job I ever had. My first day
    was the most horrible thing I could have ever gone through. As
    I walked into the back door the whole place smelled of tacos.

burritos, and every Taco Bell product there was. I didn't know anyone that worked there. I was alone and nervous. I came in ten minutes before I was to start, which is one of the many rules at Taco Bell. I sat down on a chair in the back, and when a fast ten minutes went buy, Lupe, the manager, told me to go up front.

A girl named Anna started teaching me how to make the food. There was so much to learn. How much beans to put on a burrito; how much meat to put on a taco; how much cheese and onions to put on the burrito, and how much cheese and lettuce to put on a taco.

After she went through telling me how to make every item, she made me go through it. It took a lot of correcting on her part, until I did it satisfactorily.

Anna then asked me to clean the door windows. I took my time hoping the time would pass faster.

Next she had me sweeping the floor in the front. She told me to get underneath all the cabinets. I went at it, sweeping clear under the cabinets; unfortunately I wasn't paying attention, and as I came up with the broom from sweeping under the cabinets, I heard a scream from one of the girls. To my surprise and the girl's, I had accidentally brought the broom handle right up under her dress. She happened to be taking an order at the time. She just looked at me, and I looked at her. I must have said "I'm sorry" a hundred times. I don't think she ever forgave me.

From that first day on, I was practically the only one who ever swept the floor. The broomstick incident was only the first of many.

I finally was introduced to everyone, mostly by them coming up to me and asking what my name was, and giving theirs in return. I got along nicely with everyone except Pam, the girl I broomsticked to death. I started joking around with everyone, when the managers weren't around, just to make my job easier. I ended up being known as a clown.

I was almost done for the day, when Anna asked me to do one more thing. I was to put some more ice into a square hole in the drink area. To do this, I had to take this big plastic scooper and scoop the ice cubes into the square. Of course, I'm not good at doing something for the first time and doing it right. I unfortunately didn't realize how heavy the ice was, so I accidentally dropped the ice cubes on the floor, but luckily none of the girls slipped and fell on them, except me. I didn't fall though.

Finally my three hours were up, and I knew that from this day on, this job was not going to be easy. I also knew that until I learned how to do everything at Taco Bell, everyone was going to order me around and get the best of me. I knew that if the girls kept ordering me around, I wouldn't be able to stand it, but there was nothing I could do about it. I was a newcomer, destined to be a newcomer for the next 9 months I worked there.

Publication

One of the great technological advantages we have is the ability to reproduce student writing easily. Photocopying is ideal, but if it's too costly or not available, dittos or transparencies will do. These enable the students to have a real audience, the class members, and not just the teacher. People enjoy each other's work and take it seriously. The writer, then, begins to take her own work more seriously.

We publish many papers, from many different students. The major criterion for selection is the intrinsic interest of the piece, not correctness. That comes later.

If at all possible, we collect one good piece from each student and put them in magazine form before the end of the semester. We make just enough copies for the class and a few extra for our own collection of student models.

Thanks to a grant from Lawrence Davis, the president at Laney, we publish three issues annually of a magazine of faculty and student writing called *Goodnews*. We regularly include samples of good writing from the remedial classes as well as from the advanced students. The following paper was written in the Writing Center by a basic writing student who had never written a "real paper" before. He was convinced that he couldn't write and unhappy with his attempt, so he turned it in to his instructor crumpled into a ball. Here is the final version which was published in *Goodnews:*

MY FATHER—THE MAN AND HIS WORK
by Bernard Peyton

We lived in a small farming community in northern Mississippi, and with the exception of a small sawmill in the area, and of course housework for the women, farming was the only work open to blacks in the nineteen fiftys.

My father chose not to be a farmer unlike his father before him; instead he chose to leave home at a very early age to go to work in a lumber camp, and he made that his life's work. My father was a big man who stood over seven feet and weighed well over three hundred pounds. His personality had two extremes. He could be the gentle giant that he was to me, the youngest of his ten children. He loved dogs and mules. Mules came first for they were his work. His philosophy was, "A logger is as good as his mules; his mules are as good as he treats them." So Sam and Rusty, the two giant iron greys that he was so proud of, had no complaints, and neither did Ludy and Troy, the two black and tan hounds that he had trained since pups to be "the best damn coon dogs in Mississippi," as he'd say. Or he could be as mean and distructive as a mad grizzly, like the time a local merchant called him a liar in a dispute over the balance of a grocery bill he owed. He chased the merchant from the store and left the store in chambles.

He worked very hard and enjoyed the distinction of being the best logger in those parts. He enjoyed the beauty of the forest and did his bit to preserve it, even at a time when most thought our forest land was so vast it would last forever. He marked every tree so that it caused as little damage as possible to other trees when it fell.

Being a logger didn't offer the security of being a sharecropper, which was just another name for slavery in most cases. In winter, when the weather was bad, loggers couldn't work, creating hardships for their families. It didn't matter to farmers; after the harvest there was nothing for them to do until Spring. But even that didn't lure him from his trade. Beside the genuine satisfaction he got from his work, he felt that a man could only be a man when allowed to think for himself. So he spent his winters hunting, cutting and selling firewood, when the weather would allow it, or just sitting by the fire telling funny stories or teaching me and my brothers to sing harmony. In the winter of nineteen fifty-eight he caught pneumonia and died.

General Outline for an 18-Week Course

This is not an inflexible pattern, but just an aid to clarify the general sequence:

First week: Free writings in class, 10-15 minutes.
                Student models of effective fragments.

Second week: Free writings in class, 15 minutes.
                Discussion of samples of class members' effective fragments.

Third week: Introduction of short pieces: student models.
                Focused free writings on subjects taken from free writings, 2-3 pages each.
                Begin editing exercises from student models: paragraphing.

Fourth week: Continue focused free writings in and out of class. Try to get seven or eight.
                Publish examples of interesting focused free writings by class members and discuss what makes them effective.
                Editing exercises on student models: capitalization, comma splices and run-ons.

Fifth week:	Continue focused free writings.
	Publish interesting class papers.
	Continue editing student models: comma splices and run-ons.
Sixth, seventh, eighth weeks:	Continue pattern of fifth week.
Ninth week:	Begin revisions. Select five best focused free writings of each student. Have the student choose one. Rewrite the focused free writing, working on development, organization, and elimination of major errors. Paper is graded, and specific suggestions made if student wants to tighten and correct minor errors for a better grade.
Tenth week:	Student chooses another focused free writing for revision. Revisions are graded and the best are published for the class at large and discussed.
Eleventh, twelfth, and thirteenth weeks:	Continue pattern of tenth week.
Fourteenth week:	Some students will have completed the semester's work. They are given a final grade based on their five best papers and dismissed until the final.
	Individual work with remaining students on revisions or additional exercises for special grammatical problems.
Fifteenth, sixteenth, seventeenth weeks:	Continue pattern of fourteenth week.
Eighteenth	Final exam. In-class essay on unannounced topic. Best paper of each student is published in magazine form, distributed at the final exam.

I can hear my colleagues now objecting to all this prescriptive stuff. They are not to worry. My experience as a consultant has proved to me that teachers never do what they're told to do. Instead, they very sensibly take what they can use and change the rest. But they really do want to know exactly what it is that other people do. Well, this is what I do, more or less. Unless there's some good reason to do something different.

I heard an artist once defend the paint-by-numbers kits on the same grounds. He thought the kits were reprehensible until he discovered that very few really followed the directions. Instead, finding himself with a brush in his hand and paint on the brush, each person proceeded to make his own distinctive changes in pattern and color. Finally, most lost patience with the kits entirely and struck out on their own with blank sheets of paper. I'm convinced that the teachers will take all this careful advice equally lightly.

2. *Developing Fluency*

An Experiment in Encouraging Fluency

Miriam Ylvisaker
Oakland High School (retired)

Free Flow

The idea that when working with beginners in writing emphasis should be placed on fluency prior to concentrating on form and correctness is finding increasing acceptance. Moffett, Britton, Shaughnessy all have long pointed in this direction; moreover, a number of independently formulated presentations given at Bay Area Writing Project meetings—Marlene Griffith and Smokey Wilson from junior colleges, Keith Caldwell, Mary K. Healy, among others, at the high school level—have all testified to classroom experience which verifies the sequence: expressive to transactional or poetic; diary to journal to memoir to exposition; fluency to form to style and correctness. Labels vary, but underlying theory is similar, and evidence increasingly emerges for the soundness of writing curriculum which takes this sequence into consideration.

As anyone knows who has watched a beginning writer work, difficulties with fluency amount almost to physical disability. A student's entire energy goes into gripping the pencil, body twisted and contorted, struggling to make code marks on the page. For this student is still, no matter what age, back at an elementary level when making letters was primary; one did not think about whole words, sentences, ideas, paragraphs, pages, or coherence. Handwriting itself testifies to this. It tends to be cramped; and frequently when conferring with the teacher, the student who has not done much composing will blurt out an apology, "Yes, I need to learn to write better; it looks terrible."

While the student, especially the remedial student, may sometimes think improving writing means improving handwriting, the high school writing teacher is not ordinarily concerned with this problem. We should, of course, clear up this confusion; and we should make it clear to the students that one of our primary concerns is with helping them get sufficiently detailed discourse down on paper in a reasonable amount of time. Our concern is thus with length, to a certain degree (the direction to "write about 500 words" is not necessarily a mindless injunction); but, of more importance, our concern is with the texture of prose: we want to increase the textural density of the student's prose, to combat what Francis Christensen characterized as the pervasive thinness of adolescent prose.

The experiment described in these pages was an effort to test the assumption that setting (working conditions) and response (criticism) can be organized and shaped to encourage fluency*; specifically, that a workshop setting (where students write not only for themselves and the teacher but also for the class as audience, where what they write is published for consumption by the class, and where students read what they write to the class and solicit response) and an encouraging atmosphere (an atmosphere relatively free from negative criticism and free from the threat of grades, of "grading down") will help students increase their fluency and will improve their attitude toward writing.

This was not a formal experiment. I do not have class sets of pre and post samples of writing on comparable topics composed under carefully controlled similar conditions. Nor did I administer a standardized writing attitude inventory. And, unfortunately, I did not have access to a control group. Yet I do have evidence that should be of interest to the writing teacher: pre and post writing samples from students representative of those who demonstrated change, the students' own perceptions of how they improved and of how their attitude toward writing changed, and my observations about sound teaching practices based on the behavior of the students over a six week period.

PROCEDURE

For six weeks in an eleventh grade Writing Workshop class at Oakland High School the entire work of the class consisted of the students writing and reading aloud what they had written. A copy of each piece of writing was given to each student as soon after it was finished as was possible. In many cases this was the same day, sometimes the following day, or once in a while (when nothing at school worked and I had to use commercial photocopying) two or three days following. I urged students to use dittos, a practice which prompted them to write a rough draft before preparing the ditto master. (Now and then students rebelled against composing on a ditto master—"It's too much *trouble!*" Then I simply photocopied, as I did when someone wrote something of exceptional length or wanted to include something from a journal or something written where no stencils were available.)

For the first few days at the beginning of each period I placed the stacks of students' writings on a large table and the writer distributed copies to each person; then we read aloud. However, as students began to work at their own rate and pace, it was not possible to be systematic about this. The student distribution process was often chaotic, but it served as a helpful step, because once a student had given a copy of her writing to each person in the room the next step—reading it to the class—became less formidable.

---

*I use the term fluency to include not only the notion of measurement (sheer bulk, length of sentences, and frequency of syntactic constructions) but also the notion of variety of forms (e.g., monologue, dialogue, narrative, reminiscence, diary, interview).

At first, reading aloud was structured rather formally. We sat in a circle; there were shy pauses, nervous giggles; one or two said they couldn't read but a friend would read for them. Within a few days everyone was willing to read aloud. Although I tried to confine reading time to the beginning of the period and leave the rest of the time uninterrupted for writing, students often, as they finished, asked to go to the ditto room, then returned to class, passed out their papers and read them aloud. This immediacy, this urgency, encouraged others to do the same. Each reader was asked to write a comment on each piece of writing, and to sign his name or initials. All copies, with comments, were then returned to the author.

No minimum or maximum number of pages or writings was assigned. I told students that, since it was near the end of the semester, I knew them and their capabilities well; hard work would earn high grades. We made a huge chart for one wall; next to their names students filled in a title and date for each piece of writing as they completed it.

Each Monday I distributed what came to be known as "the week sheet" —writing topic choices, primarily personal experience topics of the sort that lend themselves to anecdotal writing or opinion topics on controversial issues—things that would be interesting to read aloud and which might prompt discussion. I also kept a file box of additional topics and occasionally asked students to write topics on 3 × 5 cards and add them to the box; sometimes we read short stories or saw films for ideas; school events generated material. At all times students were encouraged to write about whatever they wished in whatever form they wished, not limiting themselves to the choices and suggestions made for them.

And finally, materials. Operating out of my own recollected childhood joy in a new pencil box full of pencils, a brand new clean lined tablet, I tried, within our limits, to provide luxury. There was a typewriter in the room, cards of different sizes, felt-tipped colored pens. If a kid forgot a pencil I gave her one and didn't try to remember to get it back. Someone gave me a gross of pencils (with erasers!); a friend got me 60 ballpoint pens for 40¢ a dozen from Arden's in Los Angeles; there was plenty of paper, lined and unlined; we were rich.

THE STUDENTS, THE CONTEXT

At Oakland High School, Writing Workshop is a non-college preparatory elective. For almost a third of the class English was a second language. Absenteeism—brief, longterm, gone-on-Fridays, absent-when-it-rains— was chronic and endemic; and school was interrupted by a nine-day teacher strike in mid-semester; this was followed by a strike of the AC Transit bus drivers. Class enrollment was 37; daily attendance averaged 25.

About half of the class signed up for it because they wanted to; the other half was made up of students who, not having shown up for programming or registration, were placed in the class—much against their wishes, as a few made clear—by their counselors. Although no students wrote really well, there were three or four who wrote freely, and should have been in a more advanced class but for scheduling reasons were forced to remain.

The writing problems in the class were extensive: from the crippling lack of control of English syntax and idiom exhibited by the English as a Second Language students to the uncertainties about sentence sense (run-ons, comma splices, fragments) and about the conventions of Standard Written English (e.g., agreement, case, spelling, punctuation, capitalization) typical of the basic writing student. The following short piece, by a boy from Viet Nam, is characteristic of the ESL students' work.*

> Shopping, friend, play, spend money. They are all I like very much. Usually I spend a lot of money when I find it in my hand. My mother doesn't want to do that, she alway sad about me. But I don't care what she said I just keep going what I like in my mind that is spend money, be nice with everyone but in one day, the sky is dark, the birds stop singing. That is the day I feel said and unhappy, because my money done, and my friends far away from me.

A second example, a short narrative, is typical of the lower-middle range of the class. An event clearly moves from beginning through middle to end, but the account is sparse in detail, not fleshed out. The sentences are short and choppy, and there are many errors.

> One night Around the corner The police and the black panther was having a shoot out. I was looking throw my window and I called my brother and sister they came and look to. The next day me and my friends went in the house where the police shot up and we left out a man was throwing bricks at people cars. The police came and took him to jail. About a week later Some men came and fixed the house back up. Then some more people moved in the house.

A third example, perhaps not so prone to error, illustrates again the lack of detail, the thinness, the barrenness characteristic of these students' writing.

> I feel that dating is alright. There's nothing wrong with it. Some parents think it's to early for their baby girls, as they think of us, to be dating. Young men and women these days are at the age of

---

*In some cases I have edited student writings to make them shorter; in all cases, however, I have kept the original punctuation, spelling and sentence structure.

15 and 16 years old when they really start dating. You can learn where you make your mistakes. Parents have to open their eyes sometimes too. Some parents don't feel your old enough, but after they find out that you are going to do a certain something anyway they go ahead and let you. I'm talking about dating. Dating you learn how to communicate with one another etc. It kind of makes me feel like a lady. Which I know I am.

WHAT HAPPENED: THREE STUDENTS

It would be gratifying to be able to report a miraculous turn-around of the entire class; that of course did not occur. At the end of six weeks those who wrote badly still did not write well, those who messed around still did so, and those who cut a lot still absented themselves. However, certain benefits did emerge, some immediately, some more slowly, and some only in retrospect.

One immediate subjective result was that the class, for me, became easier and more fun. Released from the necessity of specific day-to-day planning and free of the clerical and physical burdens that juggling several student activities per period requires, I was able to spend my entire energy and the entire class time helping students in whatever ways seemed appropriate. For the most part the routine—reading aloud, then writing—took care of itself. It was perfectly obvious when student papers were passed out that reading came next, and throughout the six weeks student interest in what was on the pages and a kind of joking good humor toward the writer prevailed. It was not necessary for me to give instructions, set tone, or maintain discipline; these things came about naturally, in a spontaneous and organic way.

I have selected the work of three students as representative of some of the changes that came about. The first student illustrates a basic change, one achieved by most of the regularly attending students: the ability and willingness to write more, to put in the details, the specifics that would make the tale or incident interesting to the class. The second student illustrates a different kind of change (one evidently begun considerably before enrolling in Writing Workshop): a willingness to compose in many forms, a releasing of a sense of drama, of a storytelling sense that shows imaginative promise. I include the work of the third student because it perplexes me somewhat. The student's output of words obviously increased; the sheer flow of his words became a force to be reckoned with. Yet what the flow reveals is a nascent pulp fiction writer, obviously weaned on the cardboard characters and predictable situations of popular culture.

Student A: This student made progress in three ways—his writings became longer, he made fewer errors, and his sentences more closely approximated the rhythms of his speech. A remedial student who had been transferred out of a regular tenth grade class and been placed into a reading class

which was rowdy and inattentive ("We didn't do nothin."), he was now, in eleventh grade, ready, in a sense, to make up for lost time. He was on both the varsity football and basketball teams and was beginning to think about college and scholarship possibilities.

This piece of writing is from the beginning of the six week period:

> During the strike I didn't do to much my usul rutine was. I would get up at about evleven oc'clock and come up to school for I would see when was practice. Every-day the coach would tell us to come to the pikett line to see when we have practic or just ask around. After I find out I would just sit on the bench outside and wast some time by just sitting around and talking. Cause we would have to meet at the school for we could go up to practice. I would come home and proble study a little and get in front of the T.V.

This account of activities is characterized by a thinness of detail (a reliance on summarizing action rather than showing it), by repetitiousness (notice how many times "practice" is referred to), by an uncertainty in spelling, and by a certain awkwardness (e.g., the clumsy "for I would see") not apparent in the student's speech. In contrast, the sentences in the next excerpt, written toward the end of the experiment, are less constrained; the piece itself is longer (one and a half pages as compared with half a page); spelling errors are not as frequent; and there is considerably more detail, indicative of an increased awareness of audience.

> When I was ten years old I played on this football team and we use to have practice after school and games on Saturday. We use to practice at fruitvale field. On are way home we would walk down the hills and catch the fifty three bus from Colige Ave. We would ride the bus all the way down to East 14th. Sometimes we would get off on foothill. We would only do this when we had some money. We would go and buy some Chinese rice and maybe something else if we had enough money. Well let's get to the good part. We got off of the fifty three bus and was waiting for a eighty going toward East Oakland. While we were waiting for the bus everybody was walking around trying to find something to do. And one of the people that was with us just happened to go down to the end of the corner by this bar. Then a couple more went down there and they just happened to look in and see some instruments. First one person when in and then everybody went on and got a instrument and started to play for a minute and then everybody ran out of the place. We did again and again and someone called the Police and they came and caught three of us. They put them in the police car and said they was going to take them down town. I was not one of the three to get caught but they told me

that the police just took them around the corner and talk to them.
And let them out.

At first Student A would ask only me for help in his proof-reading.
He always wrote a rough draft and would bring it to me when everyone
else in the class was busy (and unobserving of him) and ask me to point
out errors. I underlined, he fixed those he could (on his own or with a
dictionary), and then I looked at the paper again and told him where the
problem lay with whatever errors he had not been able to correct. Then
he wrote a clean draft. This was not a procedure I imposed on him; he
initiated it. Later he became freer about asking for help, requesting aid
from students as well as from me, "How do you spell it? How does this
sound?" he would ask; sometimes he would take the suggestions, but
occasionally I heard him say, "No, my way sounds better." Everything he
wrote was related in some way or other to sports.

Student B: This student experimented with a wide variety of forms: error
count diminished during this period. She perceived the Writing Workshop
class as one in a recent series of English classroom experiences which had
improved both her skills and attitudes towards writing.

> I've never really liked to write. When I was in elementary I hated
> English, period. I hated spelling, writing, and everything related
> with English. I don't know or remember the reason for this. In
> junior high the only reason I really went to my English class is
> because I didn't know about cutting yet. I didn't know how to put
> my ideas on paper. Whenever we had spelling tests I never re-
> ceived a grade higher than a D.

She then goes on to describe two summer school English classes which
she took when her parents and a counselor became concerned about her
lack of skills; both these classes were a positive experience.

> This year, I feel I've imporved a great deal in my ability to write.
> I really like writing now and I enjoy thinking up different ideas to
> write about. I want to keep on so I can get better. Who knows,
> someday I might be a great book writer.

Among the forms which appeared in student B's work were interior
monolog, poetry, fictionalized events, dialogue/skit material, rebuses,
concrete poetry, letters, a play which she worked on with other students,
and a fable (beginning "Once there was an alligator named Otis") in which
she transformed six members of the class into animals. She herself became
a rabbit. Student A became "the dancing bear" and, after a series of
changes, Otis achieved his goal of becoming "humble, shy, happy, and a

vegetarian." Ideas for some of these projects came from the writing topics box; others no doubt carried over from previous classes; whatever the source, she almost always changed or adapted the topic to her own wishes and purpose.

In her journal she developed a form which began with a single sentence set separately on the page, followed by the page or so of writing which the sentence evoked, as in this sample:

> "I love you.
>
> "I love you," he says. "I love you and I'll do anything I can do for you. I'll lie for you, I cheat for you, I'll steal for you, I'll even kill for you. I love you." "How can you love me if you would do all the wrong things for me, you don't love me. If you would steal for me, you don't love me. I wouldn't do any of those things for you, but I love you. I love myself more but I love you."
>
> Theres so many things on my mind. School and this boy are the main things. I really want to do good in school. Its hard some-times to stick to the things that are good for you. Some how the bad things seem to pull you away."

The next semester this student took Intermediate Composition, a university preparatory class, and earned a grade of B.

Student C: This student was a hyperactive, maverick type of kid who wrote only brief sentences or not at all when the semester began; I nagged, he joked. After the strike this piece of writing (which he read aloud, auto-matically correcting errors as he read) met with great approval from the class:

> Well It was very boring and there was nothing to do except cut and go home or harass the subs or just go get high or go down to the movies. And another thing would be to go home were were you like. And another thing that I did not like was that allmost all the subs just sat on their ass and did not teach anyone and the rest of the day was just very very dead and there were not good looking subs anyway. (illustrated with two stick figures carrying picket signs: teachers on strike)

Student C's handwriting was terrible. Then he began typing, but his typing was atrocious too. The next piece of writing, reproduced in full and exactly as typed, was greeted with comments and groans when Student C passed it out. "I can't read this;" "This is all messed up."

3 57 magnums

#$#$####$#################

IT all started at a wild party quton a yacth. there was a lot of people dancing talking and other people just getting drunk. AT about 2:00 am everybody was slowing down all the drunks were sound asleep everybody else was just re laxing and enjoying the night. WHITCHwas a coolbrezi#i#n a hot night as I walked over a copule who were laydown on the steeps I smiled IT had been a long night and it was time to go to bed but as I walked to my cabin I herd two men talking and it sounded as if one of#them wanted to kill a man so Inatura ly took a look through# the door witch was part way open.THE room was d ark and there was just a night light on and Iherd this clicking and poping sound. AND as Iwent to take a closer look I soon saw what was making the noise it s was a m an and he was holding two #### 357 ma gnums one of the worlds most powerful hand guns. WELL, I did not stick a round so I went to my cabin a nd my hart was beating very hardand I thought it would burst .WHEN I got two my room I called the captain and he told me he was going to send someone down right wa y Ifelt axs asmall relife then there was a knock on my door I went to go and open it and it was the man I saw in the dark. HE smiled in a evilway and shut the door and he slowly pulled out a 357 and Istarted to sweat and then he pulled ba ck the hammerand...357.

As soon as he began reading "It all started at a wild party..." he had total attention. Students laughed aloud about the drunks and the couple lying on the steps, but when he got to the clicking and popping of the handguns the mood was tense, and at the end of his reading there were disgruntled responses: "You can't just end it there." "What happens next?" "Did you write this yourself?" "It sounds like Chapter One of a book."

Though popular with the class, neither piece of writing was one that I felt I could respond to with genuine enthusiasm. The second one particularly was so derivative that I said nothing at all. So, if it had not been for the reading aloud, Student C could not have received the feedback, much of it positive, which he did.

At this point Student C stopped coming to class. When he reappeared after two weeks he came up to me waving his journal. "Look," he said, "I've got some more chapters. I wrote them while I was in the hospital." I looked, and indeed there they were—chapters with titles such as "The Friend," "The Street," "The Hustle"—conversation, description, event, all together in one enormous thirty-page unpunctuated paragraph.

About this time students in writing classes at Oakland High School were asked to submit statements describing their own writing processes for inclusion in a booklet to give to Alex Haley, who was coming to Oakland as part of a Scholar in Residence program. I asked Student C if he could describe how he went about writing his book (I think I wondered whether he had really done it himself) and he said, sure, he could do that.

> "My name is.... and I am writing ꭓꭓꭓꭓ a book and its called 357 Magnums. I know that there are things that I can not do and then there are things I know for sure that I can do. Such as the book that I'm writing I had a lot of problem with the charters and the places that they are spose to be at such as a man in hollywood who is a young cop. Or a young boy from New York who's parents die in a auto crash. Sooner or later it comes to me I don't know how but it does.
>
> In my story I have two young men who are plice officers and they live in Los Angles. And I hardly know anything about L.A. but I Just ꭓꭓꭓ love to use other lucocations no matter where it is. And I like to write exciting things so that they would seem real and not so fake. I sort of learned how to write my book by reading about a real life thing. And asking people who were there or do that certain thing or can.

In the course evaluation that students filled out at the end of the semester Student C made the following assessments:

Evaluate your writing now as compared with the beginning of this class:			
	Less	Same	Better
Ability to organize ideas			√
Ability to express feeling in writing			√
Ability to get ideas for what you want to say		√	
Your knowledge of vocabulary		√	
Your knowledge of sentence structure			√
Your knowledge of spelling			√
Your over-all self-confidence about writing			√ √ √

In the comment section he wrote: "I started a book in this class and I probly would have never done that at home or anywhere else. I like this class and I hope you keep it the same way always."

I would agree with Student C's self-assessment that his organization, spelling, and sentence structure improved somewhat, though in my judgment improvement was not great. The significant gain, however, is in his self-confidence, evidenced by his willingness to start a book and his manifest pride in the undertaking. Symptomatic of this change, perhaps, was a concomitant improvement in his handwriting: his words became legible, the letters larger, more carefully formed, clearer—as if for the first time he wanted what he had written to be read.

IN RETROSPECT

Forty percent of those regularly attending the class (ten students) elected (from among eight to ten other possibilities) to take another writing course the next semester. Eight chose Intermediate Composition and two took Creative Writing, both college preparatory classes. This evidence of the students' continuing interest in writing and the following summary of their course evaluations indicate that the structure of the course (more specifically, of the last six weeks of the course) did indeed have a positive influence on the students' skills and attitudes.

QUESTIONNAIRE *Evaluate your writing now as compared with the beginning of this course:*	Less	Same	Better
Ability to organize ideas		7	17
Ability to express feelings in writing		6	16
Ability to get ideas for what you want to say		8	14
Your knowledge of vocabulary		12	9
Your knowledge of sentence structure		11	10
Your knowledge of spelling		10	11
Your overall self-confidence about writing	1	8	14
Evaluate this class	Not at all	Some-what	Very
Do you think making copies of students' writing is useful?	3	12	10
Do you think having students read aloud their writing is useful?	1	5	18
How much did you enjoy this class?	1	11	10
How useful do you consider this class?		5	15

The experiment allowed certain inductive discoveries to take place, some by the teacher, some by students, some jointly.
- Once again, I realized that student discovery of error is more effective than teacher correction because it leads to the habit of revision.
- The discovery of the considerable variety of writings to emerge from

a single class was a revelation to students; and who wrote what was sometimes also revealing: the quiet girl, who wrote funny stories; the kid who
never said anything, who wrote long technical descriptions of what he
needed to learn before he could become an astronaut; the girl dressed like
a model, who wrote about childhood poverty.

• The students discovered (and I reaffirmed) the importance of questions
in critiquing writing. Students soon develop the ability to ask, when confronted with a confusing piece of writing, appropriate questions, questions
that will help the writer clarify what is not clear.

• The students recognized that writing itself is a process of discovery,
that the writer often finds out what he thinks as he writes.

Most important of all, the class procedures allowed the students to
experience, in a fairly realistic way, some of the important stages in the
writing process and, moreover, allowed me to reinforce and validate those
experiences, to connect them with the similar experiences of professional
writers. Students struggled with "what to write," saw others writing and
struggling, experienced the elation of finishing and the urgency of wanting
someone else to read what they had written.

From a student journal (describing the process of trying to write a skit):

> That day in class we were trying to get our act together but we
> couldn't think of anything, so that night when I went home I went
> in my room and sat on the bed and thought to myself. I still
> couldn't come up with anything. So I got up the next morning at
> 4:00 and turned on the radio and I just started writing and I didn't
> want to stop. I was so proud of myself, even though I left out a
> few words."

From the same journal, a note to me:

> I would like for you to get me started on that what I wrote about
> combining music and writing together. I know I can do it but I
> need a start. Or if you know someone who can get me started.
> Look around there's a lot to write about if you're serious about
> writing.

I didn't tell the students they were excellent writers, nor did they
necessarily come to think of themselves as excellent writers, but they did
come to see writing as another possible pleasurable human activity that
they not only might but could practice.

And finally, in retrospect, although I didn't notice it at the time, the
class did become a community. "We're a family," I remember a student
saying about the group at his table. The students, like members of a family,
had their squabbles, their rivalries, but they did help each other; they
cared what happened.

Writing for the Inexperienced Writer:

FLUENCY SHAPE CORRECTNESS

Marlene Griffith
Laney College, Oakland

FOR THE INEXPERIENCED WRITER it is important first to develop fluency, then to move from fluency to shape to correctness. To help and not hinder this process, the strategic place of the teacher/reader is between the writer and the piece of paper as partner, not between the piece of paper and a presumed audience as critic. By fluency, I mean the ability to write down one's observations or thoughts or feelings, to think out loud on paper.* By shape, I mean structure, form, organization, whether this be of the piece as a whole, of a paragraph, or of a sentence; it includes sentence patterns and paragraph development. By correctness, I mean such things as spelling and punctuation, the use of the "s" and the apostrophe. I am not suggesting an absolute separation of these categories; one can talk about paragraphing or organization, about the difference between "while" and "because," about periods or spelling depending upon context and need. I am suggesting that fluency is an essential prerequisite to writing, and that to help develop fluency, the teacher/reader needs initially to sit with the writer, on that side of the paper, to be a partner, not a judge, to ask for more detail, explanation, and information only when he/she really does not understand what is being said or is left hanging. In other words, the teacher/reader is interested in what the writer has to say and reads in order to understand or help the writer find what he/she has to say. This is our first function when working with inexperienced writers.

Most of what I say here I have learned from my students at Laney College, many of whom returned to school as adults who had rarely, perhaps never, "written" before. Grace, Doretha and Huey, whose work I use as examples in the following pages, came to our Writing Center, where students could write and tutors could read and we could talk to each other, usually working on a one-to-one basis. I know their work well and I print it here because it illustrates common problems of the inexperienced writer. The general principles of what is described in the following pages can be adapted to classroom or small group situations.

The goals of the following three students were similar: to write easily and well. Each, however, brought a very different set of obstacles and a different set of short-range goals. They came for a three-hour class on Thursday evenings, and none had much time for schoolwork outside the classroom.

---

*It is a phase close to what James Britton describes as the expressive mode, Janet Emig as the reflexive.

Grace, a handsome·woman in her thirties, works in a convalescent hospital and is hoping to enter the Licensed Vocational Nursing program. Asked what she hoped to accomplish at the Writing Center, she wrote, "How to take notes to spell and build a better vocabulary." The first evening she repeated that she wanted to work on spelling and punctuation. Here is her first writing, a letter of introduction:*

> My name is Grace H. H_____ .
> I like to use as a middle name my
> maden name which is H_____ .
> I work as a Nursees Aide in Walnut
> Creek. At John Muir Hospital. located
>   on Ygnacio Valley Rd.
> Ive worked the Pediatric Unite for
> Twelve years. located on the 7th floor.
> My gole is to obtain my L.V.N. Licens.
> At this point. I feel I have some
> problms. On Oct 10th Im schedule
> to go on a Toure to Iseral.
> My daughter and myself or I
> have ben planning for months.
> I'm getting very excited the
> time is aproaching very rapidly
>   to travle through the Holy Land
> have alway been my desire.
> I will leave Oakland via World air Way. Oct 10th
> there will be apperoxemy 220 other passangers
>   We will arrive in Tele-Vive
>   the following day. where we will spent the
>   night at the Sharon Hotel

After talking with a tutor, Grace wrote a second version that evening, including essentially the same material, but more connected, and indented to show three paragraphs. Lines four through six, for example, she combined to read "I work in Walnut Creek as a Nurses Aide at John Muir Memorial Hospital located in Ygnacio Valley Rd." Line ten, "At this point I feel I have some problems," she turned into an image, though perhaps a familiar one, that begins this paragraph:

> At this point I feel I am wedged
> between the rock and the hard place
> I will be leaving the class the
> first week in Oct My daughter

---

*All student work is printed as it was written, including the indentations.

and my-self will tour Israel
four fourteen days. I am getting
very excited about my trip
time is rapitly approaching iam
looking fordward to touring the
Holy Land. We are shcedule to
leave Oakland Oct 10, 77 via World
Air Way. Will arrive in Jerusalem
the following day there we will stay
at the Holy Land Hotel. We'll visit the
Dead Sea where the Scrolls were written, and
walk the shower of Sea of Galilee, too Mount
Olive, visit Jericho the oldest city in
world, and most all I will visit the tomb
where Jesus laid.

What helped Grace revise an initial list to what at least looked like a three paragraph paper isn't at all clear. The first evening of a semester is usually hectic and tutors are busy trying to get students started. The tutor who read Grace's first version may have asked for more detail, or suggested divisions, or may just have been impressed by all the information and thus been encouraging. What is clear is that Grace has notions about sentence building and paragraphing which she can use.

The second evening, she began to work with Susan, the tutor who was to work with her throughout the semester, and it emerged that one of Grace's looming obstacles was a flood of thoughts. There were so many that she found it hard to get even close to what she wanted to say or to follow any one thought. She also had no confidence in herself. Susan suggested she do some writing at home, perhaps about the trip to Israel, and noted, "We're going to work toward some security with organization and sentences."* Grace apparently followed Susan's suggestion:

For five years we been talking
about going to the Holy Land
every day I would tell my husband I would
I want to go. oh how I want to go.
I tell him I going to remodle the house,
Re do the yard Buy me furniture, buy a
car he just laugh, and say you are always

*All student work is kept in a folder that also serves as a joint and open record of the semester's work. We use the outside to record attendance, to note what the student hopes to accomplish, is working on, plans to work on next, to comment on past work. I print some of the tutor's folder entries along with Grace's work so that the reader can get a sense of the conversations that preceded and followed the writings.

going to do something. Now when are you
going to the Holy Land. for five years
we have gone through this ritural,
One sunday earyler in the year
I was sittin in Church whin the Minister
said this is your year I dont know who he
was talking to but I felt the message was
    to me. he said God is going to
bless you you will be able to do things
this year you've wanted to do for a
long time and havent been able to do
them just ask him for what you want
and start to planning, you dont have to
know where the money is coming from
just starting to planning

Now you understand the Bible say according
to (your faith be it unto you) thist Minister
dosent know me; some day I hope to meet him
and tell him how I was inspired by his message
to get back to the point. I went home
and ask my husband if he wanted to go
with me. he said so you on that kick again
I said yes, well when are you going
    I told him in Oct. of course when
he was in the Army he went to Euroup so he
said no if he would stay home and
take care of the house I could take my daughter
but what make you think you can go
what are you going to use for money I said
the money will be there. when you take that
first step of faith.
    I have wanted to go to school for a long time
but I work every day I get up in the morning
at five o'clock AM get home after four PM I felt
I just couldnt go to school it would
be too hard for, Im now going
to school three evening per week Tues, Wen, Th,
I leave work com strait to school
From 4:30 to 6:30 Tues, Th to Merritt the same day
from 7:00 to 10:00 sometime I think I meet my self
half way.
when I see Road Runner I think of myself
my time is really running out. between
my home, job, classes checking in on my
91 year old father looking after two dogs

Tutor's folder entry:

>...Grace wrote two pages on deciding to go to the Holy Land, and the
>hectic life she's leading now with work, school, home, and plans to go
>away.
>She has a nice ear for dialog so I showed her how to use quotation marks,
>both in a book and with her writing. We talked about the look of para-
>graphs; she understands the idea. She feels like she skips around though,
>that her thoughts go too fast and something comes in later when per-
>haps it belonged earlier. This perhaps relates to note taking—we might
>work on organization.

What seemed to be happening was that each idea generated another,
each detail generated another, so that Grace had clutter instead of fluency.
She felt burdened with too much to say and a need to say it all in one
writing; to narrow, focus, and develop any one idea sufficiently seemed
impossible.

This was particularly true after her return from Israel, where within a
ten-day period she had seen, experienced, and thought about much that
was new and different which we wanted to hear about. But she was
dwarfed by the material. She felt—and was—out of control. The evening
she returned after her trip, Susan was ill, and I suggested she write her
a letter and tell her about the many impressions. The tutor's absence
provided a happy accident. The letter could touch on much that was hard
to order and show many kinds of thinking; it gave Grace a familiar form
and a trusted audience.

> Dear Susan
>
>   we arrived in Israel tues afternoon
> Oct 11. entering into another country is was
> only natural we had to go through
> custom. so right away
> my daughter & I was hauled into
> security.
> my daughter was scared stiff. yonok
> the old saying where ignorent is bliss?
> I had no idea what was going on
> Security in Israle is very tight.
>   Every one we had gotten to know on
> the flight was look on whe the hauled us
> into the Security office.
> the question began.
>   For what did you come here?
>   Who did you come to see?
>   do you know any one here?

who are you with?
Are you Chathlic?
No I'm not Catholic I am Pentecostal.
eyes cast around the room what is that?

I just want to visit the Holy Land
I began to give him all of my tour
paker or scequald. I kept shuving them
in his hand.

he said oh so many papers to read.

Now after all this we didnt even open a bag.
Most of all At this time I wish to tell you about,
my mixed emotions about Israel out side
the Holy City.

there is a lot of tension between
the Arabs and Jews.
I find it very hard to under stand
why the are in const war withe each other
the Isrealies say the Arabs took their land
the Arabs say the Isrealies took their
land. I relise the has been going on
for many generation and will go on
for many more to come.
Meny American Jewes have migreated
in Israel.

But boathe the Isrealies and Arabes
give you the impression the wou lik to
leave the area. they seem to be
feed up with politic with fighting
the will do most any thing to get away.
being an out sider looking in
side you feel like they are in a
constration camp.

We visited a tirade school
very beautiful. the children live
there children with out parents, or [from broken homes]
or children from very large family
who cant afford to send there children to school.

Children go to school for free up to
age fourteen (14) there after they have to
pay so if the family cant afford send
them to school they dont get an edqucation
Every on go into the Arm at the age of eighteen (18)
But in the trad school they are
prepared for a job or college.

what ever there decision may be

I will give you more detail
about the school the the name
and whe it is supported by and
jus why I feel the way I do about
meny things you should also know
about the warm friendy side.

Tutor's folder entry:

Good return paper. Tension in Israel. Hard to write about something
you've just been through so intensely. We talked for awhile. Grace
will write some paragraph descriptions of a few of the people she
met there who gave her impressions about the tension to end off first
section. Then we will do a rewrite. Then a paper about the trade
schools "next chapter."

There is much material here for many different "papers." To develop
the possibilities, the tutor's response from this point on was almost
entirely to the information. They first talked about things in the letter
that had piqued the interest of her reader, who wanted more detail, more
information. Grace mentioned tension; Susan asked to know specifics.
This triggered conversation. Tension was conveyed by people. Again
Susan asked to know specifics.

The next writing gave a great deal of specific information on people
Grace had met, but it seemed to leave behind the idea of tension. Instead,
there is a beginning generalization about the difference between men
and women in Israel—hidden, almost lost to the reader's eye, but there.
This writing again looked chaotic, but it did not, as we had feared, lead
Grace back to the staccato, sometimes scrambled presentation of facts.
She worked this second Israel paper (following) through two more versions
and it became the stepping-stone to a main idea that surfaced from her
own experience, became focused and developed. It is all right, she learned,
to leave behind a possible topic or idea, even if half started, no matter
how promising, in order to follow another that seems to be establishing
a stronger claim.

Grace's second Israel paper:

I became very freendly with any number
Arabs and Isrealies.
on one occasion shall we call his name Isaac
stated he had a brother in the states he write
to him but useing a different name. also
he would like to marrie a Arab girl but his parents
dis prov. on another occasion he stated he

would jus leave to get away from it all.
he also request of my daughter to invite
him to the States. he expressed the fact he does
not like the Army, he want to live in peace.
his name Jacob. who ask to marrie him
that he might be able to come to the states
while another well call him John, just
wanted to talk about the affaires between the
Arabs & Isrellies.

I also met a young lady very friendly
I ask her for her address she appeared to
be a little heaseatd to give it to me
an older woman spoke up to say you
have the address at head quarter

I find meny of the female very
supercilious and some what a little vindictive.

the male is very out going while the female
is inclined to maintane troudition.
The children are very warm & friendly meny of
them have experanced a life out side the shelted
area.

one evening after a long day of touring Israel my
daughter and I was going out to dinner.

we met this hansom young Isrealie
guy about 26 years old Shalom!
Shalom! we replied as to say hello a beautiful
evening. My name is Isaac. what is you name?
beautiful lady he ask. Pinkie my daughter
stated May I see you to night he ask?
My daughter said Call me later.

Are you Americana? yes my daughter
replied. oh I have a brother in the States!

quite unlack the average young American
he also wanted to get to know her Mother also
so later that evening he call. for a visit.

he had us in sticthes all evening.
why do you let her have so meny boyfriends?

You are very unstable he said to Pinkie
you must make up you mind.
we laughed.

then he explained to us how the young girls
go to get there palms red. from the fortune teller.
and how they tell them all the things
he told her you going to live a long time

you are going to meet a handsom young man any get
married so they go off and marrie the first young
man the meet and most of the time it turn out to be
a great mistake.
to make points he got of on Religion
and his parents. he use to be Religious,
but now I dont know he stated. God must forget
about us.
Well my parents do what ever they want, then before
the Sabbath they go mic-vek the put their little
barrett on their head any go to the Synguoguy
they must think god is crazy.

    mic-vek is a type of bath they take
to cleanse their soul.

    he was so funny and we had such a good time
I think he for got his problems for a while. he
really seem to be well relax he just opened up and
talked about meny things we really didnt expect him
to talk about.

In conversation, Grace seemed to come back to her generalization about
how different the Israeli men are from the women, and this led Susan not
only to ask for more but also to suggest comparison as a form to deal with
this particular idea. It wasn't that we needed to "teach" the form; we
needed to show Grace the form to fit her content, to help her get to her
material.

    After another version of this paper that begins: "The men in Israel out
going (aggressive) while the women are very reserved and maintain tradition," tutor and student "talked an outline," and Grace took everything
home to work on it. She then wrote her final paper on Israel.

    The men is Israel portrait aggressiveness
       while the women seem more reserved
   and, maintain tradition

    My daughter Pinkie became very friendly
       with any number of young Israeli men
   and I found them to be very aggressive
   as well as couraceous.
on one occasion after visiting with a
young man name Isaac for not more than
an hour without any remorse he ask her
to become his wife, and asked me for my
blessing!
on another occasion while in conversation
with Heim for only short period of time

he assured me of his capability of giving
my daughter a rich and full life, and his
price to me would be thirty camles! Although
I had no insight at as to how I might aboard
the plane with thirty camles instead of one
daughter.
        The Israeli women are very
quiet, & modest and, appear to be inrested
in Israeli men only they seem to
stay within their own nitch and
they feel very strong about Religious
traditions they are good home makers
and maintain traditional customs

        Rachel the Wife of Jacob died in
child birth, and until this day the
young women with child visit the Tomb
of Rachel they weep, and pray to Mother
Rachel that they may birth a normal healthy
child.
        The one outstanding quality seemingly
possessed by both the Israeli men, and women,
is their profound honesty and sincerity.

Version two had a possible topic sentence, which Grace put in lead
position in version three; version four has a topic sentence and conclusion,
and what is between sticks to the focus. Grace had found an idea she
wanted, probably needed, to develop, and the papers reveal her increasing
ability to focus and select. This work was followed by a poem, and from
that point on, every one of Grace's writings had a clearly announced
opening, often detailed development, sharpening focus. The process had
not been easy, but it seemed that once Grace ordered, once she worked
out her first "topic sentence" from her own material and her own need,
all her subsequent writing had structure (shape). I am wary of generalizations, but it was almost as if she were no longer able *not* to order. Something had been mastered.

The poem is of interest here. After the final Israel paper, Susan had
suggested "a character description or a work piece or a holiday piece
(comparison) perhaps." Grace elected to compare, but in a poem.

"Think Back"

Think Back,
        To America in the days of Old
When All of Gods Children
        Did as they were told,

Back to the times when in the schools
How we all abided by the golden Rules,
    Back, to when we bowed our heads
To say a prayer,
    To thank our God for even the
Birds in the Air.

    Back to the time,
When the Church was in touch
    And the Preacher didnt use boose
Or drugs as a crutch,

    When Homo and Bisexuals
with shame, would hide
    and now they're parading
The street with Pride.

    Back upon the Court House Squear
A twenty food decorated three; would be there
    Now the say in Bakersfield town,
"no Christmas orniments on county ground".

    Back to the days
    They were oh so sweet
Remember singing, Christmas Carols
    With out fear in the street?

Thinking Back,
        Looking Back,
on the memories of my mind
        If only I could turn Back,

The
    Sands
        of
            Time.

Why did Grace choose to write a poem at this point? My guess is that after the battle she had just won, the security of imposed order offered relief. And she certainly has order here. Not only does she use the poetic genre and the rhyme, but she writes long and coherent sentences in parallel structure. The sentences, however, are almost without meaning. The poem does convey a feeling, but it is also a stringing together of clichés.

Grace has shown again that she knows about structures; she has also shown in the past writings that she absorbs vivid impression, is a keen observer, puzzles, ponders, speculates, infers, works out tentative generalizations and tests these—that she has content. But especially for the inexperienced writer, new content or new thought often results in messiness before it yields to or finds its shape—as if ready-made shapes generate ready-made thoughts. Grace's task has been to find her content, let it find/take shape, make the shape fit what she is struggling to say. The process of writing and the process of finding are here simultaneous. The struggle became easier, and the next two months' work seemed to consolidate her achievements.

We always try to work from what students have written. Noting that the poem was "about the old days, especially about the holiday season," Susan most likely suggested "a memory piece on a Christmas that she remembers as special. Why was it special? *Lots* of description." Grace next wrote three pages of childhood Christmas memories with a great deal of vivid detail and not one cliché, but again rather too rambling and all-inclusive. Her next Christmas story, however (see below), set in the present, has detail, and a beginning, a middle, and a conclusion that not only draws together what has come before but also brings it to a new level of understanding and a new level of abstraction.

My Christmas Story
Its Joys and its Sorrows

Christmas in my family was always filled with glee.
And as for me, when I grew up, I lived to see my
mother's eyes light up with surprise just as she had made
mine light up, when I was a young child.

I would turn the shopping centers up side
down, to find just <u>one</u> little thing I knew my
mother wanted, but didn't expect to get.
I would do anything to make her happy
because she was my very best friend, and I wanted
her to knowit, and feel it.
I was the year of 1956 just twenty one
years ago. she wanted a toast master, so I
felt she must have the best money could buy.
on December 21 about 3:30 or 4 o'clock in the
after noon, I took my daughter was five months
old at the time along with my two nieces who
were age two and four years old to my mother's
to keep while my sister & I Christmas shop.
I remember my mother looked very tired, but
she never complained. After shopping my sister
went by my mother's to pick the childrens up,
therefore I didn't see my mother again.
On the following morning I tried a number
of times to reach my mother by phone, but I
decided she had gone Christmas shopping. since

my attempts was to no avail.

Again along with my sister I went shopping.
we came home about 6 o'clock tired and very low
in spirit. My niece who was baby sitting for us
ran out us "Oh where have you guys been? dont
you know your mother is dead? "Please for heaven
sake we are to tired, and sick in side to hear
jokes suddenly she ran in side crying...we
knew with out a doubt then that it was true
my mother, dead.

I went into complete shock. I was unable
to face facts. My whole World had fallon apart,
for me Christmas became a thing of the past.
When any one talk I was unable to retain any
part of their conversation. When I began to
relise what was happining to me, I called my
Doctor, and knowing the relationship between
me, and my mother he was very concerned.

He sat down and talked with me at great
leinth. It was then I began to pull my self
together and face facts. I knew my mother would
want me to go on living. And how wrong it would
be for me to inflect my selfish emotions upon
my young daughter, who after twenty one years
is now my best friend just as my mother was.
Christmas will never be the same, but again
there is
> glee,
>> Joy,
>>> and Happiness

In the first finished piece of the next semester, "Why I Returned to School," Grace seems to integrate a new competence as she talks about gaining confidence. She no longer is victim to that flood of thoughts that never let her get near saying anything. This is a fluent piece of writing that describes, reflects, interprets, analyzes, anticipates; it also moves easily among levels of abstractions, and keeps its focus clear.

"Why I Returned to School"

Returning to school was an enormous step
for me.

I ve never classified myself as a brain,
but when I entered Junior High I was doing OK.

It was when my father decided to sell his
farm, and move to a brand new community, which

caused a sligh delay in getting settled in school
that semester. And before the semester ended,
I had a very damaging experience with my teacher.

It was an independent school, and every
body, but every body in that school was related
in one way or another. the school was owned,
and operated by one family, and we (meaning my
brothers and sisters) were complete outsiders.

I was so afraid of my teacher I felt like
a little mouse. her face looked like an orange
peeling, and she had one glass eye, and I was
never sure if she was looking at me or some one
else.

All day long she sat there with a hair pin
through her skirt scratching, and that glass eye
staring at what no one knew.

If I ask her to explain something to me she
would expose me to the class, and find some way
to embarrass me. I remember going up to her desk
asking her to explain a simple math problem, and
it was simple. Never the less I didn't under stand.
it. She waited until the next day, and presented
my problem to the whole class.
every one laughted so hard it made me feel like
I didn't have the ability to function like the
other members of the class.

Meny times I have enrolled in classes, and
because I have a complex about going to school
I always drop out.

I made my disecission to return to school
after over hearing an instructor informing her
studants on how one can be effected by an
emotional on set that occure in early school
years. I kept thinking about that conversation,
and remembering the experience with my teacher.
eventually I got enough courage to discuss my
proble with her. I really laid it on the line,
and left no stones unturned.

I am now looking for a solution to my
problm. I told her I had a very bad complex,
and the meny times I attempted to take classes,
and drop out. the formular she gave me seems
to work quite well. she adviced me to take one
class, and no matter tough it get stick to it
and dont drop out once "she said you complete

a class you will have accomplish an astablishment
of self satifing condivence in your self."
    The formular that instructor gave me seem
to really work for me, because in pertisipating
in this class, and several other classes. an
entire new avenue of thoughts have open for me.
Now I have courage, spunk and guts.
    I am upward bound.

Close scrutiny of Grace's work during the semester reveals that not
only essay and paragraph structure began to emerge as she achieved
fluency, but sentence structure as well. Initially, Grace used few coordinating conjunctions and did not subordinate; sentences were often
thought fragments, punctuation was omitted. For instance: "At this point
I feel I am wedged between the rock and the hard place I will be leaving
the class the first week in Oct my daughter and my-self will tour Israel
four fourteen days. I am very excited about my trip time is rapitly approaching I am looking fordward to touring the Holy Land."
    The first Christmas story, however, includes sentences such as the
following:

> My mother raised chicken and guines for laying
> eggs to sell and she would have boxes and boxes
> and boxes of eggs she kept at a moderate tem-·
> perature so they would keep fresh yet not freeze.
> About the end of November or the beginning of
> December when the price of eggs would go up, my
> mother would take the eggs into town and sell
> them. This is how she made her money, to pay
> Santa Claus.

And here are the concluding sentences of the two Christmas writings:

> [She told me] I did not have to get anything I
> didn't want to prove anything to my friends be-
> cause if I had to do that they werent my friends
> anyway they were only little busy bodys.

> And how wrong it would be for me to inflict my
> selfish emotions upon my young daughter, who
> after twenty one years is now my best friend
> just as my mother was.

The structure became more complex, the paragraphs became visible,
and the whole piece became less a pastiche and more a controlled,

deliberate piece of writing. At this point, content determined shape; need found structure.*

In some ways, our Writing Center offers almost ideal conditions. Grace worked with an experienced and sensitive tutor in a one-to-one relationship at her own speed. In other ways, the conditions sound more ideal than they are. We have few materials. We have no space for small group work, where students may function as each others' readers or work jointly on such tasks as sentence combining or more mechanical practice with punctuation or quotation marks. We do a little bit of reading each other's work when we can, but one room and much noise make that difficult. We initially had over thirty students and only three experienced tutors, and Grace herself was often so weary from a day that started before 6:00 a.m. that by the time she came to the Writing Center at 6:00 p.m., she found it hard to concentrate. Many of the "spelling" errors may well be fatigue errors. And Grace still has a long way to go. She finds it difficult to write when she is not "inspired," and she is so bound by context that what gives her a fine start often becomes an impediment. How to approach, focus, and select her material presents ongoing questions. Then there are the more mechanical problems of how to deal with direct and indirect quotations, lead-ins, transitions. But she feels better about her writing. Organization is no longer an anguished struggle, everything she says makes a point, and much includes thoughtful reflection that also moves the reader to a new understanding.

So by fluency I mean more than simply filling the page. Some inexperienced writers come with too much to say; a beginning triggers a flood of thoughts, memories, and ideas with no way to get to the material. Some have seemingly nothing to say; the first statement is also the last: "There was a lot of tension," or "Marine World was fun." What more? The first does not know how to focus, the second does not know how to open the questioning, to find the material that lies behind the statement. Paradoxically, these are the same coin. For both, the teacher/reader needs to respond to what is there, to ask the questions that will help focus or help unearth the material. The aim is to help the inexperienced writer become his/her own question-asker, to show how he/she can move from a statement to the facts or evidence, from the abstract to the concrete—or how to move from the facts and memories to the meanings. The teacher/reader's place is between the writer and the paper, and his/her function is to help the writer get a clear sense of experience, through talking, writing, thinking; a clear sense of audience, of someone out there who wants to know and hear; and thus, a trust that one's own experience, one's point,

---

*Most adults and adolescents have available a range of forms and genres. It is a mistake to think we need to start from a "beginning" just because they are inexperienced as writers. If we wish to let students find their way "back into the center of their own learning" (a phrase I learned from Pat D'Arcy), then we need to follow the student's sequence and let that teach us.

is valid, acceptable, worth saying. Sometimes it is only trust in that first audience that lets the inexperienced writer, in turn, begin to trust the validity of that inner voice.

◇   ◇   ◇

Doretha helped show us this truth. And she showed us again how complex structures often emerge once students begin to write fluently.

Doretha, also a student in our Thursday night class, was so shy in the beginning that it was hard to hear what she said; her eyes were usually down, and she used a hard-lead pencil that was difficult to read. Asked what she hoped to accomplish at the Writing Center, she wrote, "To imprould my writting ability and spelling I really needed lots help spelling and writting ably to write I should know to spell good. But I have so much problems with spelling."

She did not seem to have the notion of written sentence and paragraph structure that Grace had brought with her (cf. p.69) Doretha's first writings were often very jumbled, with wide gaps between ideas, between sentences, sometimes within sentences. Fluency seemed far off. Here is her very first writing:

Sept 14, 1977

I Doretha like very much to readed more
about other people way of living in there
countries. Because as child grown-up up. I
Love to readed and studies geograph class.
Because I felt that I did very good in my
geograph class. Because I know that the place
that I have read about I would problemly never
visit them. In one of my famlies Life class
I really learned great deal more about children's
education systems. That what I really felted In
Love with. as child growting living in mixed
neighborhood I think that what really brought
my interest in other peoples. I would like
very much to become probation office. Because
I understand children'ts really well. Because
grown-up up bring shy I felt Like I did more
harm did good to my self in the education leave

She next wrote a long, detailed piece about a childhood friend, Mary, another about a high school friend, Sheila, and then one about her recent work at Howard Junior High School.

Oct 12, 1977

I injoyed myself working with the boys and girls.
This give me opportunity to understand girls, and
boys behavior. Problems growning up. Problems
that thay are having relative with school problems.
Just thing School in the are that is more important
to function ever day Of life. In the area Language,
development mathematics reading, and writting
development.

I know that I have these problams In those are.
I do not want my children to grow up with this
type of handicaps.

That wen I decide to come back to school to
over come my handicaps. Where I would be able to
help my childern'ts grow-up intelligence.

Working as campus supervisor give time to be
with my family. Give me the opportunety to
have time to fixed breakfast for. my son and
to enjoy him before he goes to school. The
hour is just wonderful give me opportune help
my son with hes homework.
Spent time talking together as family what he
learn at school also give me a go back to
school. Learn to help my-self, and my family.
The main reason that I Love my job is because
imjoyed working. with the students gives me
opportune to be home with my family.

Conversation between Doretha and Teta (her tutor) was almost always
about what Doretha was saying or trying to say, getting onto paper what
was left in her head. "You wrote so fast," Teta would say, "because you
were thinking so fast that sometimes you left out important words. So what
did you intend to say here?" Or, "All of us who try to write léave out
words sometimes. Now I just really don't understand this. How can we
say it so it will be clearer?" They spent most of their time reading aloud
and rereading, spelling words Doretha had skipped or stumbled over
(words such as "family," "opportunity"), occasionally correcting usage
or dealing with such matters as quotation marks and apostrophes, but
chiefly filling in connections, words, syllables. The emphasis was on correcting, and Doretha often rewrote a first draft. At first, Teta read to
Doretha while both looked at the page. Eventually Doretha began to read
to Teta, and by then she often recognized her own mistakes or omissions,
and would stop and say "I left out a word here" or "How do you spell
'heavy'?"

Gaps notwithstanding, Doretha soon revealed natural powers of observation and understanding. Much of her writing was about her seven-year-old son, Savori, and about her own problems in adequately expressing her ideas. Although her progress this first semester was labored and her attendance sporadic because of transportation and child care problems, it does seem that as she herself began to trust the authority of her own thoughts, she also began to write more fully, more specifically, almost more loudly.

Nov. 4, 1977

I like very much to observe my son. while
he studies hes school work is watching television
or just playing. This would give me a chance
to study he behavior patterns. I am interested
at the different ways his body changes when
Savori is studing. His body turns and twists
constantly. Then all at once he will jump up
and run over to me, saying, "Mon, can I have
some ice cream and glass of milk?" Then Savori
will walked away laughing to him self or just
smiling. Then he will reply "Thank you Mom...."

Nov. 16, 1977

I cannot remember the exact day when Savori
father asked me. if could Savori have these
playing cards that is over hes home.

I thought about it for serveral days.
Before retured hes answear. The reason that
I throught about it first. I throught it will
be a bad image for Savori. Or give him bad
influence toward gambling. But those cards
turn out to be excellend education tools and
trainning equipments for Savori.
To learn. for esample given Savori
opportunity to learn to recognize numbers.
Also develop his mind toward concentration.
In the games that Savori and I plays. Savori
will be involved learning how to add and subtract
numbers. Savori will be thinking how much fun
its' to to be playing with these cards. He
want know that hes learning math.

Jan 4, 1977

I were at home in the kitchen part of the house
setting at the kitchen table.... I said to
myself I don't want Savori to failt in Life.
Because I want him to grown-up be successful
person in Life. I want him to be proud of him
self. Because don't want him to have problems
that I an having In School. Personly I feel
that I an force Savori to hard. He would set
there at and say to me You allway picking on me
and start crying. Then I will feel my-self
getting very mad at my-self. Because don't
want him to be like me having all the problems.
Then I will explan to him that peoples make fun
"of peoples who are not smart. Then I will
reply you can stop working. go watch your
pictures. For working so hard you can have some
ice cream or chocolate milk to drink.

I include the next two pieces, not because they illustrate any marked
improvement, but because they show such insight into the writing process.

Nov. 16, 1977

I am feeling very sad about my writting.
Because I really want to learn how to become
good writer. I am very shamed of my writting
because I am constantly leaving out words and
also miss spelling.... One of the big problam
is that I get very nerveless went I an writting.
But you know or I an going to be telling my-self
try more to relax. I will not make as many mis
takes in my writing.

Jan. 18, 1978

...But I refuse to give up. I know I have
chang some of my daily program to continue
improving my-self throught writing and reading.
I am reading more and also writing more. I can
see the change in my writing and reading. Its
also helping me with my spelling for example
in my criminalogy class. Before it were very
hard on me to reading my own writing materials.
But now in my criminalogy class. I an
able to take better writing notes also I find

my-self reading over my writing materials more
than before. I am also trainning my self not
to rush myself when I am writing; try more to
reflect on my ideas.

On her entry sheet the next semester, Doretha wrote, "I want to accomplish to be able to set down and write a good english papers without
leaving out lots of words." She and Teta read aloud together, now also
paying attention to sentence and paragraph breaks, using Doretha's voice
as a gauge. The natural breaks were often there, so Teta would ask, "Do
you think this is a different idea or a different subject? Is your mother
doing something different here?" Then, "If you think it's different, skip
a line and indent. Now that's a sign that lets your reader know you're
shifting." Doretha caught on to the idea within one evening, although it
took her considerably longer to apply it successfully.

Following is the initial draft of the first paper she wrote the second
semester:

Tonight I am going to write about my mother.
I can remember her when child growing up. I was
6 to the oldest child out of 9 childrent. In
Pittsburg, Californa where I grew up. The type
of whether in Pittsburg. Is very wind and cold.
When it rain in Pittsburg it rains very hard type
of rain. I could remember that our mother would
walk to.
    Met us at school with newspaper hats that she
had made for me and my two twins sister and brother.
Also carring coat in a hand. Our mother had to
fight her way throw the heavy rain also large
passing trucks. That came off the freeway.
Because of the rain we could not used the field
to go to school. Because of the mud. Our mother
would tell us that to be very carefull going to
school. Because we had to face the large trucks
that came out the freeway.
My sister Celestine, Ernestine, and Scipio went
to school together. When we would see the Large
trucks, we would all stop, together. Where we
could support each other and kept our balance.
    Because of haveny rains and wind, sometime
the force would move our small bodies. After we
reached home, all 4 of us would used the back
door to the home. Because there were no sidewalk,
we had to kept in our mind how our mother. Had

taught us how to walk down the mud street.
Without bring in to the house. All four of us
would stand on the back porch and take off our
clothes. and hangle them on the cloths line
that our mother made to keept us from bringing
in our weat cloths into the house.

Our mother would have us a change of cloths
to wear.

Mother would have some hot chocolate on the
stove and sandwichs on tables.
I could remember how good hot chocolate tasted.
We would drink some time two three cup hot
chocolate also sandwichs. After we complete
eating sandwichs, drinking chocolate, Mother
would tell one of the oldest childrent help us
with our home work. Then she would tell us
going and clean-up our bedroom and pick up papers
outside. After doing what Mother had said, we
would set down on the porch. and wait for the
rest of our brothers and sister's to come. We
could see the School bus from the porch.

Because we were glade to see them. Mother
would give all us a kiss ask us what we did in
School.

The periods are often in the wrong place; so are some of the paragraph
starts. But starting with "The type of whether in Pittsburg" (line four),
Doretha has most of the words, ideas, and syllables on the paper. She is
also writing complex sentences, however mispunctuated. *The error now
is no longer structural; it is mechanical.* She needs to learn not to interrupt
her own thoughts, to hear her own phrasing, to become more familiar
with the function of the newly learned period and comma. But her initially
disconnected word groups have by now become sentence patterns, and
these she seems to have taught herself.*

After a paper about her brother and father—which was paragraphed—
came this:

No Cry for Help

As a child growing up I injoyed watching.
My mother fixing breakfast or cleaning up the
house.

---

*Such learning is probably no more (and no less) than the learner's bringing to use in her
writing structures that she had gradually learned unawares. Why this began to happen,
finally, for Doretha is a central question, but one much larger than the scope of these pages.
The support she felt to write what she had to say and the assurance that writing is to be read
(by a live reader) undoubtedly helped.

I think I was about 9 or 10 years old when.
Something happened our mother. All at once she
became very sick, very weak in both of her legs.

My father believe it was due to the way she
had been balancing her meals. He explained to
her that pork was the cause of her condition.
My father did not want us to mention our Mother
condition because he felt that he would really
upset her even more. Dad explained to us that
we should go along with our daily activities.

"Don't worry your Mother.

Try to extra good children." he said.
As I can remember this start when my two sister's
and one brother were In high School. Linda and
Brutch were In Junior high School.

Nature Celestine, Ernestine and myself were
In Elementary School.

What happened to our Mother all at once?
Here leg became paralyzed. My sister's and
brother never did see or hear our Mother cry or
complain about her condition or feel sorry for
herself.

I would stand there in the kitchen with my
thumb in my mouth, watching my Mother drag her
body through the kitchen frying dinner. Pulling
and pushing her self finally make it standing
on her knees to cook washing dishes. Our
Mother went on with her daily active washing,
or Ironing our clothes.

"Our father explained to us. Let you're
Mother work as she did before because it makes
her to feel like she is still an important
member in the family she is still a woman, and
a mother."

I can remember my-self looking at our Mother
with tear in my eye, saying God please help my
Mother to get better.

I don't remember how long it took our mother
to get better.

I personlly feel that my Mother got better
because.

We in the family made her feel important
to her self and us. We did not make her feel
like she was a handicapped person. And blessing
from God.

If we overlook the misspellings and mispunctuations, and the occasional omitted word or connective, we see a piece of writing that has a clear theme, sticks to it, develops it with telling details and in a strong voice. We also find complexity of thought and sentence. Take, for example, the following:

> I would stand there in the kitchen with my thumb in my
> mouth, watching my Mother drag her body through the kitchen
> frying dinner, pulling and pushing herself, finally make it standing
> on her knees to cook [and] washing dishes.

Verbs create imagery, phrases are movingly vivid ("standing on her knees"), and the sentence itself is a model of Christensen's generative structure.*

Her conclusion,

> I personally feel that my mother got
> better because we in the family made her feel
> important to herself and us. We did not make
> her feel like she was a handicapped person.
> And [because of a] blessing from God.

is perhaps not necessary for the effect of this piece; Doretha has managed to show so vividly that she now need not comment to make her point. But these concluding sentences are necessary for Doretha, the emerging writer, because she here takes the memory she has just described so effectively to a new level of reflection, a new level of abstraction, a new distance.

This is a giant step from her first writings. She too has a way yet to go— not only in mechanics, but (similar to Grace) in being able to write as strongly outside of her own context. By this I mean that if Doretha were given a topic or idea that did not evolve naturally from her own experience (whether this is a memory or an intellectual experience), she would, I suspect, find it much more difficult to bring her own experience to bear on it, to "make it her own" by seeing how it fits into what she already knows or how it tests what she already knows.

But that is, in a way, the point of these pages. Doretha doesn't yet know *what* she knows or *that* she knows. By encouraging the inexperienced writer to write more, and with appropriate response from a trusted reader, we are encouraging the emerging writer to discover not only what he/she has to say, but also to discover that he/she has more ways of saying and thinking about things than we knew or suspected.

Experience in the doing leads to competence; competence leads to

---

*Francis Christensen, Chapter I, *Notes Toward a New Rhetoric: Six Essays for Teachers.* New York: Harper & Row, 1967.

confidence, and this progression becomes the base for further work. We are showing the inexperienced writer not how to construct a sentence or a thesis, but that he/she does, indeed, construct sentences and theses ("When it rains in Pittsburg, it rains a very hard type of rain. I can remember that our Mother would walk to meet us at school with newspaper hats that she had made for me and my two twin sisters and brother" or "The men in Israel portrait aggressiveness while the women seem more reserved and maintain tradition"). The question at this point is not "What is a sentence (or verb, or fragment, or topic sentence, or thesis)?"—except as an appropriate aside to describe or name what is there. The point is to create or generate the context that permits sentences to emerge. Sentences do not emerge when divorced from meaning and need—the need to convey to someone else, the need to make sense for oneself. And since most inexperienced writers often do not know that they have anything worth saying to begin with, a reader/tutor/teacher must know how to ask questions meant to elicit from the writer what he/she has to say, what needs to be clarified, what is worth telling (How are Israeli men different from the women? How was going to school different for you than it is for Savori?). Then, when words and sentences that carry the new writer's meaning emerge, this increased ease often frees complexity—both of thought and of structure—so that Grace can now say on paper thoughts as complex as these: "And how wrong it would be for me to inflict my selfish emotions upon my young daughter, who after twenty one years is now my best friend just as my mother was." What needs "teaching" finally becomes clear. At this point, what students don't know and need to know may be conventions—where to put capitals, the use of the apostrophe, word endings. Now instruction takes place within the context of the student's writing; the need creates the opportunity.

When and how to teach grammar is another question. We all know how very useful and time-saving it is to share the basic vocabulary that describes how language works, to know *about* such things as verbs and subjects and their relationships. And although it has been pretty well established that this kind of knowledge doesn't actually help the writing process, it provides a useful distance, a way to talk about writing; it leads to editorial control. If a student comes equipped with rules and vocabulary, and is eager to test these or get what he/she is writing "just right," fine. A good rule of thumb is to start where a student is. But grammar instruction shouldn't be confused with writing instruction. The appeal is to two different modes of thought. At this point, Doretha does not need form to generate content or meaning. Given the real limitations of time, to interrupt her momentum now with formal grammar instruction would shift the focus from fluency (what you want to say) to correctness (how you should be saying it), would be teaching the editor before the composer has emerged.

Yet most of the time Doretha and Teta had to work together, they spent on correcting. What seems to be a paradox here, really isn't. Teta's first response to Doretha's writing was always to the content. But since the page was sufficiently jumbled that Doretha herself could not read back or interpret what she had written, it made it harder to go on or to reflect on what she had just described. To achieve fluency was to unjumble what was on the paper, so Teta and Doretha worked on reading and re-reading, filling in letters, syllables, words, details, finding sentence endings, marking misspelled words, making spelling lists. Mastering mechanics can be a pleasurable sign of progress, both for student and teacher. What made all that fruitful was a shared basic assumption—shared by all three of us, and by everyone else in that room—that the editing and correcting and "teaching" were in the service of fluency, of making what Doretha wanted to say clearer, easier for her.

I think we like to assume that this is always the case when we teach "skills," or even patterns, but it isn't. Skill teaching and practice seem to take on an independent life of their own, often far, far away from writing to say something. Thus, for inexperienced writers, writing usually means getting it right, with no notion of what that "it" refers to. Put differently, inexperienced writers assume writing to be good when it's correct, regardless of what insight, understanding, or idea may be hidden behind the incorrectness.

Huey showed me this most forcefully. He also underscored what the work of Grace and Doretha had been indicating—that shape, at this point, is most often a natural consequence of content, that fluency generates and governs shape. In the course of twenty evenings spread over ten months, his writing moved from twelve lines, usually unparagraphed, to over forty lines, often paragraphed. Most surprising, however, was that his writing moved through so many "rhetorical classifications"—descriptive, narrative, explanatory, argumentative—although none of these had been taught or discussed.

✧   ✧   ✧

Huey is a thoughtful and intelligent man in his mid-thirties who read very poorly and could not spell. For the first two periods, he came and sat glued to the dictionary, rarely squeezing out more than five lines an hour. We then set down ground rules. He was not to worry about misspelled words, a hard demand for someone who has never written because of spelling. (How hard it is to permit oneself to make an error gave me some clues as to how relentlessly we teachers focus on error.) He was to make a try at whatever word was in his head and not avoid or evade or regroup to get to a word more familiar; or better still, he was to ask me, a neighbor, a tutor, anybody, or just skip the word. He was to avoid the dictionary, a time-consuming hunt that made it almost impossible to keep any idea, any flow of thoughts going. In other words, his effort was to go into getting down on paper whatever he wanted to say (fluency). When he finished writing, my first task was to read back to him what he had written. After reading, and after we talked about it as much as we could—and this was never very long, for when he finished writing on the paper he was finished with what he was saying—we worked on spelling and spelling principles, always, of course, using the words in his writing.

I think for Huey, "writing" at first meant penmanship and orthography only; then "writing" also began to mean writing his ideas. At first, he was inevitably pleased that someone else could decipher his words. That someone else could decipher his words *and* understand what he was saying seemed doubly pleasing and probably helped connect the two meanings of "writing," and helped put spelling in the service of meaning. Once he started writing more or less fearlessly, he (like Doretha) was never at a loss about what to write.

None of his writing went beyond a first draft and I never asked for a revision. Time was very limited. He had a particularly difficult boss who often made it impossible for him to get to class; several of his writings deal with that troubling situation at work. He had family responsibilities. He was sick for a while, as were other members of his family. To get his words down on paper was becoming important to him, and working on spelling took what available time there was. His writing included the following:

A process paper:	I am a detailman, a detailman is one how can take a old car and make it look like new. To start the job, you most degrease engine, we use a chenacal call RS10 we mix it whit solvent, and thin steam it off, then dry the engine whit a blow gun, thin nix you paint it and dreas it....
A character description:	My grandfarth worked in a sawmill I nevery new my dady so my grand farth tuck his place. He is a good old man and I love him as a son could love his farth. He is a very relegges man he gos to church every sunday. I can remaber on sunday how we would have to run to keep up with him, man he could walk and we had to keep up with him....
Thesis-development papers:	The Yankee was a good teme but the dodgers is a better teme, because they had the hitter.

Jackson is a good ball player, but
to me he is not worth the money they
are paing him.

I would like to talk about Ale and
Spanks. I know it was a good fite,
But Ale wanted to lose a fight so he
can be the first hadve wate to reclame
the titold 3 time....

An explanatory essay: I would like to tell about Chinese
lunar calendar. The Chinese have a
dirfferent horoscope than the one we
use. This year is the year of the
horse, upon which I was born....

An argument: I would like to know what makes a
employer thinks he can own a person
just because that person works for
him. It is a shame to see a man get
huemillyadid just because the auner
thinks that because he pays him a
sallare he can do anything he want
to that man....

A rebuttal: It's a bad thing when a black man
got to steal from blacks in order to
live just because he can't find a job.
I know you say that's not true, but in
most cases for blacks it is....

A poem (although not   I like to spik that well and true,
set up as a poem):   and whin you can't spik that know
good for you. Someone sad shete up
my frind and have a sete Oh know my
frind I want to spik, because
cmunocation is good for you. So
tall the world about your dream....

Huey wrote several personal experience papers, including a narrative
of places seen and jobs held in the army, an implied comparison between
country and city living, an account of a trip to Reno, and a childhood
memory piece about Thanksgiving. Some writings were more developed
than others, some were rambling or sketchy, but he always found a basic
form appropriate to the intention.

Much of Huey's non-writing time was devoted to spelling because that was the obstacle that kept him from transcribing what was in his head onto paper. An interesting difference between Huey and Grace is that Grace was stopped when she tried to approach her material, to focus and select, while Huey was stopped from transcribing the words in his head onto paper. The minute Grace began, she felt flooded. Much of her tutor's function was to help her find some way into that mass of material that always seemed so ready to burst forth, and help bring that flood into more manageable verbal rivulets. Huey, however, was never at a loss for shape, so much of my function was helping the process of transcription which, in his case, we called spelling.

◇   ◇   ◇

The work I show here is not *only* possible in a Writing Center with tutors, although to fill the function of the first responsive reader is more difficult in a traditional classroom. But where the ratio of students to teacher is prohibitively high, one can show that reading means wanting to understand (no easy task!) and students can help assume that function for each other and so become part of the process. They often make excellent first readers and a real audience other than the teacher/authority is immensely useful. It reaffirms that writing is to be read. It may also help student readers become better writers since it's often so much easier to see what is missing in someone else's than what is missing in one's own.

Just beginning each day with a ten-minute writing, one which gets read and responded to by teacher or classmate(s), is useful because it leads inexperienced writers back to their own language, their own voice, their own experience and thoughts, and legitimizes these. It also affirms that writing means finding ideas and transcribing what the writer has to say onto paper. What the writer has to say is within his/her experience, whether this is lived experience (memory), perceptual experience (what I see/hear/feel now), reflective experience (what this meant), intellectual experience (what I think in response to, or what I think should be), or speculative experience (what seems possible, probable, questionable). The daily ten minute writing, written to be shared, links the I to the words on the paper. It helps establish that writing is a process, not a sudden miracle.

In the view presented here, writing makes inner experience known by translating it into words and thus putting it outside one's self. But perhaps even more important for students who have academic hopes and ambitions, it makes outer experience known by filtering it through the mind's eye and I, thus letting it *be* known. A major obstacle for so many students I teach is that when they study (from a lecture or a book), when they take on ideas that come from outside themselves, they by-pass the connection to their own understanding, as if something can be known without an active knower. It's hard to think, especially about new ideas, in someone else's language, voice, experience. Genuine fluency generates and opens up access to thought.

This is true for more experienced writers as well, although then the interrelationship between what I call fluency and shape, the question of what generates what and when, is more complex. But it is especially true for inexperienced writers who need to be shown, more than anything else, how to connect their own thoughts to their own words on paper. For this to happen they need readers, real and alive, who will respond to the "what" instead of the "how." Their most frequent experience with their occasional writing has been a brief judgment, usually negative. But judgment, good or bad, correct or incorrect, is out of place here. At this point, an idea isn't correct or incorrect; it's clear or unclear. It seems important that we relinquish, if only momentarily, our judicial red pens and become question askers, that we teach our students to become question askers for each other and for themselves, and so relate the writing process to the process of discovery.

Most inexperienced writers cannot compose and edit at the same time. The editor (later the devil's advocate) stands between the piece of paper and an audience; as need arises, sometimes immediately, we may teach the emerging editor. But the responsive teacher/reader should first stand on the writer's side, work with the emerging composer, the emerging inquirer. To teach the editor his trade before the composer has emerged with any kind of assurance or authority is to confuse the product with the process.

Showing-Writing

A TRAINING PROGRAM TO HELP STUDENTS BE SPECIFIC

Rebekah Caplan
Foothill High School, Pleasanton

Year after year we make student writers cringe with the reminder to "be specific." We write in margins next to bracketed passages "explain," "describe." We extend arrows over words, under words, circling around and through words, accompanying them with the captions "What do you mean? Needs more detail: unclear." When we compose essay questions for exams, we underline the "why or why not" at the end of the question *twice* so that our students might feel the importance of that part of the response. Recently I talked with one teacher who had designed a rubber stamp which bore the words "Give an example," so that he would not have to scribble the phrase again and again.

The assumption behind this writing program is that most students have not been trained to *show what they mean.* By training, I do not mean the occasional exercises taken from composition texts, nor do I mean the experience gained by writing perhaps eight major essays over the course of a semester. What I mean by training is the performing of daily mental warm-ups, short and rigorous, not unlike the training routines of musicians, dancers, athletes, Six years ago, while teaching reading and composition in a suburban middle school, I realized the important connection between disciplined practice in the "arts" and the need for it in a writing program. My first students were eighth graders, and not knowing precisely what the junior high school student needed to learn about writing, I experimented for a while.

For approximately three weeks I assigned a potpourri of writing exercises, examining the papers carefully for common problems or strengths. I wanted to determine what the eighth grader already knew about good writing and how far I might expect to take him. It was not difficult to discover in those first few weeks of my teaching career that although students *did* write with enthusiasm and energy, not many of them wrote with color or sound or texture. In a description of a student's favorite movie I would read: "It was *fantastic* because it was so real!" For a strange person: "He is so *weird.*" For a favorite friend: "She has the most *fantastic personality.*"

The underlinings proved their earnestness, their sincerity. I attacked these "empty" descriptions, however, inscribing in the margins those same suggestions that teachers have "stamped out" for years. In class, I passed out models of rich description—character sketches by Steinbeck, settings by Twain, abstract ideas by Bradbury. I advised the students, as they scanned the model and glanced back at their own papers, that they needed to be *that* explicit, *that* good. *That* was what writing was all about. I said, "I know that you know what makes a thunderstorm so frightening. I know that you know the same things Mark Twain knows about a thunderstorm. Now what details did he use?" And we would list "the trees swaying" and the sky turning "blue-black" until we had every last descriptive word classified on the board. "And now," I continued, "you describe a beautiful sunset in the same way that Twain describes the storm."

The writings from such follow-up assignments were admittedly better, but without the prepping, without fussing and reminding, I could not get students to remember to use specifics naturally, on their own. With growing frustration I tried to examine my history as a student writer. I wanted to track down what it had been like for me to write in the eighth grade, and what it was like now. I wanted to uncover when it was that I had reached a turning point or gained a sense of discovery about language and expression. When I tried to recall my own junior high experience, however, I could not remember one assignment, let alone any instruction in writing. What I did remember was signing autograph books and passing notes in class, recording memories in diaries and signing slam books. These sorts of writings mattered the most. We cared deeply about who was one's friend and who was one's enemy, who was loved, who was hated, who was worthy of secrets, who was not. And as these issues came under judgment we based our verdict on the degree of someone's *good personality*. In fact, the supreme compliment one paid a friend in an autograph book amounted to "fantastic personality." And it is still so today.

This memory struck me as being significant. The notion that each person has a personality that is *separate* from his looks, his dress, or his wealth is a new thought to the junior high school student. I remember using that same phrase, "a great personality," with fresh, original intentions in diaries and school papers. My friends and I were intrigued by the idea of personality more than any other. We were fascinated by people's differences, yet we could not say exactly what made us like one person and dislike another. Could it be, then, that I was demanding writing that my students weren't ready to produce? It seemed crucial to respect their excitement over many of these cliched discoveries. I had to allow room for naive, exploratory generalization, but at the same time, challenge them to move beyond simple abstractions and discover what concepts like "personality" were based on— how they derived their meanings from concrete perceptions.

Next I looked at myself as an adult writer. What kinds of things did I strive for? What had I been successfully taught along the way? I surely strove for specificity. I had kept a journal for years, commenting on cycles of personal change. I usually began in a stream-of-consciousness style, listing sensations, noting the details that would explain my perceptions to myself. I wrote often, even if I had nothing to say, in the hope I would discover something to write about. I believe this ritual of writing regularly developed from my training as a dancer and a pianist. As a young piano student, I practiced daily finger exercises to strengthen manual agility at the keyboard, to prepare myself for a Bach concerto. As a young ballerina, I was forced to do leg-lifts at the bar for thirty minutes each lesson; the remaining fifteen minutes were devoted to dancing. (How we longed for it to be the other way around!) I notice that beginning artists practice drawing the human body again and again, from varying angles, using different materials—charcoals, oils, ink—to capture reality. In drama classes I attended in college, we began acting lessons with short improvisations that allowed us to experiment with emotions *before* we rehearsed major scenes for performance. In all these cases, the learning, the mastering, came more from the practice than from the final presentation.

After drawing these several conclusions about the training of artists, I decided to build into my curriculum a training program for students writing: a program that attempts to engrain craft, to make the use of specific detail automatic, habitual, through regular and rigorous practice. I created a writing program with these coordinating features:

1. Daily practice expanding a general statement into a paragraph.

2. Applying the difference between *telling* and *showing* in the editing process.

3. Practicing specific ways to select and arrange concrete details in developing an idea or structuring an essay.

What follows is a description of that three-part training program as I have used it in my classes for several years and as I have shared it with other teachers in presentations for the Bay Area Writing Project. Both in my own use of the materials and in my sharing of them with other teachers I keep gaining new insights, new ways to refine or expand the practice exercises or the editing techniques. I hear from other teachers that they too keep generating new materials, applying the two basic concepts—daily practice and "showing not telling"—in new ways. I hope that teachers who adopt the procedures described below will write to me about their experiences—their questions and discoveries.

I have been curious to evaluate the outcome of my program, for myself and for other teachers who have uesd it. I have believed from the beginning that I could see in students the kinds of improvement I was aiming for—but could these improvements be measured, and could they be seen by others? Would other readers recognize the same signs of progress I was observing? I include below (123-147) an attempt to answer these questions through three case studies of students who show different kinds of growth resulting from the daily practice program. Their work provides further clarification of the concepts taught as well as examples of how students respond to the assignments. These cases constitute a qualitative evalution of the materials: a way of showing what kinds of growth can take place in students being trained.

DAILY PRACTICE EXPANDING A GENERAL SENTENCE

Since students need the discipline of a regular routine to reinforce use of concrete details in place of, or in support of, their generalities, I assign a daily homework challenge: I give them what I call a *telling sentence*. They must expand the thought in that sentence into an entire paragraph which *shows* rather than *tells*. They take home sentences like:

- The room is vacant.
- The jigsaw puzzle was difficult to assemble.
- Lunch period is too short.

They bring back descriptive paragraphs—short or long, but always detailed, and focused on demonstrating the thought expressed in the assigned *telling* sentence. I challenge students not to use the original statement in the paragraph at all. I ask them to convince me that a room is empty or a puzzle is hard to assemble without once making the claim directly. The challenge is much like charades: they have to get an idea across without giving the whole thing away.

In order to establish the difference between telling and showing, I distribute the following two paragraphs to my students. The first is written by a seventh grader, the second by novelist E.L. Doctorow. Both passages concern a scene at a bus stop.

Telling:

Each morning I ride the bus to school. I wait along with the other
people who ride my bus. Sometimes the bus is late and we get
angry.Some guys start fights and stuff just to have something to do.
I'm always glad when the bus finally comes.

Showing:

A bus arrived. It discharged its passengers, closed its doors with a
hiss and disappeared over the crest of a hill. Not one of the people
waiting at the bus stop had attempted to board. One woman wore a
sweater that was too small, a long skirt, white sweater socks, and
house slippers.One man was in his undershirt. Another man wore
shoes with the toes cut out, a soiled blue serge jacket and brown
pants. There was something wrong with these people. They made
faces. A mouth smiled at nothing and unsmiled, smiled and
unsmiled. A head shook in vehement denial. Most of them carried
brown paper bags rolled tight against their stomachs.

from *The Book of Daniel* (p. 15)

When asked to distinguish the differences between the two paragraphs,
most students respond by saying the second paragraph is better because they
can *picture* the scene more easily. They think the people in paragraph two
are "weird, poor, and lonely," (all *telling* ideas). But this interpretation
comes from the *pictures* (their word), pictures of people wearing torn
clothing, carrying brown paper bags instead of lunch boxes, wearing
unhappy expressions on their faces. Student writers can easily discern good
description. Getting them to write with close detail is not managed as
smoothly.

I remind students that the storybooks they read as very young children are
filled with colorful illustrations that *show* the events described on
accompanying pages; the writer does not have to describe the lovely red barn
with the carved wooden trim, for the picture next to the caption "the barn
was beautiful" reveals that idea. However, in more mature literature,
drawings disappear from the pages, and the writer assumes the role of
illustrator. Language must be his brush and palette. Following such a
discussion, I initiate the daily training exercise, explaining to students that
they will expand one sentence each night from telling to showing during the
entire course of the semester.

Below are sample daily sentences. These sentences are given in no
particular order and are not necessarily linked by recurring themes.
Sometimes students themselves suggest sentences for successive assignments.
By choosing generalizations familiar to students, I increase the likelihood of
effective elaboration.

She has a good personality.
The party was fun.
The pizza tasted good.
My parents seemed angry.
The movie was frightening.

The concert was fantastic.
The jocks think they're cool.
I was embarrassed.
My room was a mess.
Foothill students have
   good school spirit.

The idea of daily writing is, of course, nothing new in itself. I know many teachers who have their students "write for ten minutes" the moment they come to class. My daily writing approach, however, is different in a number of ways. First, many teachers assign "topics" for elaboration like "School" or "Family" or "Sports." Although a topic is open-ended and allows more room for creativity, students often spend more time trying to find something to say than actually writing the composition. The type of statement I use is similar to the thesis sentence, the controlling sentence of an essay. The generalization supplies the point; the student is given the idea to support. Students are free then to concentrate on experimenting with expressions of that idea. Further, since they are all working on the same idea, they are in a position to compare results—to learn from one another.

Another departure from other daily-writing "warm-ups" is that this daily writing is done at home. Students must come to class with pieces finished and ready to be evaluated. We don't wait ten minutes while they hastily scribble some sort of solution. I want to give them time—if they will take it— to play with and think about what they are trying to do.

Finally, unlike private journals or some free-writing assignments, these exercises are written to be shared. I use the writings in much the same way as a drama instructor uses improvisation as an instructional technique. The daily sentence expansion becomes a framework for practicing and discovering ways of showing ideas. Just as drama students search for ways of expressing "ambition" or "despair" by imagining themselves in real-life situations that would evoke these feelings and discovering ranges of bodily and facial expression, my students arrive at ways of showing "empty rooms" or "difficult puzzles" by experimenting with different kinds of language expression. I instruct them very little, preferring that students find their own solutions. But finally, although the experimenting at home is free—not judged—the practice includes an important element that parallels acting instruction: the daily "public" performance. The students know in advance that some papers will be read to the class for analysis and evaluation. However, they do not know which ones. As theirs might very well be among those I choose (my selections do not fall into a predictable pattern), the students are likely to be prepared.

The "performance" or sharing of improvisational or experimental efforts is an important learning experience for the selected performers *and* their audience. The first ten minutes of every class session, then, is devoted to oral readings, not writing. I choose between five and seven writing samples which I read aloud to the class, and as a group we evaluate the density of detail.

Where did this writer have success with interesting description? Where were her details thin? This is the only time I will not comb the papers for grammar, spelling, and usage errors, for there is no time. Since we respond exclusively to content, students can give full attention to being specific without the pressure of grammatical perfection.

I grade each paper immediately as the discussion of that paper concludes. Besides assigning an A, B, or C grade, I quickly write a general comment made by the group: "great showing; too telling at the end," "great imagination, but write more." This process takes about ten seconds and then I move on to the next reading. I record a check in my gradebook for those papers not selected for reading. If students do not turn in writings they receive no credit. All papers are recorded and handed back before the end of the period, giving the students immediate response and recognition for their work. At the end of the semester I average the number of grades a student has earned in the series of assignments.

There are five major advantages to using such a daily training exercise with its follow-up sharing and discussion:

1. *Students write every day.* I do not assign sentences on the eve of exams, major assignment due dates, or holidays.

2. *I am freed from having to grade an entire set of papers each night, yet I provide a daily evaluation.* If a student is disappointed because a particular writing was not selected, I invite him to share it with me after class. This tends to happen when the student has written a good paragraph and wants me to enter a grade for this particular one, which I am glad to do. It may also happen when a student is unsure of his solution and wants help.

3. *Students selected to perform hear useful comments immediately.* They do not have to wait a week to receive response and criticism. The other students learn from the process of specifying weaknesses as well as strengths of the work and from hearing suggestions given to the "performing" students by peers and teachers.

4. *Students learn new developmental techniques and linguistic patterns from each other.* Students assimilate new ideas for specificity by regularly hearing other students' writing. In addition, they often internalize the linguistic patterns of other students either consciously or unconsciously. This process is similar to assimilating the speech patterns of a person with a different accent. After close association with this person, we may tune our speech to the inflections of an attractive or entertaining accent. I believe it is often easier for students to learn from other students who write well than from professional writers whose solutions may be out of the students' range.

5. *Students write for a specifc audience.* They write with the expectation that classmates may hear their composition the following day. So they usually put more effort into their pieces than if they were intended for their private journals or for teacher-as-evaluator.

A selection of daily writing samples follows. Two students, a remedial freshman and a college-bound sophomore, show growth and change over a two-week time span. Their writings illustrate two important results of the daily practice:

1. Students write more—either because they are finding it easier to generate more writing or because they are working harder on the assignments (or both).

2. Students gain control over a wider range of techniques.

Daily Sentence: *The new students were lonely.*

It was the first day of school and there were two new students, Dick and Dan, who had moved over the summer. They were brothers and this was a new city and school which they had come to, and in this school they would have to make friends because neither of them knew anybody or anyone.

—Freshman Student

This piece of writing is composed entirely of generalities (telling sentences). The writer explains the cause of the loneliness—a new city, new school, necessity for making new friends—but unless he shows us some foreign streets, strange faces, and unusual customs to support these reasons, he will do little to convince us. Perhaps if he could contrast "playing pool with the gang at Old Mike's Pizza Parlor" to the "eyes avoiding his unfamiliar face in the study hall," the reader might appreciate the unrealities of "new city, new school, new friends."

Here is the same student's writing two weeks later.

Daily Sentence: *The crossword puzzle was difficult to solve.*

The sixth row down got me stuck. It was plain to tell that this crossword puzzle was rough. The puzzle as it was, was made for a 12th grade level, and it made me feel as if I was in the 6th grade level. Intellectual words such as "the square root" of 1,091,056 in four digits and others. The next one was a five-letter word for phyladendron, which was "plant" to my surprise. I, as a normal person, had a very hard time trying to figure out what an Australian green citrus fruit was with four spaces. Instinctively I gave up the whole game, as it was too frustrtaing to cope with.

This section illustrates an improvement in generating examples. The writer introduces his subject by *telling* that the puzzle was tough, but immediately proves his claim with a series of illustrations—twelfth grade level versus sixth grade ability, intellectual words like square root, exotic plants and fruits that call for specialized knowledge. His writing is more enjoyable to read because of the examples he added. Notice also that his paragraph is longer but never rambles or leaves the point.

Next, the sophomore:

Daily Sentence: *The room was vacant.*

The next show didn't start for another hour. As I repositioned the spotlight in the upper balcony, the squeaks of the rusty screws seemed to echo throughout the desolate building. I walked down the aluminum stairs that resounded with the sound of rain beating on a tin roof throughout the auditorium. I then opened the curtains to the large, lonely stage which looked dark and forbidding. As I put up the sets and decorated the stage, I guess it would seem to anyone walking in, that the room was very much alive with color and objects. But to me, even the set and decorated auditorium looked bare.

In the first half of the paragraph, this student carefully constructs detail. Like many students trying to master a skill, he concentrates intensely at first, very mindful of the task. However, there comes a point, when, losing his fervor, he reverts to *telling.* With the sentence "I then opened the curtains..." he abandons his use of specifics, relying instead on vague adjectives like "dark and forbidding," or general nouns such as "color and objects."

Within two weeks, this student increased his observational skills considerably. In addition, he was able to sustain his use of vivid details throughout a much longer piece of writing.

Daily Sentence: *The rollercoaster was the scariest ride at the fair.*

As I stood in line, I gazed up at the gigantic steel tracks that looped around three times. The thunderous roar of the rollercoaster sounded like a thunder cloud that has sunk into my ears and suddenly exploded. The wild screams of terror shot through me like a bolt of lightning and made my fingers tingle with fear. Soon I heard the roar of the rollercoaster cease. As the line started to move forward, I heard the clicking of the turnstyle move closer and closer. Finally I got onto the loading-deck and with a shaking hand gave the attendant my ticket.

It seemed like I barely got seated when I felt a jolt which signified the beginning of the ride. While the rollercoaster edged up the large track, I kept pulling my seatbelt tighter and tighter until it felt like I was cutting off all circulation from the waist down. At the crest of the hill, I caught a glimpse of the quiet town which lay before me and gave me a feeling of peace and serenity. Suddenly my eyes felt like they were pushed all the way back into my head, and the town had become a blur. All I could see was a mass of steel curving this way and that as the rollercoaster turned upside down. I was squeezing the safety bar so tight that my fingers seemed to be embedded in the metal. I could see the landing-deck, and I let out a deep breath that had been held inside ever since the first drop. As the roller coaster came to a halt, I felt weak and emotionally drained. When I stepped off onto the deck, I teetered a bit to the left, but caught my balance quickly when I saw my friends waiting for me at the exit gate. I tried to look "normal," while trying to convince them in a weak voice that, "Oh, it was nothing."

Even though he makes general claims—"I felt weak and emotionally drained"—he remembers to support his feeling with specific evidence: "When I stepped off onto the deck, I teetered a bit to the left. . . ." Or, as he tries to look "normal" to prove this with dialogue: "Oh, it was nothing." This student puts himself in the experience every step of the narration. Two weeks earlier, he could not sustain such a practice.

The three aspects of the program that encourage this growth are 1) regular practice, 2) regular evaluation (teacher/class response to oral readings), and 3) effective student writing serving as models for learning. Similar growth in the writing of upperclassmen can be found in the case studies section of this report (pp. 123-147) below.

As we've witnessed in the preceding writing samples, students initially rely simply on increased use of specifics and lengthened paragraphs to improve their writing. As they become accustomed to the practice and experience some security or personal growth in generating examples, I can almost predict when an imaginative student will challenge the conventional means of developing ideas. Perhaps because the writings become less of a chore and more of an enjoyment, one student or another will "try something different," will test the limits of satisfactory elaboration. In much the same way that, after playing Hamlet every night, an actor can suddenly discover an entirely new and fresh way to express despair, so my students find, without my solicitation, original ways to express their ideas. The following interpretation of *The pizza tasted good* demonstrates one student "stretching different muscles."

I felt a little apprehensive that morning. I wasn't sure if, after so many years of separation, my brother and I could spend an entire day with one another and enjoy it. Pulling on my jeans, I tried to think of a few conversational topics that would interest us both, just in case conversation came to a standstill. I wondered if he could be thinking of the same thing. "Funny," I thought, "maybe I have no reason to worry; maybe we will have too much to talk about—maybe."

After just a few minutes on the Berkeley campus, I realized that all of my worrying and topic planning was unnecessary. C ____ and I had so much to share, so many years to catch up on, and of course, he was certainly expounding helpful, fascinating, or just plain factual information about Berkeley. He even took me to his favorite Mediterranean Cafe. Together we sipped their rich and aromatic coffee blend as he told me about the many hours he had spent there, reading the morning paper or engrossed in some outlandish novel. Of course C ____was excited. He couldn't wait to give me a grand tour of "his" alma mater. He wondered if "his" old pepper tree was still as majestic as ever, and if "his" studying area in the Botanical Gardens was still as beautiful as he remembered. The campus came alive with C ____'s nostalgic memories of his old chemistry lab in the Life Sciences Building, or the old Greek Theatre where he enjoyed Shakespeare, Bach, and Sophocles.

By lunch, I knew that C ____ and I would never be at a loss for words. More importantly, I knew that there was a strong bond between the two of us—something that even time could not erase— love. Together we sat Indian-style on the grass just below the Campenile. The stringy pizza we had purchased for lunch brought childish grins to our faces, and through the warm silence, we both knew that pizza had never tasted so good.

When I read this particular paper aloud, students attacked the writer for not having mentioned the texture of the crust or the spiciness of the sauce, but being the articulate person she is, this senior expertly defended her interpretation by asking the others whether they had ever experienced a luscious meal without the benefit of company. Had some meals simply not "tasted very good" because a low emotional state influenced one's appetite? The offense halted as students sat quiet in contemplation. They looked to me to deliver the verdict, but most students already knew the answer. We can show ideas in ways other than the most literal. Sensory experiences involve more than immediate physical sensations.

This piece of writing became an important lesson, and it came without my instruction. My experience with this training program has shown that the use of effective student composition as models for learning has more impact on the growth of other student writers than the lessons of textbooks. Students emulate the successful writing of other students more than they do that of professionals. From that moment on, in that particular classroom, many students felt compelled to "be different," to probe deeper for solutions. They were excited by this student's discovery because it was their discovery too. The following night, after I had assigned *The living room was a warm, inviting place,* many students focused on *people* making a room warm and inviting rather than fireplaces, sofas, or shag rugs.

To summarize, the daily sentence expansions provide a framework in which students can experiment and discover ways of showing ideas. It is a time for self-exploration in the attempt to attach meaning to experience; it is also a time for increasing fluency and creating a style and voice.

APPLYING "SHOWING NOT TELLING" TO REVISION

The second feature of this training program consists of using this technique of sentence specificity and elaboration to help students revise first drafts of major compositions. Whenever students work on major writing assignments—an essay related to the reading of a novel, a character sketch for a short story, a narration of a personal experience—I have them work with rough drafts in small editing groups. In addition to helping another writer correct spelling and usage errors, a student editor is instructed to search for thinly developed ideas. If a student writer fails to develop adequately an important section of her composition, the editor underlines the sentence or sentences that generalize rather than specify and writes *show* in the margin. The writer must then take the *telling* sentence and expand it for homework. Instead of the usual daily routine in which everyone has the same sentence to develop, here students use sentences from their *own* materials. As the drama instructor stops the rehearsal of a scene midway and asks the actor to approach the scene from a different perspective through exercises in improvisation, so I halt my writers midstream in their discourse, urging them to consider important elements that need focusing and elaboration. With practice, students become more effective editors, for they train themselves to spot underdeveloped ideas and non-specific language.

When a writer has elaborated her own generalization, she may decide to insert the new version into the composition. The editors in her group work along with me to help her decide whether or not the change is effective. The revisions below illustrate the process.

Seventh Grade Assignment: *Re-creation of a favorite childhood experience.*

This writer describes the fun of playing hide-and-seek with her brother. As she attempts to create excitement and suspense around being found, she writes:

Leonardo was approaching her. *He was getting closer and closer.* She thought for sure she was going to be caught.

Editors in her group suggested she *show* "He was getting closer and closer" because this sentence signals an approaching climax.
Her revision:

She could hear him near the barn, his footsteps crunching on the gravel. Next he was on the lawn, and the sounds of the wet grass scraping against his boots made a loud, squeaky noise. Next she could hear him breathing.

This writer is now *re-creating* her experience. By carefully remembering each sensation as her brother drew nearer—footsteps crunching gravel, sounds of boots in wet grass, breathing noises—she leads the reader through the experience. The showing sentences could be inserted smoothly into the original version in place of the telling sentence.

Senior Assignment: *Description of a photograph of Janis Joplin,*
60's blues singer.

One senior began:

Sitting on the sofa she looked exhausted...

Having said so much for appearances, this student went on to suggest *why*
Janis was so fatigued. A student editor thought it important for her to *show*
the exhaustion, so she underlined that sentence.
The revision:

Her eyes told of her pain—deep, set back, reaching inside of herself.
Dark caves formed where her cheeks were. Her mouth was a
hardened straight line, down at the corners.

As if this writer were the camera lens itself, she zooms in for a close-up,
examining in detail the elements that make Janis appear weary.

Sophomore Assignment: *Re-creation of a favorite memory.*

This sophomore girl describes having her first cigarette:

I slowly sucked the stick and felt a warm sensation fill my chest. *A*
chill ran down my spine as I smiled and exhaled.

The editors challenged her two ways. First, they didn't believe that anyone
could "smile and exhale" after a first cigarette. They wondered whether she
experienced any discomfort. Second, they wanted more *showing* for "a chill
ran down my spine." Her revision:

I slowly lifted my cigarette until it touched my lips. I sucked the
stick and a cloud of warm smoke filled my chest. Suddenly, I felt
nauseated and my chest felt like a time bomb ready to explode. I spit
the smoke out and coughed. My eyes began to water, but I managed
to show a grin.

This version is much more honest; the cliché "a chill ran down my spine" is
abandoned for more specific description—"I felt nauseated," "my chest felt
like a time bomb," "I spit the smoke out," "my eyes began to water"—and
finally the specific verb "managed" makes the grin believable.

Senior Assignment: *Personal essay interpreting the outcome of an*
important decision.

In this assignment, students explained the impact of an important decision they had made at some point in their lives. They were instructed to describe in detail their alternatives, then show how they came to make a choice and how the outcome affected them. This senior writer described how she chose between going to a public or private school. Choosing the private school meant leaving home for the first time. Here is the original opening paragraph to her essay:

> I was aboard the London-bound train now. In just eleven hours I would be five hundred miles away from home. Starting at my flowered overnight bag, *I frantically reflected upon the decision that I had made.* Inside I gasped, "Oh, God, did I make the right decision?" Pull yourself together," I thought, "and just think the whole thing over logically; then you'll realize that your decision was wise." Swallowing hard and trying to keep the tears away, I remembered that first day at Brechin High School.

Both her editors and I advised her to "reflect more on the decision," since she didn't give an account of her actual deliberation. "Pull yourself together" does not show us her weakness, what she's afraid she'll give in to. It only *tells* us that she's fighting something inside. Here is the writer's revision:

> I was aboard the London-bound train now. In just eleven hours I would be five hundred miles away from home. "Home," I caught myself repeating the word; how winsome and beautiful it suddenly sounded. Home, where stark white plasterboard walls were softened with woven baskets, dried flowers, and herbs that hung upside down from exposed rafters. I could smell the cardamon from my mother's kitchen, mingled with the pungent aroma of sweet pekoe tea that floated up from the shiny copper teapot. I could see a radiant and crackling fire, dancing to the music of Scott Joplin and the New Orleans Preservation Hall jazz band. I was so overcome by the rememberance of home that I jumped when the conductor opened the door to my compartment to check the ticket which was damp and crumpled in my hand. As he left, the compartment door slammed shut, and the crash of metal against metal echoed in my head. Shivering for a moment, I pulled my woolen sweater across my chest and buttoned it up.

By applying the difference between *telling* and *showing* to editing, students are more likely to be better editors and evaluators of writing. Daily oral teacher evaluation of writing has served as a model. And because changing *telling* to *showing* has become a habit, they are better able to expand their ideas into rich, vivid prose.

USING DAILY WRITING TO LEARN SPECIFIC TECHNIQUES

After spending six weeks allowing students to experiment with showing, I begin deliberate instruction in developing ideas. I begin exposing my students to methods of generating details which they may not have discovered or practiced. This is the time for them to study literary devices for revealing ideas, a time to try different stylistic techniques. By altering the procedure in this way, I make two specific changes in the daily sentence practice:

1. I assign *telling* sentences derived from what the class is studying (e.g., persuasive argument, autobiography, short story writing).

2. I require students to expand these sentences in what may be unfamiliar ways. This requirement might be called *directed elaboration* as opposed to the undirected response of earlier daily writings.

For instance, if we're currently doing a unit on persuasive argument, I structure all the *telling* sentences as opinions: *Lunch period is too short. Teenagers should have their own telephones. P.E. should not be required.* Each day we practice different strategies for developing arguments—dealing with the opposition first, saving the best argument until last—while at the same time examining published essays of persuasion. Students then have the opportunity to apply the new strategy in the assigned daily sentence.

Or, if we're practicing different sentence styles, such as the types of sentences described by Francis Christensen (1967) I require students to use certain modification structures—verb clusters, adjective clusters—in their assigned sentences.

In any case, a final composition assignment—an essay of persuasion, a character sketch—culminates the unit of study. Students write better compositions because the directed elaboration of the daily practices has given them a variety of techniques to draw on. Like the drama instructor advising the student who exaggerates Hamlet's lament, "Instead of delivering Hamlet's soliloquy to the balcony, looking up to the center spotlight, I'd like you to try that speech with your back turned, sitting in the wheelchair," I want my students to experiment with challenging and unfamiliar ways of exprssing ideas. Probably the drama teacher does not expect her student to perform Hamlet in a wheelchair in the final presentation; she simply wants the student to experience a new way of delivering despair, an experience he can apply to his final performance. In the same way, I do not expect my students to follow some exact pattern or structure when designing arguments or creating characters, just to stretch their limits and discover options.

When my students write their final compositions, when they sit down to deliver their finest performances, I want them to feel that their hours of training have paid off. I want them to gain a notion of what writers are about. And if they freeze-up in midway in the process, if they encounter the blank that all writers face, I hope they will learn to use the "art" itself as a tool of release.

The two sample units of study which follow include my instructions for directed elaboration of the daily sentences. The first is a study in characterization: the second in comparison and contrast.

STUDY IN CHARACTERIZATION
SHOWING PERSONALITY
THROUGH PERSONAL ENVIRONMENT

A six-step exercise prepares students to elaborate their next telling sentence in a particular way. This exercise is completed during a class period which culminates in assigning the telling sentence. It instructs students in the use of details to evoke character by allowing them to explore how character is revealed in their own experience of themselves and others.

Step 1. Each student is given a copy of the following chart. (Adapted from Simon, *et al.,* 1972, pp. 331-32.)

Items in my room at home	What I think these items say about me to others	What these items *do* say about me to others. #1.	What these items *do* say about me to others. #2.
1.	1.	1.	1.
2.	2.	2.	2.
3.	3.	3.	3.

Step 2. Each student privately decides on three items of decoration in his bedroom at home that he considers his favorites. These items might be a poster, plant, photograph, waterbed, record collection—anything that can be seen upon entering the room. If a student does not have a room of his own, I ask to consider the section of the room that is his.

In the first column, *Items in my room at home,* each student lists three favorite items. The student should also *describe* each possession so that someone might be able to picture it in its particular setting. For example, instead of merely listing "the plant on my desk," it is better to say, "the baby African violets growing out of an antique lacquered box," or instead of saying "my macrame wall-hanging," one might write "my macrame wall-hanging in the design of a raincloud; the colors are iridescent blue, lavender, and silver."

Step 3. In column two, *What I think these items say about me to others,* students suggest what each object might reflect about them. If students have difficulty grasping this idea, I ask them to consider *why* they like that particular item and *why* they chose it as their favorite. Each possession should be interpreted individually.

I also tell them this column is a private column; no one will see their personal interpretations. They are to be as honest as possible.

Example:

Items in my room. . .	*What I think these items say. . .*
1. my trophy collection that sits on top of my bookcase; these trophies range from football to baseball to track; they span eight years of athletic involvement.	1. I'm successful in many different sports. Others have recognized my athletic strength. I'm proud of my achievement and want people — friends — to know about it.

Step 4. When each student has filled in columns one and two, he should fold column one over column two so that column two (the private one) is hidden. Each student then asks a classmate to "evaluate" his furnishings. The responding student provides answers to the question *What* do *these items say about me to others?* In other words, by reading the descriptive list in column one, the evaluating classmate should say what he thinks each item suggests about that person. After responding to each item, he covers his response and returns the chart to its originator. The originator then selects a second person to react to his possessions. *At no time should any evaluating partner look at the interpretations of other students or of the originator.* Each student deserves original evaluations, not repeats of another classmate's impression. If students are worried that others will "peek," I give them paperclips to secure their folded papers.

Step 5. Each student compares his own interpretations to those of his classmates. I encourage each student to write something he learned from doing this activity. "Did most people see you as you saw yourself?" I ask them. "Did your evaluators' interpretations differ from your own?"

The sample chart on the following page was completed by sophomore students.

Following this exercise I ask my students, "Why does a writer bother to describe a character's room, house, or environment? Why does she take the trouble to create a setting so vividly?" Students are able to answer, "Perhaps it is because she would like to *show* a particular character's personality, rather than *tell* us about it. Perhaps she would like us to do some interpreting on our own."

After the students have connected setting to characterization, I assign the *telling* sentence *She is strange* for expansion. Although they might reveal her strangeness in many ways—actions, gestures, clothing, dialogue—I ask them to show her eccentricity exclusively through setting. Here is one junior student's solution:

> As I entered the room the warnings of the other girls in the dorm kept running through my head. I had laughed so hard at the stories earlier, but that was before I actually had seen Bessie's room. Directly inside the door was the customary extra-long desk, but she had a small-size, orange bean bag chair sitting on the end of it. Directly above it were the bulletin boards covered with a neatly arranged collection of candy wrappers. The light green curtains were held back from the window with brand new shoelaces.
>
> In front of them was her expensive clock radio, hung from the ceiling in a purple, macrame plant hanger. The large, luminated numbers could be eaisly read from the bed with blankets spread so tightly that a bobby pin would hit the ceiling if it dared to bounce on them. Above the bed was a four-by-three foot color picture of a burnt hamburger pattie, resting on a catsup drenched bun. On the other side of the room her roommate, Eve, sat watching me and my astonishment with great pleasure. To this day I see the room and smile when I hear others laugh in disbelief about the stories of Bessie's room.

Notice how her entire sketch revolves around specific possessions and decorations. Although her introductory and concluding sentences *tell* or *hint* at Bessie's strangeness with "warnings of the other girls," and "others laughing in disbelief," this writer suppports these impressions with a bean-bag chair atop a desk, curtains tied with shoelaces, and radio resting in a plant hanger.

The students enjoy creating these bizarre environments. In this sort of focused assignment, everyone wants his paper read. In a large class, I have the students form groups so they all can read their creations aloud. After sharing their writing, I hand out the following passage from *The Ballad of the Sad Cafe* by Carson McCullers:

Item in my room at home.	What I think these items say about me to others.	1. What these items *do* say about me to others.	2. What these items *do* say about me to others.
1. The items on my shelves, opposite my bed that are on the wall. I have stuffed animals on one, a couple of music boxes, and my two coin banks, and especially my Paddington Bear from England. Also, my radios, camera, jewelry box, and make-up.	1. I want all of these items to show that I love little figures and stuffed animals. I hope that people get the impression that I like keepsakes and that this shelf is the very life of my existence, my personality. There are things on my shelves that are ten years old. It is sort of a replica of my lifestory.	1. That you have been many places and like to gather things. Plus those mementos mean a great deal to you.	1. It shows you own personal objects that have and give you a lot of memories when you look at them.
2. My tape recorder always near my desk or bed, and my tape box.	2. I want people to see that I *thoroughly* enjoy music and that I might die without my tape recorder. I want them to know that I listen to music at the first chance I get.	2. That you're ready for anything and very fortunate.	2. Something that will give you happiness when you're sad.
3. A trilogy named *Lord of the Rings* that sits on my bookshelf.	3. I like to read fantasy books.	3. It shows that you like to read.	3. It shows that you are very intellectual and enjoy reading.

The large middle room, the parlor, was elaborate. The rosewood
sofa, upholstered in green threadbare silk, was before the fireplace.
Marble-topped tables, two Singer sewing machines, a big vase of
pampas grass—everything was rich and grand. The most important
piece of furniture in the parlor was a big, glass-doored cabinet in
which was kept a number of treasures and curios. Miss Amelia had
added two objects to this collection; one was an acorn from a water
oak, the other a little velvet box holding two small, grayish stones.
Sometimes when she had nothing to do, Miss Amelia would take
out this velvet box and stand by the windows with the stones in the
palm of her hand, looking down at them with a mixture of
fascination, dubious respect and fear. They were the kidney stones
of Miss Amelia herself, and had been taken from her by the doctor
in Cheehaw some years ago (p. 71).

Notice the organization of this lesson. The students wrestle with the
concept first, before they study a model. Their appreciation for style is
deepened. Having had to create a similar mood or environment, they will
value the expertise of a gifted writer. The daily sentence, then, can be used to
practice techniques for developing a characterization and to enhance
appreciation of good writing skills.

STUDY IN EXPOSITION
STRUCTURING THROUGH COMPARISON AND CONTRAST

Structuring a comparison is one of the most important lessons students
can master. History instructors frequently ask students to contrast two
decades or two leaderships; science teachers might have students compare
two chemical reactions or two life cycles. When faced with "discussion
questions" on essay exams, students can rely on this kind of structure; the
comparison/contrast pattern gives them something to *do* with the facts
they've studied.

At one point in the year I use the following practices in my English classes
to prepare students to write compositions on a major work of literature we
are studying. Since I will require these particular essays to be based on
themes of comparison between two characters, two settings, two courses of
action, I have students practice extensively with the comparison/contrast
structure, using the daily sentence to explore and to experiment.

My first assignment in this unit is the telling sentence *Saturday is different
from Sunday*. Having students compare subjects with which they are
familiar is good preparation for more expanded comparisons. After reading
aloud alternative interpretations, we share and discuss successful structures.
Here is one by a senior student:

Weekends. Just two days out of the week, yet many people live just
for Saturday and Sunday. Those two days have a distinct flavor to

them. They are both days for relaxation, or catching up on what you should have been doing during the week.

Saturday is a totally carefree day. The whole day is yours—even the night. You can party all night long, because there is still Sunday to recover. Saturday is the day for long trips. Sailing on the bay or doing whatever you enjoy. It's the day to take it easy—don't worry about it, you can do it later. Saturday night is a special time—time for parties, seeing a movie, or just laying back and watching "Saturday Night Live." Saturday is a day for doing new things, a day of deep blue skies that last forever, and nights that sparkle with stars that sparkle crisply.

Sunday really doesn't start until about 6 or 7 a.m. Saturday night holds reign until then but then Sunday manages to break out of the haze. Sunday is catch-up day, the day to do all those things you wanted to get done on this weekend. Sunday is a day for mowing lawns, doing homework, and hauling trash to the dump. It's a garden day, a day to clip back those juniper bushes that have overgrown the sidewalk. Sunday is like a sunset—things don't seem as bright as they did on Saturday, the sky is fading back to gray. It's a day of goodbyes—to people leaving, vacations that are over, memories gone by. By nightfall, Monday is right behind you—you can feel its presence. It's back inside again—recess is over.

This composition uses a typical form: an introduction showing the similarities of the two days, one paragraph devoted to Saturday, and one to Sunday. However, this student's organizational qualities go deeper; by using parallelism, he brings unity to his composition. If he mentions that Saturday is "deep blue skies lasting forever," he remembers to talk about the "sky fading back to gray" on Sunday; if Saturday is free from responsibility, Sunday is a day for obligations. Most students naturally seem to use this structural pattern—A in one paragraph, B in the other. I explain that this particular pattern is one of a writer's *options,* and we spend a portion of the period examining and discussing such a paper. Again, the lesson evolves from what the students already know how to do.

After such a discussion, I give my students a more challenging technique for consideration—the integrated comparison. Here the writer must move back and forth between her subjects in a single paragraph, knowing precisely how to disclose differences or similarities. Without becoming monotonous in this zigzag fashion, she emphasizes the major points of her comparison. The class examines a paragraph such as the following description of two unusual birds.

There are two species of Sooty Albatrosses (Brown and Antarctic) *both* of which are quite similar in appearance. They *both* have dark plumage, a long wedge-shaped tail, and long wings which are very narrow. On the underside of its body, *however,* the Antarctic Sooty

Albatross has paler plumage than the Brown Albatross, *and* it flies less gracefully. On their bills *both* species have a groove called a sulcus, which divides the lower segment of the bill; *but* the sulcus of the Brown Albatross is yellow or orange, *whereas* the narrower sulcus of the Antarctic species is blue. For nests, *both* species build up a low cone of earth hollowed out on top.

The emphasis of this paragraph is the distinguishing differences between two very similar birds. In contrast to the A-B structure, where a writer might simply list a series of parallel descriptions leaving the reader to extract the similarities and differences, this structure demands that the writer make explicit the points of comparison. In the albatross paragraph, for example, had the writer devoted one paragraph to the Brown Albatross and another to the Antarctic, the reader might have had to re-read both to extract the major differences.

Next, we examine the use of the *transitional expressions* (italicized in the model) that improve the coherence of the paragraph and make the contrasts clear. In the integrated comparison, a writer must use the expressions more frequently than in an A-B structure. So I list on the board for discussion additional expressions that signify similarity or difference:

Transitions for Similarity	*Transitions for Contrast*
similarly, likewise, equally, in the same fashion, in addition, also, too.	but, however, on the contrary, in contrast, on the other hand, while, whereas.

Finally, we discuss the economy of compiling sets of characteristics into a single paragraph. If a writer has only a few series of details, the single structure works best; a large group of details calls for more paragraphs.

At this point, after close examination of the albatross paragraph, I ask my students to imitate the structure of that paragraph. Their daily sentence becomes *There are two kinds of (fill in own subject)*. I want as precise a replica of the sentence patterns used in the albatross paragraph as possible. I want students to get the *feel* of a tightly written comparison, using transitions to disclose similarity and difference. This assignment requires that during pre-writing, each writer discover the distinguishing differences of his comparison in order to be able to imitate the albatross format. If a student falters, he can use the same transitional expressions and create descriptive phrases similar to the model paragraph ("are quite similar in appearance," "on the underside of its..."). Since many students have rarely attempted such an exercise, I introduce the assignment as follows: "If I were to ask you to imitate the structure of 'The cat ran through the grass,' noun for noun, verb for verb, prepositional phrase for prepositional phrase, supplying any subject matter, what sentence might you create?" The responses are usually quick: "The car drove down the street." "The popsicle

dripped in my hand." "The crowd cheered in the aisles." Below are two
student imitations of the albatross pattern, the first by a junior, the second
by a sophomore:

> There are two flavors of Frosted Mini-Wheats (brown-sugar and
> cinnamon) both of which are quite equal in nutritional supplements.
> They both are made from 100% whole wheat, have frosting on one
> side only, and cost the same amount of money. On the frosted side
> of the wheat biscuit, however, the sugar coated Mini-Wheat has a
> smoother and lighter texture than that of the cinnamon frosted
> Wheat biscuit, and it has a sweeter taste. On the uncoated side of the
> Mini-Wheats both biscuits have hundreds of criss-crossed wheat
> fibers; but the fibers on the cinnamon coated biscuit are darker,
> whereas the smaller fibered, brown sugarcoated Mini-Wheat is
> lighter in color. For breakfast, both flavors of Frosted Mini-Wheats
> give one a good supply of his daily nutritional needs.

> There are two ways of playing tennis (singles and doubles) both of
> which are played using similar techniques. They are both played on
> a regular tennis court, scored the same way, and require the same
> amount of skill. When playing singles, however, one needs to cover
> more area of the court due to the fact there's only one player. In the
> serving procedures, both the singles and doubles players must serve
> the ball into the same area; but the doubles players stand one at the
> end and one at the baseline while serving, whereas the singles player
> stands alone at the baseline. In order to be good, both types of
> tennis require a lot of practice and dedication.

The completion of this exercise requires each writer to read his paper
aloud, but because the paragraph is short, this reading takes practically no
time. After listening to some thirty imitations, the students have internalized
the transitional shifts that create the smooth-running texture of the
paragraph. In addition, they begin to grasp an understanding of effective
punctuation—the parentheses (Brown and Antarctic) for incorporating a list
within a sentence; the semi-colon as a useful way to join closely related
sentences which together draw a comparison or make a contrast.

The A-B and the single paragraph structures are comparison alternatives
that can be practiced and perfected. Through the use of *telling* sentences
which establish context and/or make transitions, both allow writers to
incorporate details which make contrasts more vivid to the reader. One
senior discovered a less conventional approach in a composition based
entirely on *showing*:

Saturday Is Different from Sunday

Without the help of an alarm clock, at 8:30 sharp Saturday
morning, I wake up brimmed with energy and ready to take on any

activity that floats my way. The sun is pouring bars of golden liquid in my window and the bluejays are singing merrily at the top of their musical voices. Anticipating a whole day to do whatever I want, I eagerly throw on my clothes and spring down the stairs. After a light breakfast I grab my old familiar cut-offs and my favorite beach towel, jump in the convertible, and with a delightful screech of the wheels fly off to spend a beautiful day running and laughing in the sun.

My mother is shaking me and saying, "It's past 11:00. Get up, there is work to do." With a deep groan I open my bloodshot eyes and am immediately blinded by the terrible glare of the sun beaming hot and stuffy directly on me. Very slowly I claw my way out of bed, and in a drained, limp state of semiconsciousness stumble sheepishly down the stairs. My family, faces cheerful and repulsive, is having breakfast. Just the aroma of eggs turns my stomach making me feel queasy. Instead, I trudge to the cabinet, fumble with a bottle of aspirin, and with a glass of warm water sloppily gulp three down. Then, still hung over and depressed, I sit down and stare straight ahead thinking about the agony of mowing the lawn.

The class was impressed by the vividness of this student's composition, achieved almost exclusively through concrete details. He uses other techniques, too, to give the piece a literary rather than expository tone. Although the composition follows the A-B structure, the writer doesn't identify the subject of his composition in an opening paragraph. We don't know that Sunday will be following in contrast to Saturday until we are into the second paragraph. In addition, he changes mood through careful selection of verbs. By altering the connotations suggested by the verbs in the two paragraphs—sun *pouring* bars of golden liquid versus being *blinded* by the glare of the sun; *throwing* on clothes and *springing* down stairs versus *clawing* his way out of bed and *stumbling* down the stairs—he achieves an *implied* contrast. His composition is exemplary in two ways: first, his method of comparing becomes a *third* option for students; second it shows that by paying attention to what *students* do, we can embellish our instruction. Rather than continually relying on textbooks for proper instruction, students can learn special techniques from other successful student writers.

Following examination of these three options (A-B structure, integrated contrast, and use of concrete or *showing* sentences to create implied comparison), I let students experiment on their own. As their daily sentence I assign another statement of contrast, *My X teacher is different from my Y teacher,* asking them to structure the comparison in any way they prefer. Some students use one of the studied structures, while others mix all three. Students have the opportunity to test different approaches.

By now we are well into reading and discussing a work of literature, F. Scott Fitzgerald's *The Great Gatsby* or *The Circle,* a play by Somerset

Maugham, which the class will analyze in a major assignment. Students are thinking about their essay structures as I suggest contrasting two characters, two settings, two courses of action, whatever can be compared in a specific relationship. They complete one more practice piece, however, before this final assignment. The assignment, a comparison of synonyms, is also a major composition, equal in value to all major project assignments. Besides providing students another chance to rehearse structure, it also requires them to explore the precise definitions of words, attending to the connotations of synonymous terms.

Sample Synonyms for Comparison

rebel	love	attractive	rug
revolutionary	romance	beautiful	carpet
curiosity	pride	jealousy	lady
nosiness	conceit	envy	chick
wisdom	success	hate	junk
knowledge	greatness	dislike	stuff
skinny	nuts	brainy	habit
thin	insane	intelligent	custom

One student paper in response to this assignment is included below. The case studies section of this report includes three samples of the literary essays that followed these practices.

LADY—CHICK

A lady and a chick, while both representing the female sex, have many contrasting attributes. In fact, it is not likely that one would find them together. A lady, for instance, might be found in a shaded parlour reading Shakespeare or on the veranda sipping a cool drink. A lady is respected and admired, from afar by men, and in loving friendship by women. Even her physical appearance bespeaks refinement. Her hair may be pulled neatly back from her face, revealing well scrubbed skin and clear bright eyes. She presents a soft, smooth voice at all times, no matter what may ruffle the serenity of the moment. At times, however, a refined laugh may escape from rosy lips showing pearly white teeth.

A chick represents a different group of the female sex. She has the normal attributes of a woman, but what she does with them is the deciding difference between her and a lady. The chick might be seen on a hot Saturday afternoon slinking down the street, poured into tight jeans that have seen better days. Slogans like "I'll try anything once" or "Too many men and so little time" adorn the front of her shrink-to-fit T-shirt. She, too, may be admired by men, though, in contrast with the lady, *not* from afar. The chick's appearance, like the lady's, is representative of her personal attitudes and values. She may look out on the world through frizzy, unkempt bangs, with eyes ringed with last week's eye-makeup. Whereas the highest compliment to a lady may be a whispered word from the most eligible bachelor in town, a chick receives her compliments from total strangers in roaring cars who wolf-whistle as they screech by.

 After a long day of socially acceptable activities, visits, trips to the library, cooking lessons, the lady comes home. About the same time, the chick flops down on her waterbed after a long guitar-playing session in the park. Now they both like to think a bit. If one could hear their thoughts at this moment, one may understand one very important similarity. The lady's secret wish is to be blatantly whistled at and the chick thinks how nice it would be to just once be called a lady.

This student's comparison is effective because she uses the comparison structures discussed in class appropriately. She uses *A in one paragraph (discussing the lady) and B in the next paragraph (showing the chick).* In addition she matches characteristic detail for characteristic detail (parallelism). If she mentions the lady "pulling her hair neatly back from her face, revealing well-scrubbed skin and clear bright eyes," she counters that description in paragraph "B" with the chick "looking out on the world through frizzy unkempt bangs, with eyes ringed with last week's eye-makeup."

 The writer also employs the *integrated comparison* (A, however B). In the middle of the second paragraph she shifts into distinguishing or emphasizing the most interesting differences. She begins weaving back and forth between lady and chick, saying "whereas the highest compliment to a lady may be a whispered word from the most eligible bachelor in town, a chick receives her compliments from total strangers in roaring cars who wolf-whistle as they screech by."

 Her last paragraph also uses the integrated comparison to bring the essay to an especially effective climax. She continues identifying major differences between the lady and the chick and then jolts the reader with her final ironic revelation.

VARIATIONS ON THE DAILY PRACTICE PROGRAM

 The English department of an entire school might decide to adopt the daily writing idea, only to find that after the first year, or even the first semester, the assignment begins to loose its appeal for students, and hence its impact on their writing. This is likely to happen whenever students who master a particular response are asked to go on making the same kind of response day after day.

The answer is to use the *principle* of daily practice, but to change the particular skills being practiced, regularly offering new challenges to students. The daily practice paragraph and all its associated activities from classroom discussion to peer-guided revision provides a *method* for teaching and learning, but need not be limited to a single instructional *goal*.

Here are some alternative goals, with ideas for exercise sequence which might re-direct daily practices for a period of time:

1. *Sentence-level practice* rather than writing whole paragraphs allows concentration on several specific kinds of skills. Students practice embedding specifics in a single sentence using lists, appositives, participial phrases, more precise adjectives or nouns, images, etc. Sentence-level daily practice might accompany instruction in skills such as sentence combining, metaphor, diction, denotation and connotation of words, parallel structure.

   Assignment: Teacher provides an empty "telling" sentence as before: *He was confident.*

   Challenge: Student must enrich, elaborate, change the sentence, so that the idea of the telling sentence is communicated in a *single* sentence which shows: *When it was his turn to speak, the district attorney stood up, straightened his vest, and sauntered to the front of the courtroom.*

2. *Practice in making powerful generalizations.* It is not necessary to write a whole essay or paragraph in order to practice creating good thesis sentences of the kind which give purpose and direction to exposition or argument. A variety of classroom activities and kinds of instruction could be strengthened by following them with daily homework assignments requiring students to generate one or more appropriate *abstractions* which comment on, interpret, or define a set of concrete facts.

   Assignment: Teacher provides material for shared observation, or simply a list of concrete facts. Or class develops a list of concrete details out of "showing" sentences written the night before.

   Challenge: Student must write an abstract statement or series of abstractions which provide meaning to, or explain the significance of, the collected facts. Because they are based on actual observation of a number of concrete details, these abstractions should be richer than the ordinary telling sentence students have been given in the past.

3. *Practice in focusing: practice in expressing key ideas.* The writing of captions and titles has often been used to help students identify kernel concepts and to recognize how language can be used pointedly to express ideas in a few words.

feet. The sofa had soft velvety cushions and swallowed you
 you sat in it. The walls were a light blue and had a relaxing
t. The picture on the wall was of a smiling lady who made you
welcome. The clock ticked a steady beat and gave the room a
ey feeling.

gh Craig manages to include several concrete examples—soft, thick
; soft, velvety cushions swallowing you; picture of a smiling lady on
l—he fails to elaborate other important influences which he mentions
—sunlight warming the room to "just the right temperature"; light
valls having a "relaxing effect"; a ticking clock giving the room a
y feeling." These descriptions are abstract and require much more
ative thinking to convey the image exactly. This does not mean that
abstraction needs to be elaborated; it shows rather that Craig, at this
, is limited to describing concrete reality. He leaves the more difficult
rations of feeling and sensations—relaxing effect, homey feeling, etc.—
he "safer" descriptions of paintings and couches and carpets.

few weeks later, Craig, like most students, writes longer paragraphs. In
attempt to show more, Craig is able to sustain a longer discourse:

After the meal, the dinner table did not look the same.

I looked at the table and my mouth started to water. Everything
on the table looked just right. There was a rare cooked roast, the
side dishes had their appetizing appeal while everything else on the
table was clean and neat. The pure white tablecloth, under the
gleaming silverware with plates and dishes that shined like mirrors.
After I had eaten all that I could fit in my stomach I leaned back and
glanced at the table. Everything on it had been thrown, spilled, or
dropped on the table. Someone had spilled his milk and part of the
tableclothe was wet and soggy. Some red juice had spilled over the
edge of the meat platter and there was a red ring on the tableclothe.
All that was left of the meat was a well picked bone. The pan that
had held the vegetables had a little butter juice in the bottom as
evidence they had been there. All the silverware was strewn all over
the table.

Craig is increasing his ability to elaborate abstract ideas. In his second
sentence, Craig tells that everything on the table "looked just right."
However, he moves on to generate a specific picture—rare cooked roast, side
dishes. He tells us that everything on the table looked "clean and neat,"
supporting this impression with pure white tablecloth, gleaming silverware,
plates that shine like mirrors. Even though he leaves the reader dangling with
side dishes having an appetizing appeal (abstract), he is obviously
concentrating on improving some of his abstract ideas—a definite growth
pattern. We can witness this growth again when he states that after the meal
everything had been thrown, spilled, or dropped on the table and supports

Assignment: Teacher provides a paragrapl
other stimulus before students
teacher asks students to *imag.*
essay on what happens when th

Challenge: Instead of writing the essay, stu
title, headline, or caption which c.
the experience.

QUALITATIVE ANALYSIS OF PROGRAM
THREE CASE STUDIES

The following three studies demonstrate three junior st
the Advanced Composition class that followed this trainir
the first student studied, writes below the average f(
advanced group. Carolyn, the second, represents the ave:
the final case study, is a superior writer.

Craig

Craig is a junior impressed with being in Advanced C(
disenchanted with writing. He has never felt himself a successf
in this course purely to learn "college writing." He wants to
university by mastering formulas for writing successful papers.
emerge a better writer, he will blame the teacher.

Craig is an inconsistent writer. At times I was surprised b
supportive evidence, by his immature sentence style, and by
editing skills. Compared to the attention other students gave t
Craig lacked discipline. On the other hand, there were times Crai;
strength in writing, a superior ability to capture the essence of a s
careful attention to detail. Whenever this kind of skill surfaced
upon it, encouraging him to make more use of his observational :
no matter what form praise took, Craig rejected any appreciatio
writing. Although he did his assignments, Craig was highly critical o
and the class, questioning the validity of most assignments. He ra
that doing an assignment was actually related to improving his writ
objected to the daily paragraphs, objected to the major compositions,
about grammar study, and continued complaining about the poor qu:
his writing. When his best essay was printed for distribution a
classmates, he argued privately afte class that I had made a grave er1
choosing his paper as a model because, he said, it was such poor w

Three daily writings—written at the beginning, middle, and end ol
semester—are representative of Craig's improvement in the use of speci1

The living room was a warm, inviting place.

The sun was shining thru the window. It warmed the room to just
the right temperature. The floor had soft thick carpeting cushioned

this generality with spilled milk which makes the table cloth wet and soggy, red juice spilling over the edge of the meat platter, leaving a red ring, the remains of the meat, a well-picked bone, etc. Craig is beginning to differentiate generality from specific by remembering to support several of his abstractions.

In a later writing, Craig successfully manages to detail a rather difficult idea, a state of mind. With the telling sentence *Some students are not afraid to cheat,* Craig writes the following:

> Mike walked into his first period class. The talk his father had given him on cheating was still going through his mind. His fourth period math teacher had sent a note to his parents explaining how she had caught him cheating. When his parents got it they flew into hysteria. They started to lecture him on how it was when they went to school. They told him how the kids then used the honor system and how it was unheard of to cheat. They told him that it only hurt him to cheat. His mind popped back into the present. His French teacher was passing out a surprise quiz. He had not studied that night before because he had been so mad at his parents. The teacher finished passing out the quizzes and went to her desk in the far corner away from Mike. He had pass this quiz to pass the class so his eyes started to wander towards the persons paper beside him. The lecture he had just received had allready vanished from his mind.

In this particular selection Craig must prove that the individual lacks fear. Craig's proof is the entire paragraph, built around the sophisticated use of flashback. Craig puts the reader inside the thinking of the cheater, using a series of events that build on each other to show his lack of apprehension. Each flashback moves closer to the present; each memory of cheating (and the resulting punishment—fourth period math teacher sending a note home, the heavy parent-lecturing which he remembers to show) will end up supporting the condition that Mike cares little about the consequences of cheating. As he moves into the present—the French teacher passing out a surprise quiz—and as we see Mike's eyes easily wandering toward his neighbor's paper, we understand the irony of his flashback—it has no effect on him. That one small gesture of "eyes wandering" show much about Mike in the face of his past history—indeed, proves he is not afraid to cheat.

The effects of the daily practice can be seen in the following excerpts from a major essay assignment in which close work with revision was required. Peer-group editors were searching for thinly developed ideas, and students were asked to "show" these ideas for homework (part two of the training program). This essay concerns the outcome of a personal decision. Students were asked to reflect on the reasons they chose a particular course of action in the face of an important choice. Craig wrote about choosing to go motorcycle riding when his mother had forbidden it. Here are his opening paragraph and the paragraph which holds the climax of the story. Accompanying each is the revision of that paragraph written after classmates in editing groups had suggested he elaborate.

Opening Paragraph:

> Many times I have gone against what my mother has told me, but one time really sticks out in my mind. My mom has always forbidden me to have anything to do with motorcycles. It was probably because she was involved in a really bad accident when she hit one, but I still couldn't understand why she wouldn't let me ride at least once. *Finally I decided to go with my friend the next time he went riding.*

In this final sentence Craig has leaped into making the decision without showing the reader *how* he came to decide. For a moment he stands puzzled—"I still couldn't understand why she wouldn't let me ride at least once"—and then jumps ahead into deciding—"Finally, I decided to go...."

Revision:

> Many times I have gone against what my mom has told me, but one time really sticks out. My mom has always forbidden me to have anything to do with motorcycles. It is probably because she was involved in a really bad accident about four years ago when she hit a bike and injured the rider. However, I still couldn't understand why she wouldn't let me ride one at least once. Her accident didn't affect me, and all of my friends were riding or owned bikes. I had one good friend with a bike who offered to take me with him. For a couple of weeks I thought about what I should do. I thought of both sides, and finally rationalized that to go riding would be better. After all, I was going to be riding where there were no cars.

In this revision Craig explains his rationalizations more clearly—his mother's accident not affecting him, all his friends owning bikes, his riding safely on streets without traffic. Now we are *shown* how he came to decide.

Here is the climax of the story:

> All of a sudden, I wrecked and was lying on the road. I had been accelerating down a straight stretch and was coming up on a turn. There was a little bit of gravel on the road; and when I put the front brake on from habit and started to take the turn, the front wheel locked. The next thing I knew, both the bike and I were on the ground. I quickly got up and picked the bike up and tried to start it. *I didn't hurt very much in one particular spot, but I was very shaken up.*

Students in Craig's editing group suggested he show his state of being "very shaken up" (telling sentence italicized). After all, having an accident was what he most wanted to avoid; because he thought it really couldn't happen to him, he chose to disobey his mother's command.

Revision:

> All of a sudden, I wrecked and way lying on the road. I had been accelerating down a straight stretch and was coming up on a turn. There was a little bit of gravel on the road, and when I put the front brake on from habit and started to take the turn, the front wheel locked. The next thing I knew, both the bike and I were on the ground. I quickly got up and picked up the bike and tried to start it. The first couple of times that I kicked it over nothing happened; but finally, after playing with the choke a little bit, I got it started. I didn't hurt very much in any one particular spot, but I was very shaken up. For one thing, there were a couple of soccer teams practicing on the field next to the road. I could feel the embarrassment sweep over me like a big black cloud. My hands were scraped up a little bit and had a slight sting to them. I was also shaking because I thought I might have ruined the bike in some way.

Now we know *specifically* what has shaken Craig—the resulting embarrassment from the soccer team witnessing his clumsiness, the pain from the scraped up hands, the fear he may have ruined the bike.

Craig, at this point in the course, is better equipped to make these revisions, to apply the difference between telling and showing to his own writing, because of the daily practice. In several additional essays before the end of the semester, Craig was required to go through the same revision process.

Here is Craig's best essay, written at the end of the semester. Craig contrasted two characters in Somerset Maugham's play *The Circle*.

Envy and Strife

In Act II of the play "The Circle", Lord Porteous makes several statements that show his feelings about Clive. He says things like, "Let me tell you that I don't like your manner", and "I never liked you, I don't like you now, and I never shall like you." Of course there are many possible reasons why Porteous disliked Clive, but three really stand out. Lord Porteous was envious of Clive, but Clive understood Lady Kitty, he led a more successful life, and he enjoyed life more than Lord Porteous.

Clive had the ability to understand what Lady Kitty wanted while Porteous did not. Porteous would yell and become angry with Kitty, while Clive showed grace and manners when he was around her. For instance, when Kitty lost her lipstick, Clive give it to her but he also made a witty statement about it. Porteous simply could not keep his cool when he was around Kitty. When playing patience, he could not stand to have Kitty help him, and he became so angry when she did that they had a terrible argument. They ended up not talking to one another for half the night. Clive controlled his temper though; he calmly accepted her when she was around. For example, when Kitty asked him if he wanted her to come back to him, Clive calmly told her that he didn't care for her anymore. Most men would have become at least a little emotional.

Besides the fact that Clive got along with Kitty better, he also had a more successful life than Porteous. By running away with Kitty, Porteous sacrificed his almost certain position of prime minister. Because of the divorce scandal with his ex-wife, Porteous went from a high political position to nothing in a few short years. Comparatively, Clive did lose a little over the scandal, but not nearly as much as Porteous. Clive just disappeared from the public eye and still had a fairly successful life. He also did not have as much to lose as Porteous. Clive lived very comfortably and did a lot of traveling, visiting the higher society of Europe. Porteous, on the other hand, just went to live in an old secluded castle which he owned; and although he had plenty of money, he was thrust down to the lowest social class. Also because of Lady Kitty, Porteous did not have many real friends.

Besides his relationship with Kitty and his social status, Porteous also disliked Clive because Clive had more enjoyment in life. While Porteous was constantly fighting with Kitty, Clive was having affairs with many different young women. Although Clive was very upset when Kitty first left him, he soon decided he was not going to let it ruin his life. He would start an affair with a young woman and break it off when the lady reached the age of 25. Meanwhile, Porteous had to suffer with the company of Lady Kitty for 30 years. Even though Porteous loved her, they were always bickering and having little arguments which made his life miserable. Porteous was not as happy or satisfied as Clive.

Because of his envy, Lord Porteous did things that we, as normal people, might do. For example, when he refused to speak to Lady Kitty it was because he was jealous of her relationship with Clive. Many times when a guy is jealous of someone his girl friend knows, he expresses his resentment by refusing to speak to her. He will usually say it is for some other reason, but if he looked deeply enough into himself, he would find that it was because of jealousy or envy.

Craig elaborates the jealousy of one character over another with careful use of example. Not only is his thesis insightful and rather sophisticated, his rich use of dramatic evidence shows Craig's growth in attention to detail—especially to abstract ideas, in this case "jealousy and envy." Although there are weak, underdeveloped segments—like choosing to paraphrase the action of the play instead of using direct quotations ("when Kitty lost her lipstick, Clive made a witty statement" or "Porteous and Lady Kitty were always bickering and having arguments")—he manages to find a variety of examples that when totaled, support the notion that one character is indeed jealous of the other.

Finally, here are the pretest and posttest essays Craig wrote for the research experiment, laid side by side, so that we might examine the kind of writing skills Craig had gained:

Pretest Essay

Score 9

Describe something from which you learned a lesson.

I was wet fly fishing. I had filled my clear plastic bobber with water, tied a fly to the leader and proceeded to cast the rig out and reel it back in. My friend was with me but he was just watching. He had never really learned to fish but he was going to help me land the fish since I didn't have a net. Twenty minutes had passed and we were both getting tired of fishing. It was midafternoon, about 3:00 o'clock so the fish probably weren't feeding anyway. Then all of a sudden I had a strong strike. I had the fish hooked and started to reel him in. He fought very hard and would swim towards me to make me think I had lost him since my line went slack. Then I would reel in some line and find out I still had him. Finally I had him very close to shore, his back stuck out of the water because I had him so close to shore. I told my friend to grab him in the middle of his body so that he wouldn't get away. My friend started to grab the line with one hand because since he never went fishing he didn't know that was wrong. The next thing I knew the hook had come out of the fishes mouth and had come up to where my friend had a hold of the line. He almost got the hook in his hand but he let go of the grip he had on the fish so he could get the hook out of his hand. We had lost the fish and it turned out to be the only bite I had that day. I have learned from that experience to never trust someone to do something right that they have never done before.

Craig begins by incorporating close description (filling the plastic bobber with water, tying the fly to the leader, casting out the rig). When he gets his "catch" he again shows the feeling—the fish fighting very hard by swimming towards him to deceive him, making his line go slack; the fish losing his battle when Craig sees his back sticking out of the water. However, when we get to the most crucial part of his story, the learning of the lesson, we become somewhat lost because he does not clearly show us why or how his friend did not know what to do with the catch. After he tells his friend to grab the fish in the middle of his body, the friend "grabs the line with one hand because since he never went fishing he didn't know that was wrong." Craig doesn't tell us what was wrong. The next thing we know his friend accidentally loses the fish because the hook almost gets caught in his hand, and Craig learns he should have released the fish himself.

Although Craig does use some close description to show the novice fisherman's error, he is not clear in showing us the correct way to get the fish so that we might understand his friend's blunder. In addition, for the learning of the lesson to have impact, we need to feel the importance and thrill of catching *that* fish—a feeling Craig fails to convey. Rather than a slow building of excitement or suspense around making the catch, Craig rushes through to the climactic moment—"twenty minutes had passed and we were really getting tired of fishing." It is hard to believe this catch really matters.

In Craig's posttest essay his growing skill is evident:

Posttest Essay

Score 11

Describe something you enjoyed doing as a child.

A Detective, racing against time, attempts to solve the puzzle of the crime before it is too late. He races around town in his red sports car always one step behind the criminal. Then, out of the blue he solves it, right before your eyes. You can never understand how he seems to put the pieces together the way he does but they always seem to fit.

Now I'm on space colony three, trying to prevent an explosion from destroying everybody while the enemy attacks from all sides of the ship. The enemy fighters whiz by at terrific speeds, our anti-matter guns trying to hit them with their deadly energy bolts. Finally the enemy ceases the attack and we complete our mission of exploring a new planet.

The cool sea breeze blows through my hair as it whips away the fishy smell of the ship. Suddenly the lookout shouts and signals that a French ship is ahead, full of treasure and gold. Our pirate ship prepares to broadside it as we prepare for a fight. We come along side the ship, our cannons blazing, a fire breaks out on the ship as we hurry to get the treasure before it sinks with the ship. After the fight, everyone celebrates the treasure that we have just captured and we prepare ourselves for another raid.

All of these scenes can be found in my imagination as I would read books on subjects like these. The excitement of a pirate ship to the thrill of solving a crime. The number of books is endless. I enjoyed laying down with a good adventure book as my usual dull life had the excitement of a book.

In this final piece of writing, we see Craig's attention to sensory detail pervade the entire composition. In addition, he begins with the course of his memory, putting the reader immediately within this pastime. This technique of plunging the reader right into the action is far more sophisticated than introducing the memory with a telling sentence such as "I was wet fly fishing" in the pretest essay. Craig learned this technique in two different ways during the semester: 1) hearing other student writers use the technique during the daily oral readings, and 2) writing to my lesson on "moving right into the action" as a narrative techinque.

Going further, Craig now gives his attention to paragraphing, showing a growth in singling out and developing the major ideas of his essay. In his pretest essay he combined numerous ideas—setting, situation, climax, resolution—in a single paragraph, devoting little time to the elaboration of any one description. Craig now paragraphs the detective, then the astronaut, then the pirate, demonstrating the effects of daily paragraph practice.

Carolyn

Carolyn is a junior who has average writing ability and sincerely wants to improve. She does all homework assignments, does them on time, studies diligently for tests, and usually puts much time into composing essays. She's the sort of student who always achieves A's in English for being conscientious, but she really has no special flair for an especially interesting writing style.

Here are three daily writings representative of Carolyn's growth in use of specifics. Like Craig's, these are illustrative of work done at the beginning, middle, and end of the semester.

Those girls are snobs.

I can't believe those girls! They strut around school like they own the world. They'll never condescend to speak to anybody who isn't a member of their select group. They might honor you with a quick hello, but never carry on a conversation with you. If by great chance they speak to you it's usually to let you know how inferior you are. They prefer to live in their own narrow world, too bad they don't realize how much they are missing.

Carolyn's paragraph is almost entirely built of abstractions. "They strut around like they own the world" is a cliche. They speak to you only "to let you know how inferior you are" is telling. We need some direct dialogue here, some snatch of conversation. "They prefer to live in their own narrow world" needs examples like "every girl in the group wears a dress on Mondays, jeans on Tuesdays, has feathered-back Farrah Fawcett hairdos," etc.

Several weeks later Carolyn shows *She seemed frightened:*

The chatter of gossipy girls hit me as I opened the door. There were about twenty young noisy girls scattered about the room. They all seemed to be enjoying themselves: talking with friends, eating popcorn, playing cards, or drinking rootbeer, all except one girl. She sat quietly in the corner of the room studying the rest of the group. When one of the girls came up to her from the side she jumped like a frightened bunny. She quickly turned to see who had tapped her on the shoulder. The girl asked if she wanted to play cards and without hesitation she said no and turned sharply around. She studied everything in the room. She seemed to be picking apart everything and everybody with her dull eyes. She kept a tight hold of her sweater trying to keep everybody in her sight. I went up and offered her some popcorn, she replied with a short and quiet "No, thank you" and went on with her scrutinizing of the room.

This piece of writing shows marked improvement. Carolyn remembers to support general claims with "pictures." "They all seemed to be enjoying themselves (abstraction), talking with friends, eating popcorn, playing cards, drinking rootbeer (specifics)." Amidst all this pleasantry sits the lone girl who seems frightened. Carolyn shows this through "jumping like a frightened bunny" when being approached from the side, turning quickly to see who has tapped her on the shoulder. She also "kept a tight hold of her sweater, trying to keep everyone in sight." Carolyn even uses dialogue to convey the girl's shyness and fear—saying a quiet "No, thank you" to popcorn.

Here is a daily writing from late in the semester:

Car advertisements are unrealistic because advertisers promise misleading gas mileage, they imply that the cars come fully equipped, and they get better gas mileage on the highway than they do in stop and go traffic, but car advertisers only give the very best mileage. They don't give you the mileage for when you have the air conditioner or heater on, or when you drive in the mountains, or when you are stuck in five o'clock traffic. They claim that their cars have the best mileage, but they don't tell you if other cars have the same. They forget to point out the costs of the extras: the radio, air conditioner, the power brakes, the clock, and the power steering. They don't tell you a car is like a pizza. The more toppings you want, the more you have to pay. The more comforts you want, the more you have to pay.

The car advertisers appeal to your emotions instead of your common sense and knowledge. They have a woman in a sexy dress tell you how good a car is instead of a mechanic who knows something about cars. Advertisements are often misleading by having rich, pretty or handsome people do ads implying that you will become rich and beautiful if you buy their car.

Carolyn is not only writing longer compositions, she is also increasing her attention to detail and example. Each abstraction of her thesis—misleading gas mileage, implying cars are fully equipped, giving silly reasons for purchasing—are all supported with specific examples—not to mention mileage change due to air-conditioner or heater use or driving through the mountains; not mentioning extras, specifically radio, power brakes, clock (she even makes an artful analogy, comparing the extras to extras on a pizza); having a sexy woman sell the car in place of a knowledgeable mechanic.

Carolyn's work with revision in her editing group also reveals her improvement in specificity. Here are two excerpts and their revisions from her "essay of decision." She had to decide whether to give up gymnastics, a favorite extracurricular activity, to meet the demands of college preparatory classes and marching band. The first is the opening paragraph of her essay, the second is the actual deciding.

Opening Paragraph:

> A sport which I have always enjoyed doing is gymnastics. Even though I'm not Olga Korbut or Nadia Comaneci *I can do a few stunts and enjoy doing what I can.* I have been participating in gymnastics for about six years intermittently. In my freshman and sophomore year I was a member of the Foothill Gynmastics Team. We lost every meet. But that didn't matter, we still had fun. Each year I would say, "Well, I'll just have to do better next year." This year was going to be my year.

In essence, Carolyn is "telling us" that she's been involved in gymnastics for a long time and has thought it much fun. However, where is the real enjoyment, the real skill? If her essay will concern giving up this beloved sport, we need to believe her attachment to it. Her peers suggested that to make us believe her dedicated involvement she *show* what stunts she could do.

Revision:

> Gymnastics has been an important part of my life since I was ten years old, and I've loved every minute of it. The exercise has kept my body limber, while the hard work and frustration of learning a new move have always been outweighed by the satisfaction of achievement. Even though I'm not Olga Korbut or Nadia Comaneci I'm content with a mastery of such basic moves as cartwheels, roundoffs, turns, rolls on the beam, or a pullover on the bars. The challenge of not being able to do more difficult moves gives me an insentive to work harder.

In this passage we see the benefits of having been involved in gymnastics— keeping her body limber, allowing her new goals to set and conquer; we see the basic exercise she has mastered: cartwheels, roundoffs, turns, rolls on the beam and pullovers on the bars. We have moved from fun, enjoyment, and achievement in the original version to specific causes of those feelings.

Next Carolyn debates whether to continue in the sport:

> Considering how much time I would have to spend with band and *how much harder my classes were going to be,* I realized that if I was on the team this year my schedule would be just as bad, probably worse, than last year. I had to decide whether to continue with a very hectic schedule this year or not to go out for the gymnastics team.
>
> *I didn't go out for the team.* Even without being on the gymnastics team I still don't have time to do all that needs to be done. I miss doing gymnastics and losing all the meets. When I told the coach I was not trying out for the team she said, "I was hoping you would get over the high bar this year." Getting over the high bar was going to be my personal goal for the year. Now that goal won't be met. I've finally accepted the fact that I can't do everything.

Carolyn fails to do two things: 1) show the rigor and strain of her upcoming year ("how much harder my classes were going to be") and 2) show how she came to decide not to go out for the team ("I didn't go out for the team.")

Here is Carolyn's revision:

> I tried to imagine what this year would be like. I knew my classes would be more difficult. I'd be taking U.S. history, Advanced Comp., Advanced Math, Marching Band, Physics, and French 3. I knew I would have to spend a lot of time on my homework to maintain my 4.0 g.p.a. Being on the gymnastics team meant practice everyday for two hours and meets twice a week. Band practices would be scheduled almost every afternoon and sometimes in the evenings. Performances would take up Friday nights and all of Saturday. The pieces were not fitting together very well. My schedule was going to be even busier than last year. My big problem was to decide whether to try this ridiculous schedule or give up the gymnastics team.
>
> My mom and boyfriend helped influence my decision. My mom knew better than I how much time I would have to devote to the band and she was opposed to my joining the gymnastics team. I value her opinion highly and knew that she was right. My boyfriend is always upset with me for being too busy even though he's in the band too. I knew he would really be furious if I added gymnastics to my already hectic schedule.
>
> Gymnastics has been eliminated for this year, but it hasn't helped much. I still don't get enough sleep, practice the piano enough, study enough, or spend enough time with my boyfriend or family. I

miss being a member of the gymnastics team, I even miss losing all the meets. The coach's reply when I told her I wasn't going out for the team was "Oh! I'm going to miss your floor routine. I was hoping you would get over the high bar this year." Getting over the high bar was going to be my personal goal for the year. Now that goal won't be met. I've finally learned that I can't do everything, at least not this year.

Clearly, Carolyn has composed a much richer piece of writing. We are shown exactly what will constitute her academic coursework. We are shown the amount of time each activity, gymnastics, school work, and band, will take up. The elaboration of the time elements in conjunction with her mother and boyfriend's feelings show us how she came to make her final decision.

Carolyn's essay of comparison for *The Circle* reveals further progress:

TIME CHANGES ALL

Best of friends often are as alike as two peas in a pod. They think, do, and say the same things. If one friend thinks the boy next door is cute, then the other friend also thinks he is cute. One often sees best friends looking at each other at the same time when somebody says something they think is strange. But as the years go on, even the best of friends drift apart. They drift like ice blocks in the seas, slowly forming their own shape. So it is in W. Somerset Maugham's play *The Circle.* Over the years Lord Porteous and Clive Champion Cheney, who were once best friends, changed greatly and are now different in appearance, disposition, and social status.

Thirty years before the setting of the play, Lord Porteous was one of the best dressed men of London. Clive admired Lord Porteous and describes Porteous to Elizabeth, Clive's daughter-in-law, as very nice looking. He points out that Porteous had the yellow hair and blue eyes that everyone envied and a fine figure to top that. But now thirty years later, Clive is the one with the fine figure. As the narration describes Clive, he is a tall man, in his sixties and bears his years with grace. He still has a fine head of gray hair. He is very well dressed and one can tell he makes the most of himself. Lord Porteous, on the other hand, can be described as elderly. Even Clive tells him that he is aging. He has no hair, has false teeth, and wears eccentric clothes. He complains about his false teeth while Clive tells how healthy his are. It is no wonder that Porteous refuses to go and says he hates exercise when Kitty, his mistress, asks him to go for a stroll. His once fine figure is gone.

Clive is a man with an easy-going personality. While Porteous is very gruff and snappy, Clive doesn't become upset even when he finds out that his ex-wife and her lover are going to be in the same house as he. But Porteous becomes outraged when people talk while he is playing bridge. Clive himself says that he has a naturally cheerful disposition and Porteous implies that his disposition has been soured at no fault of his. Porteous scolds Kitty and tells her that she ruined his career, as Clive speaks to her softly and tries to comfort her.

Clive and Porteous were both once very active in politics but now neither are. They both are still very rich, but they lead very different lives. Clive travels all around Europe spending time in Paris whenever he wants. He has a new mistress, always a younger woman, whenever he fancies one. Porteous, on the other hand, lives in France, where there are no sanitary conveniences, and among loose ladies and vicious men. Lord Porteous isn't accepted into high society because he lives with a woman to whom he is not married. People are snobs to Lord Porteous and no longer look upon him as a well known figure.

It is funny to see what time does to people. The closest of friends can become enemies and thoughts once shared can now be argued. So it was between Clive and Porteous. Time aged them both in its own and different way. Clive is still young at heart. He tells Kitty that he still has his wild oats to sow. While Porteous became a stereotyped figure of an old man—he is bald, has false teeth, and has become very grumpy with time. No one can really predict what time will do. One is often surprised at the outcome of how time changes people.

Besides Carolyn's rich use of example to support her thesis—Porteous and Clive, who were once best friends, greatly changed in appearance, disposition and social status—she creates an analogy to show how time changes people: "They drift like ice blocks in the seas, slowly forming their own shape." We are reminded of this comparison once again at the finish of her essay. "No one can really predict what time will do. One is often surprised at the outcome of how time changes people." With this use of analogy Carolyn shows she can use several developmental techniques at once to show contrast. The intermittent use of examples in the body of her essay supports her creative comparison.

Carolyn's growth is documented, finally, in her pretest and posttest essays:

Pretest Essay

Score 8

Describe something you enjoyed doing as a child.

When I was younger my sister, Lynda, Lisa, Lori, and I would play house by the hour. Lynda, Lisa, and Lori lived across the street from us so we were always together. It may seem strange, but we had a name for what we play. When we played house; we played

"Your Highness." The named evolved from another game we played which became house. We would set up elaborate houses, or so we thought, in our garages. The houses even had separate rooms. We spent half our time setting-up and cleaning up.

"Your Highness" involves one family. The members of the family were: a dad, which was I, Lynda was always the mom, and older and younger daughter which were Lisa and Peggy, my sister, respectively, and last but not least Lori played the teenage son. Now what we know about how parents treat their kids; we thought everything. Of course the kids would argue, and the parents sent them to their rooms, and that would settle everything. Then they were the outside family arguments like "Why does Lynda also get to be the mom?" complained Lisa. "Because I'm older." replies Lynda. Oh, well you can't please everybody. But a couple little arguments never stopped us from playing.

Eventually we stop playing "Your Highness." I guess we just thought we were too old for such silly games. Now when ever the five of us get together we laugh about our silly but fun games.

Although Carolyn outlines the principles of the game "Your Highness"— someone was the dad, the mom, the younger and older daughers, the teenage son—she doesn't reconstruct actual episodes. She tells us that the kids "would argue" and be "sent to their rooms" to settle disputes—but we do not see the actual arguments—the colorful vignettes that show kids imitating parents and their children in conflict.

Carolyn's posttest essay shows maturity in description:

Posttest Essay

Score 10

Describe something from which you learned a lesson.

During my freshman year in high school I started going with my first boyfriend. We were very close. We would see each other at school, go out, talk for hours on the phone and tell each other our inter-most secrets. After seven months my feelings started to change. My boyfriend didn't seem as special anymore. I wanted to be around other people more. It seemed like the bar that held us together had turned to string.

My problem was that the feeling wasn't mutual. He didn't feel like anything was different between us. I thought for a long time about how I was going to tell him. I'd see him at school and want to tell him, but I couldn't. I tried calling him but every time I picked up the phone I got a lump in my throat and my hands would shake, so I'd hang up feeling like a rat.

Finally I got up the courage, all of it from deep inside myself, and told him how I felt. I felt like a wicked person. It was like telling an

anxious child that there would be no Christmas tree or presents this
year. That was the hardest thing that I had ever done. It was even
worse than telling my mom I broke her crystal laddel.

Because his feelings weren't the same as mine he pleeded for me to
take him back. When he looked at me he had the expression of a
little lost puppy. On a bus trip down to L.A. he played a tape with
all "our" songs on it. He begged me again to accept him back into
my heart but I couldn't. Why couldn't he respect my feelings?

I don't think I have ever gone through something as upsetting as
our after brake-up. I never wish that kind of pain on anyone, not
even my worst enemy. Even though it hurt very much, I learned
something very valuable. No matter what one's feelings are, one
should always respect another's feelings. If one doesn't he can really
hurt the one he cares for.

Carolyn enjoys using comparison to show her emotions. She does not give
the actual change in feeling through concrete examples, but summarizes her
feelings in terms of analogy, a technique Carolyn obviously came to
appreciate and cultivate during the course of the semester. Carolyn chooses
an appropriate technique, also, for conveying difficult emotions (abstractions) which can often be best described through comparison. Like Craig,
she learned the impact this technique can have through 1) hearing other
compostions daily, and 2) learning the technique as an optional strategy
(part three of the training program). Carolyn shows her once-close relationship as a "bar, turning to string." When she tried to confront her boyfriend
about her feelings, we see her failure to be strong—feeling lumps in the
throat, hands shaking, hanging up the phone, the analogy of feeling like a
rat.

When she finally mustered up courage, she "felt wicked, like telling an
anxious child there would be no Christmas tree or presents" (another
analogy). It was even worse than telling her mother about the broken crystal
ladle (symbolizing her boyfriend's fragile state of mind).

The boyfriend's reaction is also put in terms of comparison—"expression
of a little lost puppy." Finally, his resulting reaction of playing their songs to
her on tape in order to win her back becomes the "symbolic gesture" (the
showing) of how blind he was to her pain in having to be honest. Although
her conclusion struggles in its explanation of the lesson learned, her use of
analogy throughout as a means of description shows a maturity in writing
style.

Lisa

Lisa entered Advanced Composition already appreciating the importance
of specificity in writing. She practiced consistently the use of specific
examples in narrative as well as expository compositions. Her daily
paragraphs, when read aloud, drew admiring responses from the class, and

her major essays usually surfaced as models of excellence. Certainly Lisa's writing contained weaknesses, in organization and editing, for example; but the natural ease with which she incorporated specifics contrasted sharply with the struggles of others. I was curious, then, about what impact the training program might have on an already gifted writer.

Here are three daily writings taken over the course of the semester.

The autumn weather reminded me of other autumns.

I am always caught by surprise when the first autumn weather blusters in. Week after week of Indian Summer days roll by and then one day I feel a crispness in the early morning air that tingles in my lungs, or a gust of cool air brushes past my cheeks and lifts the hair off my forehead with an unexpected puff. Each smell that wafts on the breeze brings with it visions of times gone by that are as sharp as the air.

I see myself as a child walking home from school kicking through leaves and dragging a stick, anticipating the warm sweetness of chewy fresh baked cookies. I remember the feel of cold glass against my squashed nose as I watched the rain donning each leaf-bare tree with diamonds. Once again I hold a thick mug in my hands and smell the rich hot chocolate as it's steam warms my nose and fogs my glasses.

Notice Lisa's precise verb selection to convey feeling—days *roll* by, air *tingling* lungs, *brushing* hair and *lifting* it, smell *wafting* on the breeze. She uses additional effective verbs in paragraph two: *kicking* leaves, *dragging* a stick, rain *donning* each tree with diamonds, cocoa steam *warming* the nose, *fogging* the glasses. This attention to word choice is one of Lisa's strengths that reveals her attention to detail, her close observational skills.

People make a good party.

Over in the corner sit two people involved in an animated discussion. One wears the electric colored silks of a disco and the other jeans, a cotton plaid shirt, and glasses. By the punch bowl a well groomed girl in polyester pants fills the dip bowl and playfully slaps away the snitching hand of a boy with hair to his shoulders and patched Levi's. Beneath the bookcase a boy points out pictures of birds in a dusty old volume. On the couch a boy in a letterman's sweater watches. All throughout the room ironic looking groups cluster, reform, and spread. No one's eyes are downcast, no pained expressions adorn the faces of those present. Each person accepts and learns from the other's ideas and attitudes and no one is bored for very long.

Lisa subtly creates characterization through clothing, costume. Rather than *tell* us we have a socialite, a carpenter, a secretary-type, a hippie, a bookworm, or an athlete at this party, she *reveals* their personalities through their dress—a crafty use of description.

Re-creating a television commercial: Chanel No. 5

The scene is simple, the background, black, the foreground,— well, the foreground is Catherine Denuvieve, stretched out on her side, dressed in black, her long blond hair lacquered into place over white shoulders. She stares at us searchingly, persuasively, and the camera-man succumbs, moving in for a tight shot. "I like being a voman, I can be strong if I vish, or I can be gentle, and let my man take over. I like very much dis-(pause)-dis freedom." We are now seeing only her eyes, large, liquid, and alluring. Every male in the room from 9 to 90 is at attention, breathing heavily and popping their eyes. She reaches down and runs a well polished finger over a bottle of amber colored liquid, the subject of her clincher statement. "You know, dis f-r-r-r-r-agrance is vat it means to be a voman— Chanel #5, soft, but strong and capable." She pauses, again, and seems to have suffered a severe memory loss, for she shrugs her shoulders and again we here "Chanel no. 5, vat it means to be a voman." At least we girls hear it, and the boys have grabbed their wallets and run out of the door.

Lisa employs many techniques to show this characterization: 1) careful verb choice (*stretched* out, hair *lacquered* into place, *staring* persuasively as the cameraman *succumbs* to her pose); 2) close description, precise adjectives (*black* background vs. *blond* hair, *white* shoulders, eyes *large, liquid, alluring; well-polished* fingers running over a bottle of *amber-colored* liquid); 3) direct quote ("I like being a vo-man; I can be strong if I wish" etc.); 4) *reaction* by others—the boys have grabbed their wallets and run out the door, proving her hypnotic effect.

In examining Lisa's work with longer pieces of writing and revision we see that even a talented writer has room for growth. Here is her "Essay of Decision" in its entirety, a description of her deciding to run for eighth grade class treasurer. Note the underdeveloped segments.

THE RACE

Early morning, a morning like so many other dreary 7th grade mornings. I stumbled into my classroom and dropped into my seat. Still half asleep I rested my chin in my hands and stared off into the deepest darkest corner the room had to offer, whereupon I promptly sank into a semi-catonic state.

The room become somewhat quieter as the morning bulletin began to drone over the P.A. system. "Good morning" a very unenthusiastic voice greeted us. "This is the morning bulletin for

May 24, 1975, I idly wondered why she felt compelled to tell us that tid bit of information, what were we expecting, a bomb threat? She went on, and on, and on...then, "Elections will be held for next years officers on June 8th. Intent-to-run forms can be picked up in the office starting today."

Hmmm, what was that about elections? "RUNNING FOR OFFICE", I had always imagined it literally, a big race with giggling cheerleaders and heavyweight jocks trotting far out in front and me panting behind them all. The thought was so unpleasant, that I dropped it. Besides thinking was always painful for me at 7:30 A.M.

As the day wore on, however, I found the subject popping into my head at random moments. Just suppose, I said to myself, just suppose someone had a gun in my back and was forcing me to run for something, not that I'd *want* to of course, but just suppose. What would I choose? President would take up too much time— same with Vice-President. Secretaries have to have good handwriting—strike that one. *Treasurer. "Treasurer." I whispered to myself. The word tasted good.*

But it soon tasted bitter. What was I doing? Letting stupid fantasies drift too close to my safely guarded reality. It would never do letting my well ordered life be jostled by something as unpredictable and risky as running for office. *Wait a minute, wasn't "well ordered" just a synonym for "boring" in this case?*

I looked around me to see my peers. Some seemed so cocky and self-assured, others sat crouched against the walls eating soggy tuna fish sandwiches with an air of martyrdom. "My potential subjects", I giggled.

"But I have no time!" my insides squealed, coming back to reality. The granite-willed side of me came to the fore. I gritted my teeth yes, I *could* give up Woody Woodpecker re-runs.

Imagination began to canter, trot and then run. Lisa, treasurer, maintaining razor sharp columns in neat ledger books. Lisa, treasurer, earning millions and bringing the school out of a financial slump. Lisa, treasurer, travelling to Washington at special request of the President to show the Secretary of the Treasury how to handle his books. And, choke, Lisa, treasurer, tripping on the speech platform at an assembly, and stuttering during a grimy-penciled campaign speech.

Awakening painfully from my reverie I found myself sitting on a bench smack in front of the office. A sample intent-to-run form staring me in the face.

I felt like I was on the point of a towering mountain with deep chasms on each side. A chance-taking something that had been pushed way down deep for so long, flickered, and caught flame.

I reached for the silvery knob and flung open the door, the race had begun.

In this essay, Lisa again demonstrates her inventiveness with language; again she reveals that she is capable of colorful descriptions. Her weakness in this essay lies in her failing to tie together the steps of her process—1) being attracted to office, to 2) giving into weakness (her boring place), to 3) making the move to run—into a conclusion about herself. Since her "boring place" is what moves her to take action, she needs to show that restless place. She also tells us that this place is "safer," but fails to show why—an essential element in explaining the decision process. Finally, she never really makes a point about herself, never comes to a conclusion. She hints at one by mentioning "I felt like I was on the point of a towering mountain with deep chasms on either side. A chance-taking something that had been pushed way down deep for so long, flickered, and caught flame." However, she does not show us what this "chance-taking something" actually means (an abstraction that demands elaboration).

Here is the revision of that essay:

THE RACE, REVISED

It was early Monday morning, a morning like so many other dreary 7th grade mornings. I stumbled into my classroom and dropped into my seat. Still half asleep, I rested my chin in my hands and stared off into the deepest, darkest corner the room had to offer, whereupon I promptly sank into a semi-catonic state.

The room became somewhat quieter as the morning bulletin began to drone over the P.A. system. "Good morning," a very unenthusiastic voice greeted us, "This is the morning bulletin for May 24, 1975," I idly wondered why she felt compelled to tell us that tid bit of information. What were we expecting, a bomb threat? She went on, and on, and on...then, "Elections will be held for next year's officers on June 8th. Intent-to-run forms can be picked up in the office starting today."

Hummm, what was that about elections? "RUNNING FOR OFFICE" I had always imagined it literally, a big race with self confident super-achievers, and extremely organized secretary types trotting far out in front, and me panting behind them all. The thought was so degrading that I dropped it. Besides, thinking was always painful for me at 7:30 a.m.

As the day wore on, however, I found the subject of the elections popping into my head at random moments. Just suppose, I said to myself, just suppose someone had a gun in my back and was forcing me to run for something, not that I'd *want* to of course, but just suppose. What would I choose? Secretaries must have good handwriting—strike that one. Treasurer. Visions of *me* as a super-achiever, incongruous as they seemed, began taking shape. For the first time, I saw myself as really achieving, becoming and doing something worthwhile. The picture was so rosy that the word almost tasted good as it rolled off my tongue in a self-conscious whisper.

But it soon turned bitter. What was I doing? Letting stupid fantasies drift too close to my safely guarded reality. It would never do—letting my well ordered life be jostled by something as unpredictable and risky as running for office. Up at 6:30, I was showered, dressed, and breakfasted by 7:15. Once at school, I went to and sat through the average "expected-of-7th-graders" classes. After school, while others ran off to practices or meetings of some sort or the other, I went home to homework and the Brady Bunch. Wait a minute, wasn't "well ordered" just a synonym for "boring" in this case?

"But I have no time!" my insides squealed, coming back to reality. But the granite-willed side of me took over, and I gritted my teeth. Yes, I could give up Woody Woodpecker re-runs. Imagination began to canter, trot and then run. Lisa, treasurer, maintaining razor sharp columns in neat ledger books. Lisa, treasurer, earning millions and bringing the school out of a financial slump. Lisa, treasurer, travelling to Washington at special request of the President to show the Secretary of the Treasury how to handle his books. And, choke, Lisa, treasurer, tripping on the speech platform at an assembly, and stuttering nervously while reading from a creased and well worn sheet of binder paper that holds her laboriously written campaign speech.

Awakening painfully from my reverie, I found myself sitting on a bench smack in front of the office, a sample intent-to-run form staring me in the face.

I felt like I was on the point of a towering mountain with deep chasms on either side. One side was a haven from all that was risky and uncertain. A place where I could dwell safely, without heavy responsibility. A place where no one might mock my puny efforts. But the other side offered new opportunitites and new challenges; added responsibility and added priveleges. Things that may lift me up or tear me down, but things that would *move* me!

A chance-taking something that had been pushed down deep inside me for so long, flickered, and caught flame. I reached for the silvery knob and flung open the door. The race had begun.

The most striking aspect of Lisa's revision is her conclusion about herself. This time Lisa examines her own debating to learn something about her decision-making process. Because she takes the time to think about (elaborate) the importance of a class officership—"a real achievement, doing something worthwhile"—and weigh that consideration against her safer place of boredom—"up at 6:30...breakfasted by 7:15...classes...homework...the Brady Bunch"...she concludes that she needed to take action, that remaining "on the fence" too long is not something she easily tolerates. As students like Lisa practice drawing out their ideas, as they're pushed to explain their feelings to themselves, effective conclusions like Lisa's are indeed possible.

Lisa's comparison essay, written in response to reading *The Circle,*
follows:

THE CIRCLE

In England, when children are quite young, they often play a
game nick-named "hoop-n-stick." The equipment for the game
consists of a dowel-like rod, a foot or so long, and a large circular
hoop. The object of the game is to keep the hoop rolling, and this is
accomplished by hitting it every so often with a sharp rap from the
stick. One must take care, however, not to hit it so hard that the
hoop topples, or so softly that the hoop receives no impact and
therefore begins to fall to its ultimate demise. The ideal is a short but
jolting rap that supplies the circle with fresh energy to keep toddling
down its intended path. Life in Somerset Maugham's play, "The
Circle," resembles this game in goal, in equipment (figuratively)
and, ultimately, in outcome.

It is essential to hoop-n-stick experts to keep the hoop up and
rolling. In "The Circle," also, the players' goals are somewhat the
same. Arnold and Clive's outlook on life—if only, they wish, life
would keep on a smooth and steady course towards the prime
ministership or at least great political power. *In fact, throughout
most of the play there is an undercurrent of straining to keep things
on the up and up.* Only totally acceptable behavior fits into this
socially sterile atmosphere. Even Lady Kitty and Lord Porteous—
notorious "hoop jostlers," themselves—have become confined by
their own rules and commitments. It isn't until Maugham allows us
to see some deeper facets of his characters that we see that the hoop
of their life is about to receive another jolt.

For centuries, women have known that the best way to keep a
little excitement in life is to make sure that her man is a little unsure
of his position. Some women go as far as to request that their man
be downright jealous. Lady Kitty is one of these. In act III she says
delightedly..."Hughie, you may throw me down the stairs like
Amy Robstart; you may drag me about the floor by the hair of my
head; I don't care, you're jealous. I shall never grow old." First -
actions - and the jealousy they bring are Lady Kitty's "stick." She
uses them to speed things up when the hoop begins to wobble a
little. Elizabeth, on the other hand, uses her frail features and woeful
eyes to make a man begin to jump around and sweat a little. In act
II, Elizabeth's constant threat of crying nearly pushes Teddie over
the brink during their very emotional scene. Clive uses a different
stick altogether. His reserved, man-of-the world way of speaking to
women makes them painfully aware of their naivate and feel as if
they haven't a leg to stand on.

Act III of "The Circle" is one big wobble after another—not only
in the hoop of the characters lives, but in our own emotions.

Maugham makes us really relate to Arnold and his plight and then, like a fickle schoolgirl, makes us feel like not giving Arnold the time of day. Where ten minutes ago reason and the cool prevailed, now love and roses are all that really matter. *Through Maugham's masterstrokes, though, the story, (and our emotions) like their wobbling counterpart, manage to stay upright.*

On a grand scale, we can see the entire game laid out before us. Stick in hand, Mr. Maugham sets us out rolling with Kitty's jolting emancipation, and,just as the Cheney-Porteous-Lutton hoop is beginning to wobble and falter, makes us believe again in the power of love by using Elizabeth and Teddie to upright it with a perfectly dealt flick of the wrist.

Lisa's subject for comparison is delightfully original. She makes concrete the abstract image of the cyclical order of men's lives. By comparing the repeating sequence of family action to the "hoop-n-stick" game popular in England, Lisa creates a clear visual connection for the symbolic "circle."

On the other hand, Lisa neglects important elaboration in the body of her essay. Perhaps having become so enamored of her own inventive thesis, she fails to see her lack of development in supporting that thesis. In other words, the *idea* is the seller of the essay, not the supportive argument.

The sentences *italicized* show weakness in development. In the second paragraph Lisa needs to show additional examples of the characters' "straining to keep things on the up and up." If the total action in Maugham's play can be likened to "keeping the hoop rolling," then Lisa needs more instances of that sort of endeavoring.

In the next-to-the-last paragraph, Lisa admits the wobbling of the hoop, but then merely *tells* us that Maugham "manages to keep the action upright." Lisa needs to draw on specific courses of action that reveal the steadying of the game.

This essay is certainly no set-back. Lisa has an exciting thesis, an idea that certainly in itself *shows* the central abstraction of the play, i.e., "life is like a circle." Growth in developing ideas need not be limited, then, to X number of examples in a given paragraph; growth in developing ideas can show up in the vividness of a thesis. Continuous work with evaluation and revision combined with an emphasis on being specific can, over a period of practice, train the writer to be more consistent in all area of development.

Lisa's pretest and posttest essays were scored identically—each a *10*. There seemed to be no dramatic change in her ability to generate and interpret examples in a timed writing exercise. Rather than examine these essays here, trying to distinguish subtle differences that might render one more effective than the other, I am including her final essay for the course.

Students were assigned to take a "mock" University of California Subject-A Exam, an essay exam used for placement of entering freshmen in University Writing courses. The exam requires the students to respond to an essay question based,on a reading of a non-fiction piece of prose. Students in my class were given an essay by John Ciardi titled "Is Everybody Happy?" an essay suggesting that true happiness is found more in the struggle to achieve happiness and less in the final accomplishment. Lisa's response is an agreement with Ciardi.

SUBJECT-A EXAM: FINAL ESSAY

Throughout life, people of all ages try to avoid work. Children whine and cry about helping with the dishes or clearing the table, causing their parents great exasperation. Teenagers, watching T.V. in their comfortable bedrooms, shout to their parents that they're doing their homework when asked to take out the trash. An adult, in the peak of health, calls in sick, another takes a two-hour lunch to catch the "unmissable" pink carnation sale at Macy's, and they both generally "serve time" against the day when they can ultimately retire and stop going to work completely. Isn't it ironic then, that this same individual, after he has been handed the symbolic gold watch, is likely to become depressed, feel useless, decay mentally and keel over from a heart attack within five short years. It is only through diligent effort and meaningful expenditure of energy that we can attain happiness.

A mountain climber, tough and seasoned, is confronted with a seemingly unscalable sheer-rock cliff. He considers the weary muscles he must force on, the sweat he must shed, and even the life he must place in danger, to get to the top. But he responds to the challenge, because that's why he's there, to attempt the extremely difficult. When he comes home, he thinks not of sitting passively at the peak of the towering mountain he set out to conquer, but of each steep, treeless incline, each narrow edge and each threatening talus. The conquering, then, is not in the final resting state, but in the overcoming of each smaller trial. As Ciardi states it "Effort is the gist of it."

Why are there jigsaw puzzles? A beautiful picture is exploded into 1,001 tiny pieces and swept into a box which the public buys for six or seven hard-earned dollars. This Joe Public takes home, dumps the 1,001 tiny pieces onto a rickety old card table and can't wait to commence putting it together.Our jigsaw junkie will walk about bleary eyed, miss dinners, and stagger to bed at three in the morning 'til he presses the last piece of blue sky into place. And then what does he do with this picturesque scene? Does he shellac it and hang it on his wall? No, he crumbles this masterpiece of time, effort and energy into 1,001 tiny pieces and stashes them in a box, on a shelf, under his tennis racket with the broken string.

A wife keeps dinner warm till 9:00 for her husband who's been held up at a meeting, a father works overtime to earn enough money to take his family on vacation; a child gives half of his precious peanut-butter and liverwurst sandwich to a chum; a teenage girl loans her cherished "electric-blue" disco dress to her best friend for "the big date;" and night after night a tired mother reels out of bed three or four times to feed and diaper her newborn infant. One would think these people might feel angry, upset or used, but on the contrary, as they give deeply of themselves, *their love grows deeper.* When the other person ceases to need us, to come to us, to desire us, we begin to feel useless, unessential, and dispensable. Our own ego suffers, and we find ourselves pulling away from those we may have loved the very most.

Happiness is in the slope not the summit; in the solving not the solution; it is in the service, not the reward. Those who escape work will find that they have only escaped happiness.

3. *Beginning*

Formative Writing

WRITING TO ASSIST LEARNING IN ALL SUBJECT AREAS

Virginia Draper
St. Mary's College of California, Moraga

More and more writing instructors are urging their fellow teachers in other disciplines to care about, to pay attention to students' *writing abilities* rather than simply respond to the *content* of students' papers and examinations. These often weary writing teachers mention that there's little point in encouraging a student to improve her writing ability if no one else on campus demands good writing. It's also common for those other instructors to complain about students' papers, and either ask the English department why they're not "doing something" about this campus-wide crisis of inadequate writing or ask their English colleagues to recommend a "good writing handbook" to help them to identify student errors. But attempts to improve students' compositions, as well as increase teacher and student satisfaction with writing, will have limited success if our efforts to improve students' written expression remain focused only on the final *products* such as the paper, the essay, the answer—products designed to exhibit the student's knowledge for the purpose of awarding a grade. Instead, we need to expand our critical and instructional concerns to include the entire *writing process.*

To consider how to expand the concept of writing beyond that of product, take a moment to think about your writing process. Think of the steps you go through when preparing an article for publication, a paper to be read at a conference, a letter to a colleague, even a proposal to add a teaching assistant to read student papers if you've been giving more writing assignments.

From your own experience, you know writing to be a multidimensional activity initiated by a need or desire to amuse, to share an idea or insight, to convince or persuade someone to do something. If the writing is to be publicly evaluated, you probably discuss your ideas with others, make several drafts and revisions, even get an editor to help before you are satisfied and are ready to send the final product to the appropriate reader(s). As a process, writing involves:

Pre-writing   research, talk, notes, questions, journal observations, etc.

Formulation   identification of audience, purpose, and tone; identification of major ideas, supportive details, effective order; perhaps the design of an outline.

Transcribing	the combined mental and physical acts necessary to get words onto paper in sentences, paragraphs, and sections.
Reformulation	reordering of argument or narrative; sharpening focus, often assisted by a sympathetic reader or editor if the paper is important.
Editing	proofreading for grammatical errors and syntactical awkwardness; polishing style for readability and interest.

The ease and satisfaction with which you accomplish each of these tasks depends upon the quality and quantity of your recent writing, your familiarity with the subject matter, your motivation, the existence of support or encouragement when needed, and your insights into your idiosyncrasies and ways of getting beyond the writing blocks all writers experience.

With the assistance of recent research on acquisition and use of language by Piaget, Moffett, and Britton,[1] and on the nature of the composing process by Emig, Shaughnessey, and Haynes,[2] many of us who teach writing to *all* kinds of college students believe that in order to improve the *products* of students' writing, we must support and develop students' understanding and practice of *all the tasks of the writing process.* Particularly, students need activities in pre-writing, formulation and reformulation which have often been ignored or misconstrued by other teachers. In mid-semester of my freshman composition course at a non-selective four-year college, I recognized the importance of working with students throughout the writing process and developed writing activities consistent with recent cognitive and learning theories (Cross, Chickering).[3] I also realized that because the writing and learning processes are closely related, writing activities could be designed to assist students' learning in non-composition courses.

We need to expand our use of writing as a method to enhance learning rather than use it solely as a measure of acquired knowledge. Therefore I propose to show how writing can assist learning in all disciplines and to suggest to the non-writing teacher some specific writing activities to increase teacher and student awareness and practice in the early steps of the writing process. I am convinced that this awareness and practice will not only improve students' writing, but also increase learning and teacher satisfaction.

Formative Writing

Students can write on the first day of class and on the last; they can write during and outside of class. They should recognize that writing is one extremely valuable way of learning, of *finding out* what one knows and thinks, as well as *showing* what one knows. Writing is a way to explore and question, as well as to gain control over and exhibit knowledge of subject matter. Writing engages the imagination, intellect, and emotions and encourages articulation of those attitudes, skills, and values necessary for effective learning in most disciplines. It is a unique learning activity because it allows the student to capture thoughts and data for future reference, contemplation, and synthesis. At the exploration stage of learning, writing can be more self-exploratory than speaking because interruptions can be self-controlled. In the formulation stage, it can be more disciplined than speech because of the necessity to make meanings clear for a distant and perhaps unknown reader. It is a way to individualize and personalize learning because each student is able to respond at her own level, to ask her own questions, to attempt her own definitions, formulations, generalizations, and theories. Shared writing can establish responsible and fruitful dialogue between students and between student and teacher. Experiences with various kinds of writing not only expand and improve the student's academic learning, but also give her a process for future adult learning. If the goal of education is to assist the student to find meaning in this world, writing can help the student discover methods to identify and expand meanings and a voice, or several voices, to articulate this meaning.

To develop students' use of writing in these ways, the instructor can design activities that integrate writing and the learning of subject matter. Besides the term paper or written product, which for many students is not a satisfactory vehicle for the expression or discovery of meanings, teachers should introduce students to the writing process.

The activities associated with the beginning tasks of the writing process could be called *formative writing.* I have borrowed the term *formative* from the field of evaluation, where practitioners distinguish between *formative evaluation* (evaluation for the purpose of assisting and refining the development of a process) and *summative evaluation* (evaluation for the purpose of summarizing or giving a final judgment).

Students may already receive formative evaluation from practice quizzes before the final exam, comments on rough drafts of papers prior to revision, and diagnostic tests. Grading is the primary measure of summative evaluation. Usually permanent, the results of summative evaluation go beyond the evaluator and the evaluated to the Registrar and onto transcripts and do not usually motivate learning by indicating fruitful avenues for growth. Formative evaluation is not public; it is used by the evaluator and the evaluated to define strengths and problems and to shape practices and goals.

We offer students too little formative evaluation of their writing or their learning. Term papers and exams, by their normal end of semester submission dates, almost have to be subjected to summative evaluation. Teachers could be providing the student with formative evaluation of and through writing. The purpose of formative writing, like formative evaluation, is to assist the student to shape and develop *her own language,* her thoughts through language.

The audience for formative writing can be the student herself, another student or groups of students, or the teacher in the roles of knowledgeable assistant, sympathetic reader, or resource person. When responding to formative writing, the instructor is not a judge or grade-giver. The audience, no matter who it is, should be concerned with assisting the student to clarify, form, shape, and develop by commenting upon the interesting, challenging and positive aspects of the communication, by asking questions, by offering suggestions and resources for the student's further investigation. If a teacher is not comfortable with this non-judgmental role (it may take some practice and reorientation), students can write for peers, a teaching assistant, or friend as well.

Formative writing is not to be measured by editorial or professional writing standards; it is not to be graded, but responded to. The person responding should be aware that in the beginning stages of forming or developing one's thoughts and ideas, certain formalities of standard written English are not of primary importance, and attention to them may impede the fluency which characterizes exploration and creating thinking.

In formative writing, readability should not be a major consideration of the student. That comes later in the formulation, reformulation and editing stages. Too often the student's awareness of the reader's (usually the teacher's) evaluation inhibits expression of her own ideas and meaning.

Free-Writing and Focused Free-Writing

The following two paragraphs by the same student exemplify this problem of writer inhibition and introduce the varieties of formative writing appropriate for college classes. The first sample is the introduction to an argumentative essay on a topic of the student's choice; the second, a five minute free writing response to the question: "What should the students at the College do with a recent gift of $200,000.00?"

I. The majority of Americans in California feel since they have been granted an adult life status at the age of eighteen by law, they should be granted at the age of nineteen to drink alcohol just like the capability of adults at the higher level. Being granted adulthood status we should look at the basis of legal responsibility to determine legalizing nineteen year olds to drink alcohol. The nineteen year old since he/she is growing up to adulthood life, structures and coping with the society which they live should be looked at with the highest degree.

II. I will spend the money of $200,000.00 partially. I'll invest half of the money in the bank and spend the rest on my wedding, car, a beautiful house. The rest I would put in a fund for my kids so when they get older they will have money to go to college of their choice.

I would really invest on stocks and bonds to increase my interest rate. I also would give some of this money to a charity fund to help other minorities like myself to go to college. S.M.C. would really be world famous if they really did give each person $200,000.00.

I would go to Mexico and buy land and have a huge ranch with lots of workers working for me. I would have a big business in Mexico and in the United States with the investments.

My wife and I will still be working hard to obtain money because the taxes haven't been declared yet.

The second sample is an example of formative writing (focused free writing, to be precise). No audience was stipulated for this assignment, and the student did not reread or revise the passage. The first was written for the teacher as audience; the student expected the paper to be graded and believed it should meet the criteria for an argumentative essay with a minimum of mechanical errors. The student had three weeks to work on his argumentative essay, and I'm sure had done some revision of a first draft.

I would have expected a student who could write as fluently in five minutes as he did to have written a clearer paper when he had time to think and revise. Why, I wonder, are his syntactical problems so severe in the first passage yet absent in the second? I was amazed at the differences in clarity of expression and syntax between the two writings (I had received them in the order presented) and was challenged to help this student express complicated ideas with the same clarity and reduction of errors he exhibits in the formative writing.

One way to help is to use the student's formative writing as a basis for essays. He needs to begin with and retain the fluency which characterizes the second passage, to hear his own writer's voice *before* he becomes concerned about the reader's expectations. The difficulties with the formal introduction stem in part from his conscious use of academic language which he has read and believes appropriate for this kind of essay, but which impedes his expression of argument and meaning. He has an internal editor which dictates a certain vocabulary while stifling his own voice.

Peter Elbow *(Writing Without Teachers)* points out that while editing is necessary, many problems arise when editing goes on at the same time as producing:

> ...The habit of compulsive, premature editing doesn't just make writing hard. It makes writing dead. In your natural way of producing words there is a sound, a texture, a rhythm—a voice— which is the main source of power in your writing.[4]

This student was editing as he produced his argumentative essay. The editor was absent in the second writing activity.

Elbow recommends the practice of "free writing" as the first task for any composition in order to explore ideas and discover structure. Exercises based on Elbow's concept of free writing and its several variations are one kind of formative writing I recommend for use by college teachers and their students in all disciplines.

Usually free writing is done during a set period of time. The instructor emphasizes that the purpose of the free writing is to generate a flow of words and thoughts without concern for polished phrases or mechanics. The writer is not to worry about spelling, punctuation, grammar, complete sentences, or paragraphs. He is to write, keep writing, and if a block occurs, to repeat the last written word again and again until another thought comes.

I have used free writing at the beginning of class, giving students the opportunity to bring to consciousness and focus the thoughts and emotions swirling in their heads. This use of free writing sometimes contributes to a greater openness and attentiveness during the class that follows.

"Focused free writing" occurs when the teacher asks the student to respond to specific topics, such as an idea, poem, lecture, event, passage or quotation. The time limit and the same "ground rules" apply. The writing may be strictly private (for the writer's eyes only) or it may be exchanged with another student to expand each one's concept of the topic. It may be read by the instructor to serve as a guide for her future lectures or remarks. The instructor may want to identify ideas that would be valuable to expand into a future essay or recommend books or articles or other sources to the student.

If an instructor uses free writing in any form, she should tell students before they write who might read the writing. As all writers know, the prospective reader affects the degree of self he is willing to reveal.

When free writing is to be shared, the instructor will want to spend some time establishing a climate of trust both between herself and the students and among the students themselves if they read each other's works. Teachers and students may have to learn the kinds of responses that encourage ideas. Some instructors permit only positive comments, those that emphasize the interesting aspects of free writing, then introduce other responses, such as questions about meaning and clarity. Peter Elbow has specific suggestions ("Giving Movies of Your Mind") for reader responses to the question, "What happened in *you* when you read the words *this time?*" He reminds us that application of standards of right and wrong, or good and bad, are inappropriate to free writing. The activity is generative, not corrective.

Focused free writing can provide the instructor with information about the students, or if read by other students, provide a basis for classroom discussion. For instance, free writing on the first day of class on the title of the course or textbook might inform the instructor of students' expectations, fears, hopes and prior knowledge relating to the subject. Focused free writing on a concept read about or explained in a lecture can reveal gaps in students' knowledge or understanding. A required writing focused on a reading assignment could be used to initiate discussion between small groups of students at the beginning of class. These small group discussions may be summarized for the whole class. Once students are accustomed to doing this kind of activity, they can be asked to do free writing outside of class.

Focused free writing, if it is to be read by someone else, encourages an external dialogue: student with teacher or writer with reader. For the teacher, there are several advantages in establishing this dialogue as it addresses two major sources of teacher dissatisfaction identified by James Bess: "the difficulty of defining, of *ascertaining and interpreting evidence of* changes in students" and "the requirement that most persons have for a sense of continuity—for an environment that affords some personal stability..."[5] Teachers frequently react to these difficulties by resorting to teaching modes which allow little variation from expectation. Unfortunately, these teaching modes obscure the teacher's perception and solicitation of "cues that their efforts are productive."[6] By establishing a dialogue between teacher and student, focused free writing provides these cues and allows students to articulate the changes they experience or to express to the teacher difficulties they might have with the course content.

By having students' writing available for reflection outside the pressures of the classroom environment, an instructor can give close attention and written responses to the personal communications of the students. The instructor has a way to encourage and enlarge upon students' thoughts. He can query students' ideas and ask for a response and can enjoy observing students play with ideas. Free writing (focused or not) is the play before the hard work of shaping a paper for a reader's eyes. It allows both student and teacher to develop a personal style which makes the reading of writing enjoyable.

Questioning, Note-Taking, Journals

Besides activities which emphasize fluency of expression and thought, the instructor can encourage other kinds of free writing. For instance, while exploring a subject of interest, a writer usually jots down questions on a napkin, a matchbook, a notebook cover—curiosity intrudes at the most surprising moments: this habit is characteristic of good writers and good learners. As most good essays begin with the desire to respond to original and challenging questions, students should be encouraged to ask and record their questions. During a lecture, students could be given note cards to write down any questions that occur to them during the lecture. At the end, the note cards are collected, delivered to the instructor, perhaps written on the blackboard, and responded to. Because the questions may be related or repetitious, this procedure has an advantage over taking questions from the "floor." Putting the questions on the board gives students an idea of the variety of curiosities of the class. If time runs out, the instructor might try to match a questioner with a student who could provide an answer, or return to the questions at the beginning of the next period.

Instructors could ask for written questions on reading or outside assignments. Using this method in an English literature class, the teacher wrote all questions on the board. After some discussion and grouping of the questions, students selected the three they wished to discuss that day. Discussion may also focus on why a particular question was asked, thus encouraging students to discriminate between questions of fact and opinion, of major or tangential importance, of widespread or individual interest, and to locate common and particular concerns. If students are not required to put their names on questions, this procedure eliminates students' fears of asking stupid questions. Often after a few sessions, students gain confidence, and a sense of trust is built among the participants so that students no longer see questioning as perilous and begin to ask questions and give responses more willingly.

Taking notes and keeping a journal are other kinds of formative writing. I've noticed students don't take many notes in class anymore, and it troubles me. This practice of recording and synthesizing is a necessary developmental stage of good writing. Besides recommending that they take notes, instructors can give students models for practice by handing out outlines of lectures with questions, asking students to respond to the questions in writing during the lecture and to hand them in.

In smaller groups, a student could be assigned as a recorder and given a specific notebook to summarize discussion, list questions, or note levels and kinds of individual participation. In my composition class, we formed small groups of five to seven students, and each group elected a recorder who took "minutes" of the discussion. These minutes served as a record for me, a summary of the group's progress for them, and were a boon for the many absentees during a severe month of the flu. Because the student who takes notes benefits more than the others, the responsibilities of recorder should be reassigned from time to time.

I've also asked a student to record major topics and questions during discussion on the blackboard. At the end of the session, students are asked to review the material on the board and write a summary of the discussion. A comparison of the summaries often reveals diverse interests and approaches.

Good notetaking bridges the pre-writing and formulation stages of the writing process; it connects the flow and collection of ideas, thoughts, and experiences to thinking structures. Another way to help students practice this connection is to have them identify patterns or make generalities from lists of related data or observations. Then ask them to write a paragraph including the generality with supporting details. This activity might be done before or after a lecture and used as the basis for discussion. By sharing these kinds of writings with other students, they will begin to acknowledge and appreciate the variety of responses and interpretations that results from different interests and backgrounds.

For some, keeping journals is similar to free writing; for others it is a data collection or organizing activity. A journal can be used to record feelings and emotions. Instructors might investigate the journals of writers in their disciplines, show these to students, and ask them to keep similar journals for a few weeks. If journal keeping is unstructured, each student might be asked to review the journal entries from a month's writing in order to classify the recordings into self-defined topics, such as generalization or detail, fact or opinion. Students could also select their best journal entries to read to the class or show to the teacher.

Writing About Assignments

Connelly and Irving are convinced that "the single most wide-spread *external* cause of bad writing is bad assignments."[7] Charles Cooper echoes this conclusion: "In the Writing Place, the drop-in writing tutorial program in the Learning Center at Buffalo, we're still surprised at how much of our time is devoted to clarifying writing *assignments.*"[8]

Therefore, whenever possible, I ask students to respond to assignment directions by restating the requirements, describing what seems easy and difficult, and jotting down any questions. This response is particularly useful for essay assignments as it encourages the student to plan the task and reveals problems with the assignment the instructor may not have foreseen. The instructor also has an opportunity to comment, directing the student toward a more meaningful approach and a better paper.

For instance, I use the following activity to motivate students to think about a paper assigned for another course. They are free to choose the assignment they wish to focus on, and I have found these questions are appropriate for most compositions:

1. Restate the assignment in your own words.
2. Who is the audience for your writing? How much does he/she know about your subject?
3. What are the reader's expectations?
4. What form will be appropriate for this writing?
5. Free write (5-10 minutes) on the assignment or your topic.
6. What questions do you have about this assignment or topic?
7. What do you need to do (pre-writing activities or formulation activities) before beginning to transcribe?

In response to number four, the teacher and student might discuss a variety of appropriate forms. Pointing out that instructors "assign writing in order to encourage the students to gain imaginative control of the material they want to teach," Peter J. Connelly and Donald Irving suggest that teachers consider a variety of forms: journal, epistle, note, essay, and report. These forms serve different purposes for different students and assignments. And by introducing students to a variety of forms, we can help them write something different from the usual report.

In the reformulation stage of writing, I ask students to give written responses to their own papers. After reading the first drafts of a set of argumentative essays, I have students answer the following questions:

1. What *question* does this essay try to answer?
2. What is the answer to this question? Respond by completing this sentence: "In the essay the writer (asserts) (maintains) (argues) that..."
3. What are the major reasons supporting this assertion? Respond by completing this sentence: "To support this thesis, the author makes the following points:..."
4. What conclusion(s) does the author make? Respond using this sentence beginning: "The author concludes..."

This activity serves several purposes: the students write about themselves as writers; they learn a way to approach and summarize other writers' essays; by examining their own writing, they are able to see the need for connections between generalizations and details, between thesis and support, between the whole essay and conclusion, and to spot organizational weaknesses or imprecision. The resulting revisions were, in most cases, quite improved.

Writing and Learning

Except for the last activity, all these writing activities relate to the pre-writing and formulation stages of the writing process. Students do not spend much time in these stages though professional writers do. Teachers do not give much attention to them, but they are essential to good writing.

In "the mess and privacy of the behavior called writing," Shaughnessy identifies a "sequence of concentrations that seem implicit in the act of writing."[9] She recommends that instructors provide students with needed help by sponsoring activities to encourage these concentrations:

- Getting the thought—recognizing it first, and then exploring it enough to estimate one's resources (motivational and informational) for writing about it.
- Getting the thought down—proceeding, that is, into the thick of the idea, holding onto it even as the act of articulation refines and changes it.[10]

Most student writers are unaware of "the writer's way of composing," of the "deliberate process whereby meaning is crafted, stage by stage." This ignorance contributes to the major problems in students' writing: lack of development, syntactical errors and awkwardness, illogical assertions, and voiceless prose.

Besides informing students of these stages, we need to encourage the student to *write* (not just talk, though conversation should be abundant also) during these sequences because by writing the student develops the essential dialogue between "writer as creator and writer as reader."

This dialogue is most commonly found in writing in the reflexive mode as this mode is defined by Janet Emig *(The Composing Processes of Twelfth Graders,* 1971). Although most school writing is *extensive,* that is writing to communicate, to influence others, to argue a point a view, Emig asserts from her review of professional and high school writers that most good writing begins in the reflexive mode wherein the writer addresses oneself or a trusted audience. Emig found that when high school students wrote in this exploratory mode, they spent longer on pre-writing activities and made more frequent reformulations. By limiting school-sponsored writing to writing in the extensive mode, teachers in fact encourage the detached reportorial writing that is so boring to read, and truncate the process of writing into a mechanical activity.

Britton, et al, define three modes of writing: expressive, transactional (writing to get things done) and poetic.[11] They maintain that practice in the expressive mode, from which the other two spring, is essential because "in developmental terms, the expressive is a kind of matrix from which differentiated forms of mature writing are developed."[12] My term, *formative writing,* corresponds to Britton's expressive and Emig's reflexive. *Formative* seems to me to relate more directly to the purposes of writing in the college classroom and to the uses of writing to assist learning, not just to improve writing.

Clearly, these formative writing activities contribute more to the student's mastery of learning *processes* than to the learning of *content,* and this emphasis is certainly intentional. I am disturbed by research results such as those reported by Chickering and summarized by K. Patricia Cross in *Accent on Learning:*

> Chickering found that a majority of students said that they spent much more time memorizing than they did analyzing, synthesizing, applying, or evaluating. Thus, the research gives a picture of present institutions of higher education placing too much emphasis on the student as a "storage tank" and giving too little attention to the education of the student as a fully functioning human being capable of using knowledge to moral and social ends. (p. 142)

Between the acts of memorization and analysis, synthesis, application, and evaluation, between the acts of gathering data and taking notes and transcribing an essay, there has to be time for exploration: for tentative beginnings, expansion, playing with ideas, trying out different roles and hearing different voices, for the suspension of accountability in favor of experimentation and flexibility. During this time, these writing activities can serve the student and teacher.

Formative writing offers opportunities for teachers and learners to explore choices, use experience, discuss ideas, communicate frequently, and evaluate formatively.

Why should the non-writing teacher design and sponsor formative writing activities?

• Because we have reason to believe that these writing activities will produce better writing.

• Because these activities give the teacher an opportunity to interact with the student during the learning process in ways that are satisfying to the teacher, providing support, motivation and assistance.

• Because these writings cue the teacher to students' interests and problems.

• Because these activities create and support conditions necessary for effective learning: self-defined approaches to knowledge; active involvement with the material and in the learning process; opportunity for timely response and feedback from a variety of sources; formative evaluation as a basis for further exploration and growth which may reduce fear of failure and create a willingness to risk.

Clearly, I dismiss as unnecessary and unprofitable the two most frequent reactions to the writing instructor's plea for other instructors to take some responsibility for improved student writing: more papers and an increase in instructor's marginal editing or proofreading marks.* The traditional concept of composition as only a product has ill-served teachers and students. Rather we need to develop writing activities based upon recent investigations into the writing process, research on writing improvement and learning theory. On the other hand, the composing process, like learning, requires formative activities: exploration, development and discovery. Therefore, the integration of writing and learning promises to enhance both.

---

*To deter any impulses to take out the possibly outdated College Rhetoric or Grammar Handbook in search of appropriate correctional symbols I would ask potential wielders of the red pencil to recall their reactions and responses to papers returned by an instructor. Did we respond to the AMB, ?, or AWK by asking the instructor what was meant and then revise to make meanings clearer? Probably not, either because nothing really depended upon our doing so, or we received the paper after the instructor had left campus for a deserved vacation. We may have recognized our ineptness by these teacher comments and grade, but had little foundation for improvement unless further practice was required and necessary to succeed in the course. The effectiveness of various kinds of teacher comments has been challenged by research reported in Haynes (1978).

Footnotes

[1]Jean Piaget, *The Language and Thought of the Child,* trans. M. Gabain, (London: Routledge and Kegan Paul, Ltd., 1926); James Moffett, *Teaching the Universe of Discourse,* (Boston: Houghton Mifflin, Inc., 1968); James Britton, *Language and Learning,* (London: Pelican Books, 1972).

[2]Janet Emig, *The Composing Processes of Twelfth Graders,* (Urbana, Illinois: National Council of Teachers of English, 1971); Mina Shaughnessey, *Errors and Expectations,* (New York: Oxford University Press, 1977); Elizabeth Haynes, "Using Research in Preparing to Teach Writing," *English Journal,* January 1978, pp. 82-88.

[3]K. Patricia Cross, *Accent on Learning,* (San Francisco: Jossey-Bass Publishers, 1976); A. W. Chickering, *Education and Identity,* (San Francisco: Jossey-Bass Publishers, 1969).

[4]Peter Elbow, *Writing Without Teachers,* (New York: Oxford University Press, 1973). p. 6.

[5]James Bess, "The Motivation to Teach," *Journal of Higher Education,* XLVIII, 3, May/June 1977, p. 248.

[6]*Ibid.*

[7]Peter J. Connelly and Donald C. Irving, "Composition in the Liberal Arts: A Shared Responsibility," *College English* (37, 7, March 1976), p. 670.

[8]Charles Cooper, "What College Writers Need to Know," unpublished address to the Department of Literature, University of California, San Diego, April 5, 1978.

[9]Shaughnessy, *op. cit.,* p. 81.

[10]*Ibid.,* pp. 81-82.

[11]James Britton, Tony Burgess, Nancy Martin, Alex McLeod, Harold Rosen, *The Development of Writing Abilities (11-18),* (London: MacMillan, 1975).

[12]*Ibid.,* p. 83.

Appendix

Examples of Formative Writing

The samples of students' writing included in this section show the college teacher a variety of formative writings. Each student was responding to specific directions which are included. The design of each assignment may not correlate directly to the activities suggested in this paper, as I adapt activities to the class, course, and student. They are all, however, designed to provide me as teacher and the student as learner with concrete evidence of what the student is thinking, and to indicate, wherever possible, where the student is headed. They are also designed to engage the student in the various tasks of the writing process, so that he becomes aware of the purposes and possibilities of each to develop form and compose.

Students know that this writing will not be graded or edited but that it is required to fulfill the demands of the course. They also know that this writing will be read thoughtfully and in some cases used for class discussion.

The writing samples are divided into two categories:

I—Formative Writing for Formal Composition
II—Writing Without Formal Composition as a Goal

The student writing samples have been typed as they were written without corrections, sometimes with my comments as I made them on the original papers.

I: Formative Writing for Formal Composition

The following assignments and students' writings were required as part of the composition process of an argumentative or persuasive essay (probably the most frequent form of academic writing in all disciplines) during a freshman composition course at a four-year private, liberal arts and business college where over half of the students major in business-related disciplines. The students who wrote these samples scored below 500 on the SAT verbal test.

When designing assignments for a long term paper based on independent research, an instructor in a discipline other than composition may not have the time to require and respond to each one of these activities. But they are suggestive of the possibilities of formative writing that students may find helpful when writing a formal essay.

I have omitted the two traditional pre-writing assignments: notes and outlines. Students were required to take notes on notecards according to a recommended form, and, usually after the first draft, they were asked to make an outline. Some students spontaneously produced outlines, or perhaps made outlines according to some prescription they had learned in high school English classes. My reason for omitting these two kinds of writings is that they usually do not reveal the student's thinking *in process.* Notes often are mere transcriptions from reading; outlines represent the results of thinking. The writing assignments here have one thing in common that notes and outlines do not: they are dynamic or dialectic activities. That is they show interactions between details, ideas, writer and self, writer and others, a kind of movement which generates rather than reifies thought.

A. Creative Exploration (adapted from Susan Miller, *Writing Process and Product.)*

B. Logical Exploration (adapted from Ray Kytle, *Clear Thinking for Composition.)*

C. Focused Free Writing (adapted from Peter Elbow, *Writing Without Teachers.)*

D. Diary of One's Own Composing Process

E. Proposal for a Research Paper

F. Developing a Thesis for an Audience
Stage One—Pre-draft
Stage Two—Post-draft

G. Author and Reader Response to a First Draft
Evaluative Summary
Critique

A. Creative Exploration

Directions to Student:

It seems to me that there are two kinds of exploration of any subject you might want to write on: I call these creative exploration and logical exploration. They are not always completely separate, but we can separate them for the purpose of your practice and awareness. I strongly recommend that you do the creative exploration first.

1. Free write on your topic or idea for at least five minutes. Read what you have written and summarize the focus or center of gravity in one sentence. Free write on this sentence for five minutes or more and write a second one sentence summary. (Keep doing this as long as you wish!)

2. What is the one thing you would say about this topic or idea if you could only write/say one sentence?

3. What is the most prevalent or frequently expressed opinion/idea/thing that people say about this topic? Do you agree or disagree?

4. What is your basic feeling (not thought or idea, but real feeling) about this topic? What is the opposite of this feeling?

5. What is this topic like? Give an image, metaphor, simile to show what this topic is like.

6. What is this topic unlike? Give an image, metaphor, or simile.

7. What colors, people, setting, objects do you associate with this topic?

8. Repeat #2 trying to incorporate some of the answers you have given for #2-7. Remember: sentences can be very long.

A. Creative Exploration

Creative Exploration

"A parent's best defense against inappropriate programs and commercials maybe to watch T.V. with the kids."

Sacramento Bee

By Barbra Riegelhaupt

I think parental control is a definite must when it comes to children and television. There are too many shows and commercials on these days which have harmful effects on kids. If the program is complex in any way, the parent should be with the child explaining what and why things are happening. I think T.V. should not be used as a main entertainment devise. The hours which it is being watched should be limited. If a parent is not around, it should be stressed that the child watch only what programs you allow when you are there.

1) Parental control is necessary when it comes to children and T.V.

2) T.V. has many harmful affects on children

3) Children spend too much time in front of the "tube".

4) Concern, indifferent

5) Cookie dough being mixed

6) A bridge

7) bright colors, children, Chestor Aarron, family room.

8) T.V. has many harmful affects on children mainly due to the fact that they spend too much time in front of it without parental control.

B. Logical Exploration

Directions to Student:

Analysis is the process of logical exploration. You will analyze your topic from various points of view, asking questions suggested by that point of view, and then classify these questions. Your classifications may include: types, sources, effects, purposes, form, function, advantages, disadvantages, definition, characteristics, cause, effect.

B. Logical Exploration

Logical Exploration

Subject: January term

Points of view	Classification

1. What is the Jan. term?   Definition

2. What is the purpose of the Jan. term?   Purpose

3. What is the outcome of the Jan. term?   Outcome

Subject: Outcome of January term

1. Are there actually outcomes of the January term?   Existence of outcomes

2. What kinds of outcomes?   Kinds of outcomes

3. Are the outcomes beneficial or disadvantageous?   Benefits or Disadvantages

Limited Subject: The beneficial and disadvantageous
outcomes of the January term

1. What is meant by "beneficial" and "disadvantageous"?   Definition of Terms

2. What are the types of beneficial outcomes?   Types of benefits

3. What are the types of disadvantageous outcomes?   Types of disadvantages

C. Focused Free Writing

Directions to Student

The purpose of "free writing" is to record all the thoughts, details, questions, anything you have in your mind that relates to your topic. Write without regard for "correctness" (i.e., spelling, sentences, grammar). Write for a specified time (12 or 15 minutes is suggested). Free writing can be used at the beginning of your planning when you are trying to find a focus or during the writing of drafts when you experience a writer's block.

C. Focused Free Writing

---

15 minute free write   4/2/79

It seems that Homosexuality is a topic most people have opinions on and yet have no desire to discuss it.

I have talked to guys from my floor and I get the same answers. "Homosexuals are queers," "if someone I knew told me he was gay I would punch him out," queers are not worth shit--where I come from (Pasadena) me and my friends take BB guns and shoot at them as they come out of the gay bars on Colorado Blvd."

These guys have their opinions on homosexuals but as soon as you say lets talk about homosexuals instead of using emotive language to prove that something i wrong with homosexuals why not try to find out about homosexuality. My replies were--your sick, I am not queer and don't care to know about gays. Yet these same guys talk about gays in jokes.

When I told the guys I was doing a paper on homosexuality I was told I was sick, queer and that I should see a doctor.

Some of the guys left my room and to this day refuse to notice me to talk to me. I feel that one of the reasons for the reactions received had to do with the idea that I was trying to find out about a subject that was not suppose to be explored by anyone who was not gay. I was going to prove the statements made against gays were true or whether they were false. I guess I was suppose to except the statements as true.

A friend named Peter told me in confidentiality that I should not explore this area because it could effect me and the consequences of this happening would cause our friendship to end.

I have gotten a feeling that men feel that homosexuality is a "disease" that contagious from the people I have talked to and from the books I have read. If I start talking to gays then I will become gay.

People should look at homosexuality as part of the person and not as the whole of the person. Their is more to a man than his sexual orientation.

In our society we accept the idea of the puritans long ago--that we are good upstanding peoples with a fear in God as long as we keep homosexuality quiet everything is okay but as soon as it is brought out in the open, havoc starts. Right away peoples mind think negative thoughts. They judge Homosexuals without hearing their side. Well in the paper I am allowing to hear the side of the Homosexual. I want to understand were he is coming from.

The people I have talked to live in a world of fear. They are afraid of being "found out" for their whole life would be in jeopardy. I talked to a man named John (fictional name) he works in the Financial District in S.F. he is vice president of a corporative management, has a family and all the fringe benefits of his position. He told me if anyone found out he was gay he said he would lose his job, his friends and even his family. John is only one of many people who have to live this way.

I say this is outrageous. A person should not have to live his life in fear--full of anxiety that no one find out the secret. When talking w/ John he told me he loved his wife and kids but that a piece was missing. A piece he found only with another man. John said he had a hard time admitting his homosexuality. He told me how could he be homosexual when he was very athletically inclined homosexuals were suppose to be very feminine. It took him 15 years to realize that he could be gay and be athletic. He asked me if God approved of what he felt. (I had told him were I went to school and that I was thinking of joining the priesthood) I told him that I could not answer that for him. I did tell him that I felt God is understanding, loving and full of mercy. I told him that the question asked, he must ask God himself and pray. I told him that I was sorry for him. He left then with another guy.

This is the type of thing that angers me. How our society suppresses and forces people to lead a double life in secret. Who are we to bring such judgement to other people?

> What a feeling, perceptive response you have — and you are trying to deal logically with emotional, subjective, perhaps illogical issues which is difficult.
>
> Notice by the way, how fluent, personal and clear your writing is!

D. Diary of One's Own Composing Process

Directions to Student:

Every night (one or two exceptions would be permissible!) write in your diary noting anything you did, thought, or said that related to your composing this theme. Record also your feelings about how the process is going. Try to be aware of when, how, and why you experience blocks, relief, what helps, what seems to hinder your thinking, writing, and exploration. Set aside at least five minutes each day for this recording.

D. Diary of One's Own Composing Process
    (Selected Entries)

Writer's Diary

March 24 -- Wednesday

The topic I have chosen for myself is Homosexuality→ Why Homosexuality?
With so many people giving their opinions on Homosexuality, what causes it and
what type of person is gay. This is an area which is an important topic/issue
in our society. I want to find out the other side of the gay life--the gay
life as seen from the gay individual--the one who is living the gay life.

March 22, 1979 -- Thursday

I went to the Library in Moraga, and went over a few books on Homosexuality.
--I feel I need to learn as much as I can about Homosexuality before interviewing a person whose sexual preference is for his/her own sex.

I have a few books that give brief mention of Homosexuality I read these books
and took down a few notes.

March 26 Monday

The David Kopay story left a very important imprint on me.
I saw how a man had to cope with the idea that he could be a homosexual
and also a football player was very hard for him to except. Kopay says
that he plays a rougher game of football as a way (means of giving off his
sexual energies. He also says that football is considered the macho-macho
area that cannot be effected by homosexuality. The fact is that homosexuality
is in football. David and others in football are gay and must learn how to
deal with it.

Still reading for Money or Love....This book gives insight to the idea that
homosexuality can be learned--even forced upon.

April 5, 1979

I talked with my romate about Homosexuality. He feels that gays become gay
when as a child they did not become guided correctly as far as sexual development is concern. I partially agree with this statement.

April 25

I read parts over again "the Homosexual and the Church" I feel that the
church has taken a view of understanding--trying to understand the homosexual
as a human being. The church in representing Christ who shows mercy on all
and loves all. Homosexuality is a personal thing. Each person who reaches
the conclusion that he is gay must take (and does take) time to sit back, and
look at the situation this way way they can better understand their sexuality.
See where their homosexuality is at in other words is it just in sex that
the same sex is preferred or is it in all aspects of living--a friend, a com-
panion who you want to spend the rest of your life with? The person who is
gay must look at these things before making anh hasty decision before reaction
to the truth of his homosexuality.

May 9

Had a meeting w/Jean came to the conclusion that what we are seeing
in my paper is that through the proccess we can see that the issue is broader
than our prejudices! --try to write the paper over again.

E. Proposal for a Research Paper
    Directions to Student:

PROPOSAL FORMAT

 (Respond to the following on a separate piece of paper--preferably typed.)

1. Are you going to examine a problem or explore something? If a problem,
    identify the problem and its parts or related aspects. If exploration,
    identify its parts or related aspects.

2. Why are you personally motivated to focus on this topic for your Long Theme?

3. What do you think you might gain from doing this exploration or from
    examining this problem?

4. What resources are you planning to consult? (List at least 8--four of which
    must be reading; others may be interviews, observations, visits or activities.)

5. Looking at your topic as objectively as possible, what questions do you have,
    or might others have about this topic? (Come up with at least six.)

6. Do a 10 minute (or more if you want) focused free write on your topic.

E. Proposal for a Research Paper

March 20, 1979

Proposal Due

Title IX

1. I am going to examine the problems that were felt about Title IX and I am going to narrow my topic to a more of a less broader subject and narrow it down to the problems and effects it will have upon the Intercollegiate Athletics here at this college. Will it be good or bad? is there resentment felt or will Title IX ever go into effects. *WAtch either...or thinking*

2. I am personally motivated on *to examine* this topic because I've talked to women here at this college who play intercollegiate sports who have complained that things are unfair, a sample would be: All the women's games are played with in the State of California, while the men's basketball team has traveled to Hawaii, New York, and all over. Allso disputes over athletic equipment, and use of the gymn, so on.

3. It definitely would be a topic that would be informative for my own personal knowledge, I've heard a lot of complaining of unfairness of this topic by the women athlete here at school. That what Title IX is supposed to be is not carried out, at all, and probably never will be.

4. 1. U.S. News - July 10, 1978 pp. 79-80 Womens Sports Boom.
   2. Sports Illustrated 48 34-36 March 20, 78 Women in Sports
   3. Time 54-60 Je. 26, '78 Too Far To Fast.

4. Encyclopedia - general information on passing of Title IX.

   Interviews   Activity Observation
   1. Coach Joe DeLuca   Women's Basketball game
   2. Coach McDonald   Men's Baseball Team
   3. Coach Manini   Women's Softball Team
   4. Alice Duffy   Men's Rugby Team
   5. Shari Otto
   6. Anette Chiara

5. 1. What is Title IX
   2. Is it a good or bad law? Upon small college, compared to large univ.
   3. Is it working, has it accomplished anything or has it ruined things.
   4. What is the effect upon this college?
   5. Will it have any devastating or make amends and bring the mens and women athletic departments closer.
   6. How do athletes and coaches feel about this.

6. Free Write

I found that Title IX was a law that was passed eight years ago I can admit there has been a change but only in the bigger schools. Because things are more noticeable thére. Here at this college very little has changed, the men still have priority over all athletic money and facilities. Things have improved slightly but nothing widely noticeable we do offer a few scholarships offered for women compared to men who have alot of money and can even go out of state for recruiting.

F. Developing a Thesis for an Audience

    Stage One - Predraft

    Explanation to Student:

When the student is ready to begin writing the first draft, I assign a kind of rhetorical "Square" which encourages the writer to see the relationships among audience, purpose, form, and style and how these concerns relate to the topic, focused topic, question the essay attempts to answer, and thesis statement.

F. Developing a Thesis for An Audience

    Stage Two - Post-draft

    Explanation to Student:

After turning in the first draft, I ask the students to give a overview of the draft. This overview forces the student to observe and judge clarity of expression, focus, purpose, and modifications of the original intent of the essay.

F. Stage One: Developing a Thesis for an Audience

Child Abuse - Square

Audience

General public - 5 in my group
interested in child abuse.

Purpose

To inform those people interested about
child abuse and the causes for it.

Inform my group about the "vicious
cycle."

Topic: Child Abuse

Focused topic: The causes of child abuse

Question: What causes the actual abuse of children?

Thesis: Although child abuse exists in all societies, and economic
lifestyles, usually the causes for the abuse are, in most
cases, (similar.)

nice

such as...

Style

Definition and example and
possible case history.

Form

Beginning - definition and statement
of issue.

Middle - actual causes and possibly case
histories.

End - summary and a possible

F. Stage Two: Developing a Thesis for an Audience

Title: My Kind of Plan

Topic: The General Management Plan for Yosemite

Focus Topic: My Defense of The General Management Plan

Question: Should The General Management Plan Be Supported?

Purpose: To defend the measures which have been outlined in The General
Management Plan.

Thesis: Even if the Draft General Management Plan does recommend drastic steps, suc
as the removal of more than one hundreds structures, and would cost
millions of dollars, I support it since it proposes steps to elimanate the
majority of the congestion, urbanization, and overcrowding that are
destroying the eco-systems in the park.

G. Author and Reader Response to a First Draft

   After the first draft is completed, I asked that the first drafts be
reviewed by both the writer and another student. Directions for two kinds of
review are included in the samples: Evaluative Summary and Critique.

EVALUATIVE SUMMARY

Use this form and write one paragraph reviewing this essay:

Author

Essay

Reviewer

In   (title)   (author)   hopes to   suggests
                                                  prove   argues
                                                                  maintains
that   (thesis or main argumentative point).

(Author's last name)   supports this thesis/point by

(list major points of the paper that support the thesis).

(Take two or three sentences to comment upon the believability of this argument
or point, problems you see in the argument, and/or strengths of the argument or
essay).

After reading   (author's essay, title), I   (state what conclusions or

opinions on this subject you now have).

                         sign your name_____

G. Author and Reader Response to a First Draft
   Evaluative Summary

Summary

A World Without Sound

In "A World Without Sound," (the author)   suggests that the problems
of the deaf child should be examined with more knowledge and a better understanding. She feels that they should be acknowledged for what they are, and
accepted into our society. Although in the past these handicapped children
were referred to as "deaf-mutes" present-day technology has taken big steps
such as the development of hearing aides. Society is also helping the deaf
by making available special schools for the deaf including guidance for the
parents. (The author's)   essay is convincing because of her style and
the way she presents her topic. Her personal experience in the beginning of
the paper adds insight and makes for an interesting start. Through examples
and good arguments, she explains her topic well, proves her thesis, and leads
into her conclusion. After reading this paper, I now have a bit more insight
about the problems of the deaf child. "A World Without Sound" is an interesting
paper to read.

G. Author and Reader Response to a First Draft
Critique

Title: _Title IX and it's affect on_   (name of college)

Author: _____

Reviewer: _____   Date: _April 25 '79_

After you complete your critique and evaluation, return this paper to
the author.

CRITIQUE

1. Read the essay carefully. Circle the thesis statement or main ideas.
2. Read the essay a second time. Make marginal notes if you want:
   (✓) fine point or idea or image; (?) unclear; (M) more wanted.

3. Write a one or two sentence summary of the essay which includes the
   main point and supporting points. _The main pt. I thought
   you were trying to pt. out was the
   major affects that Title IX had on
   schools in general and then how_ (name of college)
   has been affected.

4. In what ways is this argument convincing or weak? (Cite specific
   points, sentences, words.) _Your title painted out
   that you were going to study the
   affects Title IX had on_ (name of college)
   _your paper it seemed to me —1
   did not become specific enough about SMC_

5. What questions do you have that the author would have to answer before
   you could agree with the author's thesis or argumentative point?
   _I would want to know how the
   athletes feel and also the spectators
   of the sports._

6. Note to the author (suggestions, response, reactions): _I think
   that your paper is quite interesting.
   You should try to get more female
   interviews and maybe narrow your paper
   down to title IX's affect on SMC
   more_

II — Writing Without Formal Composition as a Goal

A. Exploration of Subject and Personal Goals

B. Written Response to Assignments: Identifying Problems and
Questions for Class Discussion

A. Exploration of Subject and Personal Goals

This assignment can be used to discover students' prior knowledge about a subject and to find out individual expectations of what the student hopes to learn or thinks he/she needs to learn. These writings can also:
- guide curricular design (assignments, discussion, etc.);
- support self-motivated and self-designed learning;
- provide a record for comparison with what the student actually learns by the end of the course.

I used the writings which follow as the basis for small group discussion (seven students): students read their writings to each other before beginning to discuss poetry. After sharing this information, each student knew what others in the group had studied, had some notions about what each one could add to the group's future discussion about poetry, and knew what each expected from the study of poetry.

Directions: Please write out your answers to the following:

1. Past Experience: Describe your formal (school) or informal experiences with poetry.

2. Preferences: Name those poets and poems you prefer or dislike.

3. Expectations: What are some of the things you expect to do, happen, or learn during this semester's study of poetry? What do you expect of other students in the class? of the teacher?

4. Personal goals/hopes: What do you personally hope to read/do/learn/ "get out of" this study of poetry?

5. Achievement: If possible, suggest ways you can achieve these personal goals.

A. Exploration of Subject and Personal Goals

English 10B

1. Past Experience - Poetry 〈 Formal - School
                                  Informal

2. Preferences - Name, poet, styles

3. Expectations 〈 Teachers
                   Student
                   Content

4. Personal Goals

5. How Achieved?

1. My last experience with Poetry was in Grade School (8th grade), and I'd
    rather not remember those frustrating times. The teacher felt that there
    was but one universal interpretation and you can just imagine as eighth
    graders trying to discover it. It was like trying to pick a needle out of
    a haystack.

2. I prefer not to read the usual sing-song, rhyme, poetry but blank verse. I
    feel meaning deteriorates in rhyme form. (At least for me anyway.)

3. Expectations/Personal Goals
    When I enrolled in this class I expected our work on poetry to include a
    tedious line by line analysis approach, on an individual basis. I really like the
    idea of working in groups and playing on each other's interpretations. I feel
    that a student can be a leader if we work in groups and this would suit me a
    lot better.

B. Written Response to Assignments: Identifying Problems and Questions
for Class Discussion

Written responses to assigned readings can be structured by the teacher
or unstructured, essentially free writing. For structured responses, I have
asked students to respond imaginatively (e.g., write a letter explaining this
poem concept, report to another student who hasn't read this assignment, pretend
you are the author and summarize this passage); definitively (e.g., choose the
three most important words in this passage/poem/essay and define them); or
personally in a narrative or record (e.g., record all the thoughts, feelings,
questions you had while reading this poem/passage/story the first time, then,
reread the passage and record your new thoughts. Did they change? deepen?).
After writing these kind of responses students review their writing and identify
problems posed by the text or ones they have. Usually, I ask that these problems
be shaped into questions which are presented in class for discussion.

The student writing samples which follow are unstructured responses to the
novel, Wuthering Heights. The questions were to be: "ones you believe
important to discuss and answer in order to discover the purpose/meaning/value
of the work."

Though not directly coordinated with the development of a formal essay,
this kind of writing often reveals the seeds of an essay (most essays are
explorations of a problem). I always note those "seeds" in the margins.

B. Written Response to Assignments

The first thing that I really began to wonder about was the type of narration that Bronte used in "Wuthering Heights". She gave the story line through Lockwood, but he become a listener and Nellie becomes the main narrator of the story. I couldn't quite understand why she used this unique method at first. But then I realized that it seemed as if I was having the story told to me rather than me just reading it.

I enjoyed the way all of the peices fell together, like the colors of a painting. Each chapter brought on new developments which moved me ever closer to the situation which existed upon Lockwood's (and my own) arrival at Wuthering Heights. The novel starts with several surprizes: the multiple Catherines, the ghost, Heathcliff's and Harton's true identities, and the strange moods of the characters. Slowly all of these changes become understandable as Nellie tells of past events, Bronte then seems to be predictable since everything is now falling into place. But she doesn't allow her imagination to fail us. The story takes a unexpected turn just when it appears that Heathcliff has completely suceeded in avenging the world. It is at this point that the surpizes begin to reappear: Heathcliff's inability to enjoy his revenge, Hareton's devotion to Heathcliff, and of course Heathcliff's strange death.

One difference which I quickly noticed between this novel and modern day novels, was the lack of outward action in "Wuthering Heights", since the majority of the novel was told through 2nd person. This made everything seem like memories in my mind. I just finished reading "The Day of the Jackel," which seemed like non-stop action.

B. Written Response to Assignments

Wuthering Heights   5/18/79

Yellow Paper

The first few chapters expose the keys to the plot very slowly. We
meet the troubled Heathcliff--he is so very rude! Its easy to immediately
dislike him, but I feel also especially sorry for him. His loss of Catherine,
even after all these years, still torments him. We see the consequences of a
great and deep love that suffers the separation of death. How different is
Heathcliff from everyone? Despite our valiant attempts to mask our sorrow,
are we not tormented always by lost loves? Why does love remain so difficult
to attain? The obstacles are endless. Forces intervene and disrupt--as
with Catherine and Heathcliff? Her development at the Lintons into a graceful
woman (with a strong will!) was at odds with the stagnated maturation of
Heathcliff--resulting in the other marriage and his flight from the Heights.
Catherine's subsequent illness--emotion has power over our entire being.

Heathcliff returns, now very wealthy. Does he feel that his new status
can bring Catherine and him together? I wonder at this--it seems to degrade
their love if money can bring them together. Or is this just more practical?
Heathcliff becomes driven to acquire both the Heights and the Grange. Possessing
both would symbolize to Heathcliff that he has also attained his Catherine--
also a great revenge. But it is an empty one. He remains tormented, dying a
sorrowful man.

The narration is an intricate one--why does Emily Bronte do this? It passes
from the mildly obnoxious Lockwood who knows nothing to the perceptive Nelly Dean

who knows everything. How important is the narrator to a story or novel?
Crucial or irrelevant?

As the story ends Catherine Linton and Hareton are in love, and few
obstacles confront them. Heathcliff has lost his spiteful spirit and does
not interfere. Emily Bronte is here perhaps trying to end on a more hopeful
note--love can survive and develop peacefully! Some justice exists, allowing
lives to emerge from past tragedies of past generations happily and hopefully.

1. Should we pity or hate Heathcliff? What drives him throughout his life?

2. What does the novel have to say about love? Is it worth suffering through?
   Can we logically put our hopes in it?

3. Why does the narration switch? How important is viewpoint in a novel?

Mapping the Writing Journey

I

Mapping and Thinking

Marilyn Hanf Buckley
University of California, Berkeley

From any perspective, writing is the most difficult language process.
The demand that writing makes of logical thought and deliberate language
provokes students—whether in elementary school or college—to moan
as if inflicted with pain whenever the assignment is to write. Many otherwise active students experience a temporary paralysis of both mind and
muscles when they are requested to confront a blank page. With pens
poised in hands, ideas frozen and locked in place, anxieties increasing
and rapidly diminishing their already small store of confidence, students—
both bright and lackluster—protest to whoever will listen that they would
rather be doing something else, anything else than writing. Well intended
teachers who advise "Just get going" are, unfortunately, of little help
because that is the very thing the students can not do. We hope, in the

pages that follow, to offer some suggestions for helping students solve the problem of how to get going.

A prewriting technique many teachers have found useful is called *mapping,* a preparation—if you will—for the writing journey. Most students would agree that the success of a journey—be it a backpack trip in the Sierra mountains or a trip to Ashland, Oregon, for the Shakespeare festival—is determined, to a large extent, by the care or lack of care in planning. And so it is in writing. Even though mapping is helpful to all students, it is especially beneficial for those students who have never developed procedures or strategies for thinking through *what* they will write about and *how* they will go about it. The excessive energy that these students spend on initial decisions about organizing and beginning their writing leaves them with little vigor for the more important tasks of making meaning with groups of words. When applied, mapping provides students of all grades with a simple, relatively quick way of organizing an intellectual plan for their linguistic journey. Most students, we must admit, will never cease complaining about the difficult process of writing no matter what activities, techniques, or procedures are developed by talented teachers. Mapping, even though an exceptionally effective process of organizing ideas, will probably only soften the groans.

To write well is to think well. The interrelations between thought and language are readily observed whenever students' writings resemble a riot of ideas as in a verbal collage, with improvised and premature knots of confusion intricately wandering through five paragraphs. Obviously the student's thinking is confused. No amount of noun and verb agreement or exercises in the sixteen uses of the comma will help. Problems resulting from disorder and nonsense are only ameliorated by the imposition of order and sense. The single reason why writing can make the exact man, as Bacon suggested, is that writing, if it is to be effective, depends upon that consistency of reasoning one finds in logical thinking. Most teachers know that controlled and limpid discourse comes from writers who are lucid and exacting in their thinking. Their real problem, most teachers admit, is *how* to guide students through their initial untidy tangles of confusing ideas to a level of writing which is clear and coherent. The technique of mapping helps in this pursuit in that it teaches the three most important thinking skills: recalling ideas, organizing ideas, and structuring ideas. If students use mapping, these three cognitive skills which are basic to writing can be readily practiced and to some degree perfected.

RECALLING IDEAS

Students do not write writing, they write ideas. The greater the quantity and diversity of ideas that students can choose from, the better. Before students can decide upon a thesis statement and select a particular audience, they need to bring to the surface of their memories all ideas

associated with the topic. Working in small groups, students freely associate or brainstorm about the topic, producing a great quantity of words
and phrases, some valuable, some not. Students are reminded that during
free association, no judgment of worth or relevance is made. Emphasis is
on divergent thinking, fluency of ideas, diversity and creativity. At first
students need encouragement to have confidence that they know a lot
about the topic and should resist early closure of brainstorming until the
group's list is abundant with possibilities. So that everyone can quickly
accumulate a plethora of ideas, each group shares with the class, inviting
others to take freely from the list. It matters not which student generated
the words; writing is difficult and everyone needs help and support from
everyone else. Very early in their relations, the teacher proposes: language
is the human experience. The more we can realize the range of possibilities
in our language, the more we can develop our humanity. But development
is difficult, and we owe one another an intense loyalty. The class is a
community of scholars, collaborating with each other—raising questions,
proposing answers, suggesting revisions or rewrites, encouraging others to
take risks in language or discouraging another's empty, bombastic verbosity.

If students protest this initial step of brainstorming for ideas in small
groups and sharing with one another, suggest that they compare writings
done without these techniques with those done after using the techniques.
By comparing the two products, many students will soon realize that if
they do not remind themselves of what they know about the topic *before*
writing is begun, they will probably not recollect those ideas during the
act of writing when the mind is preoccupied with whatever language task
is at hand. The slow and many times tedious process of writing is out of
touch with the swift racing of thoughts. If ideas are not to be lost, they
need to be anchored down, made visible, available, and accessible to the
writer. However, quantity of ideas, no matter how rich, is of little use
unless the ideas are organized and categorized into groups and labeled.

ORGANIZING IDEAS

Any classroom of students can produce an overflowing list of ideas.
But just as the students could not carry dozens of books without dropping
all of them, they can not mentally carry dozens of ideas. The mind prefers
order to chaos, clarity to confusion, and tidiness to disarray. When
students arrange separate and discrete ideas into groups, patterns, or
logical units, they create a system which is friendly to the way their memories work.

If students ask two questions—*which of these ideas go together?* and
what shall I call that group?—they will translate their list of words into
categories of meanings that complement the topic. Again, if students
share in small groups and give and take from each other, they will have a
greater range of possibilities for each student to choose from. A group of
students is always wiser than an individual student. But even if the students

all write the names of their categories on the chalkboard for everyone's potential use, the task of writing is not yet accomplished.

The students are now ready to move from a general topic to a specific thesis statement. By overviewing the categories and all the ideas connected with them, the students can each select one that they individually want to write about. At this stage the teacher guides each student to decide upon a thesis statement and the purpose of the writing and to establish a particular audience for the piece. Ideally students will then share their decisions in a small writing group to get some response from others regarding their choices.* Now the student is ready to brainstorm individually about his thesis, bringing out of his memory all related associations. This step is done easily and quickly because of the work done in the initial group brainstorming. As with all lists of diverse ideas, the student categorizes his own list. These categories establish the principal parts of the thesis. In many cases, the categories will become the separate paragraphs of the writing. Selecting categories and arranging them in a sequence will enable the students to then structure or map their ideas on their topics.

STRUCTURING IDEAS

On a blank piece of paper, the student draws a large geometric shape— circle, square, and so forth—in a central position for the thesis. Extending from the center are as many lines as there are categories. Branching from the categories are several levels of smaller lines which represent the supporting details. It is best to use one sheet of paper so that the student can intellectually appreciate a comprehensive overview of the journey about to be taken.

Being able to see at a glance how her writing will begin, develop, and conclude enables the student to visualize the whole with all its related parts. Students gain a sense of confidence and control when they complete a comprehensive map. Every idea has its place and every place is indicated on the map. Some students think of mapping as an advance organizer; others say that the map is their ideational scaffolding. Whether organizer or scaffolding, the map helps the student to do what every text on writing advises: organize ideas.

It is not only the student who gains from mapping; the teacher does also. As students map, the teacher can move around the room and can *see* the students' proposed structures of ideas, the previews of events to come. At this prewriting stage the teacher can question, advise, share ideas, and applaud the students' designs. Readily visible are the students' decisions—the thesis statements, their main categories, the supporting details for each category in hierarchical order, and the sequence progressing from beginning to end. Usually the teacher has to wait until the writing is turned in before she can be a thoughtful listener or interested reader. Map making as a prewriting process provides the student with opportunities for dialogue with the teacher or another student. The map, a graphic, schematic arrangement of ideas, can be shared with other students in the writing group, providing an opportunity for the authors to explicate their proposed plans. As teachers well know, the more thinking and talking before writing, the better the chances for writing to flow gracefully from central to subordinate details, clearly establishing the substance and the sense of the composition for its readers.

The technique of mapping can be grasped in a single lesson. Students need only to respect a few principles: a map is visual, one can easily *see* the development of ideas; the ideas flow from main or primary ideas to secondary which in turn branch out into tertiary ideas and so forth; each idea has a place and is related to and interrelated with the whole. Each map is unique, shaped and structured by its author. No two maps in a class are alike because no two students think alike and mapping is a process of thinking. Once students and teachers engage in mapping they become curious about its rationale and ask, why does mapping work?

RATIONALE

To map is to engage in a thinking process involving two types of symbolic expression: *presentational* or non-language expression such as art, and *discursive* or language expression.* As human beings our unique, distinguishing attribute is our extraordinary innate ability to translate experiences symbolically. The philosophy of symbolism began with Kant and was developed by Cassirer, but it was Susanne K. Langer who skillfully explained, in *Philosophy In A New Key,* why our most primary instincts direct us to make meaning through symbolism. Our natural, innate propensity to symbolize provokes us to dance for joy and for rain; to decorate walls, caves, and clay water jugs; to design skyscrapers and coats of arms; to weave blankets and baskets; to compose etudes, symphonies, and rock songs; and to write epics, love sonnets, essays, and stories. Symbol making is the definitive human activity. It is not only the way we think; it *is* our thinking. Even casual introspection will reveal to us that no aspect of our lives is exempt from symbolizing. After a day of continuously sending and receiving symbolic communication in work and social affairs, we toss our weary bodies onto our beds at night, only to engage in a riotous show of symbols in our dreams.

Dreaming is presentational as is the visual aspect of mapping. While engaged in mapping, students become artists and make pictures of their ideas; they illustrate, so to speak, their ideational intentions. Most students, particularly in secondary schools, are seldom invited to exercise their powerful and creative visual intelligence. To see is to think visually. The visual image is as much a thought as is the verbal image. In the preface (p. *v*) to *Visual Thinking,* Arnheim writes that "artistic activity

---

*See M. Buckley Hanf, "Mapping: A Technique for Translating Reading Into Thinking," *Journal of Reading,* January, 1971, p. 225.

is a form of reasoning" and the "truly productive thinking in whatever area of cognition takes place in the realm of imagery." It is interesting to note that our creative thinking is called "image" and "tion" or *imagination* and that when we truly understand we often say "I see" or "I see what you mean." If our mental roots are in the image, this may explain the speed and delight with which students learn mapping.

In mapping, students can be thoughtful architects of their own intellectual blueprints. Even though it is presently fashionable to speak of the right hemisphere of the brain as the seat of spatial, sensory, wholistic thinking ability (Ornstein, 1972, Rico and Claggett, 1980), we do not need to be current to validate our proposal. The visual image has always been a powerful and persuasive means of communication and, of course, historically was the prerequisite for writing. The tale of cave paintings, hieroglyphics and cuneiform "picture writing" as the portent of writing is a tale told many times. Young children intuitively begin scribbling ideas and drawing messages as their own self-imposed readiness to formal writing. Berger, in *Ways of Seeing* (p. 7), comments: "Seeing comes before words. The child looks and recognizes before it can speak." If we respect developmental theories of intelligence, then students should first *see* their compositions and use this visual production as a foundation and a guide to saying and writing compositions. Many benefits accompany visual thinking: the student can see, for example, the whole as well as all its parts as one perceptual unit of thought. Apprehending the whole or the *gestalt* contrasts with verbal intelligence, which is lineal. Ornstein proposes that lineal or verbal intelligence is only one type of thinking. He writes:

> The lineal sequence of events is our own personal, cultural and scientific construction. It is certainly convenient, and is perhaps necessary for biological survival and the development of a complex technological society—but it is only one of the many possible constructions available to men (p. 220).

By presenting the *gestalt,* the map presents, through its branching, an intellectual progression of major and minor ideas complete with relations and interrelations among the many parts. Also visible in the map is the sequence of events proceeding from beginning through development to conclusion. Another impressive attribute of the map is that the picture is easy to hold in memory and equally as facile to retrieve.

Conquest over memory has preoccupied philosophers throughout all ages, as Yates tells us in *The Art of Memory.* The picture has better staying power than the word, but both images need a structure or a pattern to connect the discrete bits of details. Descartes advocated connecting images with one new image that united all. Descartes' "new image" is the visual structure of the map. If a student can recall the primary categories

of the map, all details within these categories—a complex array of details—
will be retrievable without mental burden along with the categories. All
the details of the categories "ride free" by attaching themselves to a
larger unit. Bruner, in *The Process of Education,* writes: "Perhaps the
most basic thing that can be said about human memory, after a century
of research, is that unless detail is placed in a structured pattern, it is
easily forgotten." (p. 116) Ease of understanding and ease of remembering
are among the many benefits of mapping which help explain its extraordinary effectiveness as a presentational symbolic activity. The map,
however, is also verbal, and presents the students with all the advantages
of the discursive or language symbols.

DISCURSIVE SYMBOLS

In mapping, the mnemonic power of the visual is reinforced by the
verbal labels signaling each category. That is, the label or name acts as a
category which orders, regulates and pulls together similar associations.
It is the label that triggers the mind to recall all the details subsumed in
the category. Miller, in "Information and Memory," explains this principle:

> Our memories are limited by the number of units of symbols we
> must master, and not by the amount of information that these
> symbols represent. Thus, it is helpful to organize the material
> intelligently before we try to memorize it. The process of organi-
> zation enables us to package the same total amount of informa-
> tion into far fewer symbols, and so ease the task of remembering
> (p. 549).

Packaging information, to use Miller's term, is a feature of organizing.
But there is more to writing than organizing. For example, there is the
role of oral language.

When a student writes, he is talking to himself. How well he can control
his inner speech to say in an efficacious manner what he intends to say
is dependent to a great extent on how well he uses oral language. Oral
language is the powerful prerequisite to written language as Loban's and
others' research substantiates. Frequent and consistent practice in oral
language, including expressive, narrative, and transactional, is the best
preparation for fluent written language. In "A Guide to Developing an
Oral Language Curriculum," I suggest a sequence of four steps: brainstorm
to generate ideas, categorize and order ideas, draw a map and structure
ideas in an effective sequence, and talk out the composition. It helps
many students to see *in detail* the composition before or after the talking
out. Getting a good fit between visual and verbal images usually results
in vivid, strikingly clear writing. If students use their maps to guide them,
they can practice visualizing—in meticulous detail—their compositions.
Their objective is to produce a discourse replete with striking, vivid

details of characters, actions and settings. After these visual productions, students—again using their maps as guides—talk out their compositions, attempting to find intense verbal images to match their visual ones. The oral composition is told to a partner who listens and responds. Because oral language is rapid in comparison with writing, students can quickly gain a sense of where they are going in their verbal thinking and how well their language is performing. John Cheever comments, in the preface to *The Stories of John Cheever:* "My favorite stories are those that were written in less than a week and that were *often composed aloud"* (p. x, emphasis added). Imaginative instruction in using oral language effectively will do more to improve writing than grammar books will ever do. If students can orally tell a tale or persuade or describe an event or argue a proposition, then there is some hope that they will put up a good intellectual fight when they confront the most difficult process of language— writing.

In summary, a process called mapping is an agreeable way to encourage students to organize their thinking. This graphic scheme—mapping—is both visual and verbal and hence has all the advantages of those two symbolic modes: the presentational and the discursive. In Part II below, Owen Boyle discusses in detail many types of maps and uses of mapping in written composition.

II

Mapping and Composing

Owen Boyle
University of California, Berkeley

WHAT IS A MAP?

A map is a graphic representation of a written or oral composition including only key words. Using a map, students organize ideas; produce and receive information; and think, imagine, and create a product uniquely their own. Mapping aids composing and comprehending because it teaches students to differentiate among primary, secondary, and tertiary ideas; it is a simple and useful procedure for organizing speaking, writing, listening, and reading activities.

When students make maps of books, essays, or lectures they discover that the process makes the work accessible to them for long periods because retention becomes easier. Mapping can precede and improve oral discussions which are important in preparation for writing. Because I believe the language arts must be integrated, this paper illustrates ways to use mapping in speaking, listening, and reading as well as writing, but the emphasis is on writing.

Mapping and the Brain

An argument can be made for teaching mapping because the process seems to integrate functions of both hemispheres of the brain. Recent research on the right and left hemispheres of the brain suggests that these two hemispheres process information differently.

The simplistic model in Figure 1 below generalizes from a complex field of research. Because this research is in its infancy, teachers should be cautious when they make generalizations based on studies of the two hemispheres. Generalizations sometimes made from recent brain research are that the left hemisphere is intellectual, analytic, linear, verbal and sequential, and that the right hemisphere is intuitive, synthetic, holistic, nonverbal and spatial. James Morrow cites Theodor Roszac in warning of the risk of overgeneralizing:

> It's a staggering—and not automatically warranted—leap from the right hemisphere's documented visual-spatial talents to assertions about the locus of art, metaphor, holistic insight and intuition (Morrow, p. 75).

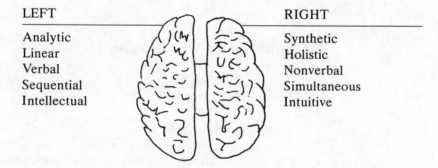

LEFT		RIGHT
Analytic		Synthetic
Linear		Holistic
Verbal		Nonverbal
Sequential		Simultaneous
Intellectual		Intuitive

Figure 1
Research on the Processing Roles of the Left and Right Hemispheres of the Brain

Some teachers have related brain research to the learning modalities of students, stating that some students have a predominantly left-hemisphere learning style and some have a predominantly right-hemisphere style. The theory is that the student who learns best in left-hemisphere modes will usually process information sequentially and analytically, while the right-hemisphere learner will process information holistically by synthesizing. It is too early to know how helpful this view of human learning will ultimately prove to be, but we do know that humans learn in varying and complicated ways and that teachers need to use as many techniques as possible to reach all students. It may be that there really aren't as many *slow* learners in our classrooms as there are *different* learners. Teachers who use mapping for the first time will discover students writing copiously who were previously unable to generate more than a few words. This power of mapping, as Marilyn Buckley pointed out in part I, comes from combining the visual with the verbal.

Review:

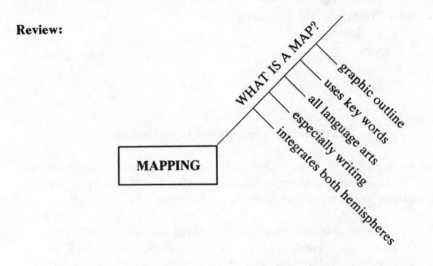

ADVANTAGES OF MAPPING

Many students begin with linear maps, then learn to use other non-linear maps to show relationships between ideas and/or characters, including mandala maps and mobile maps. The following pages contrast these kinds of maps with a section from a traditional outline.

READING INSTRUCTION TECHNIQUES

    I. Word Recognition
      A. Context Analysis
      B. Sight Words
      C. Phonic Analysis
        1. Consonants
          a. Single
          b. Blend
          c. Digraph
          d. Silent

2. Vowels
    a. Single
    b. Digraph
    c. Diphthong
  D. Structural Analysis
II. Comprehension Techniques
  A. Locating Information
  B. Remembering
  C. Organizing
  D. Predicting and Extending
  E. Evaluating
III. Fluency
  A. Oral
  B. Silent

Figure 2
A Portion of a Traditional Topic Outline

A topic outline such as Figure 2 above is the simplest kind of outline. Even so, learning how to make such an outline is difficult. Here is only a part of the instructions from a book on writing:

> Main divisions of an outline are designated with Roman numerals (I, II, III...), secondary divisions with capital letters (A, B...), subdivisions under these with Arabic numerals (1, 2, 3...), and still further subdivisions with small letters (a, b, c...). Each subdivision is indented further. Never have one division or subdivision without a corresponding one; i.e., never use a *I* without a *II*, an *A* without a *B*, a *1* without a *2*, an *a* without a *b*. You may, however, have subdivisions under one major division and not another. You may also, of course, have more than two divisions or subdivisions.

Many students struggle with this form for weeks or months while they might have learned mapping in a day; several of the sample maps that follow are the first attempts by students whose ages range from seven to sixteen years. Mapping is easy to learn and helps students see the relationships between characters, setting, and ideas in stories they have read; and because they can see these relationships, they are better prepared to write about them. Seeing the whole structure of an essay or story gives students a new power in their writing; students who simply paraphrased stories or essays in the past begin to write about ideas they cull from their maps. Elementary students use maps to aid learning in all the language arts; college students use them to prepare for written and oral exams; professional authors such as Douglas Hofstadter *(Gödel, Escher, Bach)* and Tony Buzan *(Use Both Sides of Your Brain)* use maps to plan their books (see pp. 26-27). College professors use maps to help teach writing and reading. Teachers of deaf students use maps because they are visual.

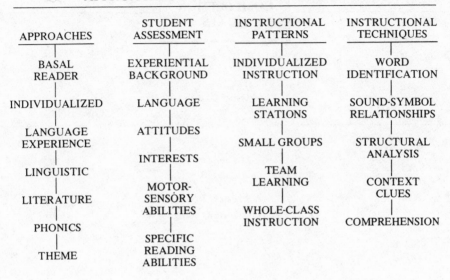

APPROACHES TO READING INSTRUCTION

APPROACHES	STUDENT ASSESSMENT	INSTRUCTIONAL PATTERNS	INSTRUCTIONAL TECHNIQUES
BASAL READER	EXPERIENTIAL BACKGROUND	INDIVIDUALIZED INSTRUCTION	WORD IDENTIFICATION
INDIVIDUALIZED	LANGUAGE	LEARNING STATIONS	SOUND-SYMBOL RELATIONSHIPS
LANGUAGE EXPERIENCE	ATTITUDES	SMALL GROUPS	STRUCTURAL ANALYSIS
LINGUISTIC	INTERESTS	TEAM LEARNING	CONTEXT CLUES
LITERATURE	MOTOR-SENSORY ABILITIES	WHOLE-CLASS INSTRUCTION	COMPREHENSION
PHONICS	SPECIFIC READING ABILITIES		
THEME			

Figure 3
A Linear Map

A first step away from a topic outline is a linear map (Figure 3) which really is just an outline without indentation and numbering. Students may want to do a linear map before exploring the other possibilities of mapping, but they should recognize its inability to show the interrelationship of ideas.

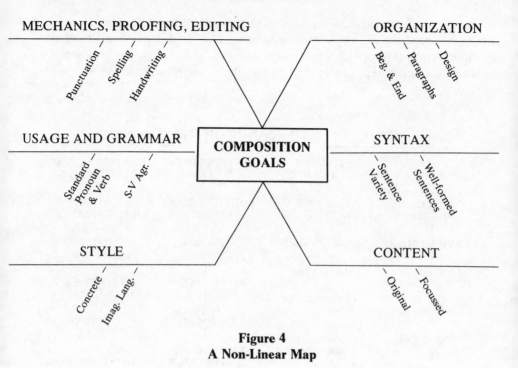

Figure 4
A Non-Linear Map

The map in Figure 4 breaks away from the linear approach. Students who map their thinking in this way find it easy to retain and review pertinent information, and they find that, when planning an essay, they can start with a simple map which grows organically as they make discoveries about their thinking.

Below and throughout the book are examples of maps which represent first attempts by students. These maps were selected for the wide range in ability and age of their authors, and they illustrate how easy it is for students with varying abilities to learn mapping.

The map in Figure 5 below illustrates a seven-year-old girl's first attempt at making a map for composing. The map was planned orally; first the teacher illustrated how maps work by mapping a sample letter, then the girl and the teacher talked about what the girl wanted to say to her grandfather and grandmother. The teacher made a few suggestions, but the map was formed and written by the student. The girl used the map to start her writing; as she made discoveries about her subject she enlarged her map. The map aided her in fluency, helped her make discoveries about her subject, and facilitated form.

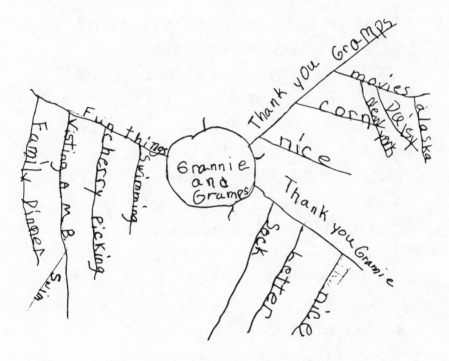

Figure 5
Map for a Letter by a Seven-Year-Old

Dear Grannie & Gramps
Thank you for writing
me that letter.
Thank you for being
sonice to me while we
were visting you.
My mom figured that
you woud send my
sock because she coudn't
find it before we left.
Could you call Antie
Louie and tell her
that ~~that~~ the pictures
are on there way.
Gramps It was fun
planting the
corn with
you.
I enjoyed
your moveis

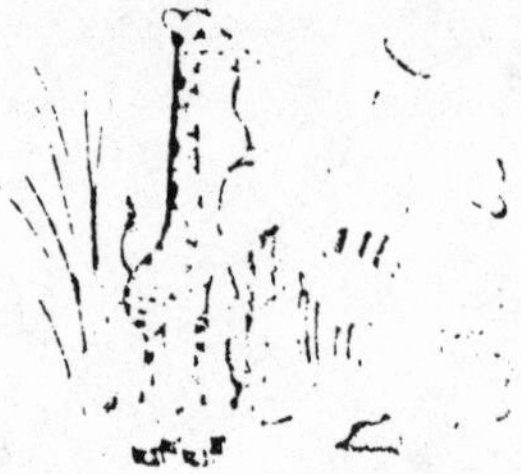

Figure 6
Letter Based on the Preceding Map

In *Writing Lessons That Work* W. R. Hudson explains what mapping did for one of his beginning writers in intermediate school:

> The work below is by a student who tested out in the lowest percentiles. He was in my class the previous year and he did not do at all well. At no time did he ever write over three lines, and those lines were often incomprehensible.

Figure 7 below is the student's map. It is followed by the five-paragraph essay he composed based on the map.

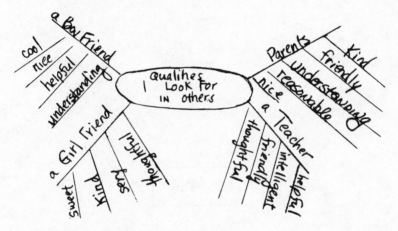

Figure 7

What qualities do I look for in a iadeax person. Like a girl friend and Boy as a friend and a parent and a teacher.

in a girl friend sweet and kind and sexy and thoughtful and loveaby she love all things and she is helpful and theses things I look from a girl friend.

in a parent kind and friendly and understanding reasonable and nice these are the thing I look from a parent.

in a boy as a friend cool and nice and helpful and understanding these are thing that I look froma boy as a friend.

in a teacher I think that they could be helpful and intelligent and friendly and thoughtful that what I look from a teacher

Mapping vs. Outlining

Mapping can be a prewriting, revising, or postwriting activity assisting students in organizing, composing, and evaluating compositions. Mapping has six advantages over outlining:

- Mapping is easy to share.
- Mapping illustrates relationships.
- Mapping presents a whole structure.
- Mapping is personal and idiosyncratic.
- Mapping is easily learned.
- Mapping moves students from fluency to form.

Mapping adds a visual dimension to our students' linear thinking; through using this visual method, combined with their verbal abilities, students gain a power greater than the sum of the two parts.

Review:

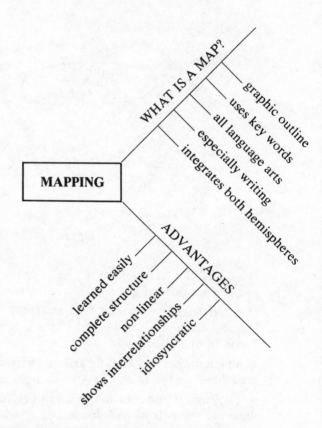

HOW TO MAKE A MAP

To help students get away from linear mapping it might be useful in the early stages of instruction to have them think of a map as looking like a spider. The body contains the main idea, the legs the secondary ideas and so on. The map below illustrates this approach. Later students will find this form too restrictive and will develop maps shaped like trees, baseball caps, or elephants, depending on their topics.

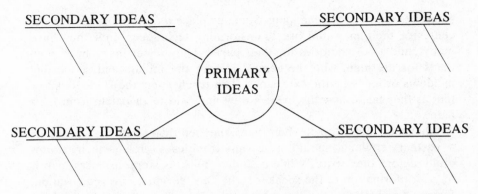

When introducing mapping to students it helps to let them take a common topic such as *sports* or *soap* and generate as many words as possible relating to this key word. Next, they take their generated words and organize them into categories. These words are ready to be placed into a map with the topic in the center, categories on the legs, and key words attached to each category. Now students are ready to write. The map will help them write with an ease they haven't known before.

Mapping For An Autobiography

A useful first assignment to familiarize students with mapping is to have them make a map to plan the writing of an autobiography. Using a known

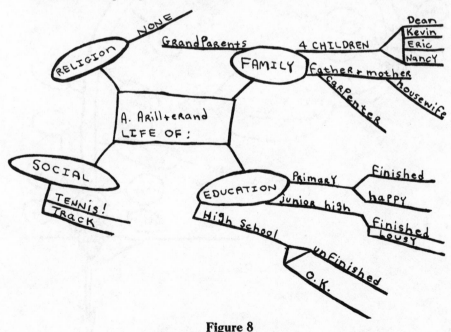

Figure 8
Map for an Autobiography

subject facilitates their mapping. Students place a controlling idea in the center of their map and use brainstorming techniques until they have many childhood memories for their paper. They select their "best" incidents for the map, with the central idea in the middle and supporting incidents or ideas on the extensions. The teacher lets the students know that as they make new discoveries they may add to or delete from their maps.

When students complete their maps, they tell their stories to a group or a partner; students should have opportunities to relate their stories orally before they write. While a student tells his story, listeners map it to give information to the speaker so he can reevaluate his organization. Figures 8 and 9 are maps representing the first efforts of two high school students. One is more creative than the other, but each follows the rules of mapping to make an autobiographical map which is unique.

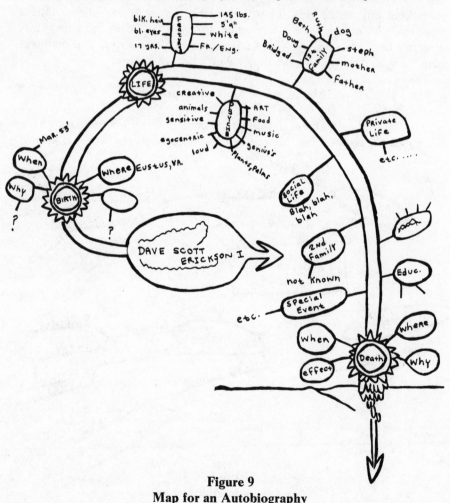

Figure 9
Map for an Autobiography

Group Work and Mapping

It is often useful, in introducing mapping to students, to permit them to work in small groups of two to four. Mapping gives students opportunities to share their thoughts and knowledge. Through group work students become less egocentric because they are writing for and getting information from an audience. The students work through their first drafts and revisions in groups before the teacher reads the papers. Because a map is visual it is easy to share, and students find maps easy to talk from when giving oral presentations.

Review:

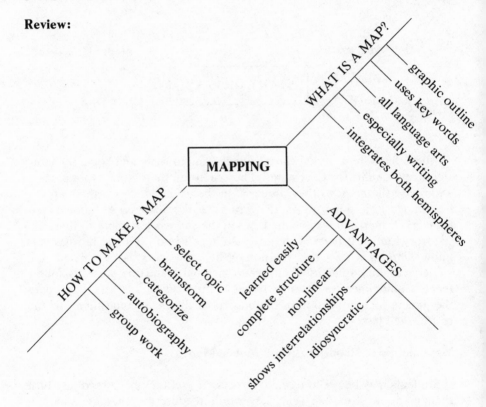

THE USES OF MAPPING

There are three principal uses of mapping: mapping for composition, for notetaking, and for comprehension.

Mapping for Composition: How to Compose an Essay or Story

When students map for a composition, they read about their subject if they need information, brainstorm, and categorize words and phrases, discarding unneeded words. After students have completed the first steps, they map their information to indicate primary, secondary, and tertiary ideas; then they use their maps as outlines for writing. When they have written their essays and checked them in small groups, they can remap them to see and to evaluate the complete structure.

Mapping a Short Story or Play

Students may work in pairs to develop short stories or plays, using a map to facilitate the organization. The map helps students focus on the central theme and its relationships to plot, characters, setting, and point of view.

All students think about what they are going to write and begin selecting significant details for their maps. They each tell their stories to a partner and revise the maps as they proceed. In the example above, the map is a beginning; it is adjusted as the writers make discoveries about their subjects. A map can also be made when the story is complete to illustrate the story's unity. If parts of the story do not fit into the map, the students know there is a need for revision. When the story is completed, the students make copies for their group members, and the students follow teacher guidelines for revising. After a final revision, students prepare the papers for publication in the classroom library or tape them for the rest of the class.

Maps and Book Reports: Using a Mobile Map

Students may be asked to map a story or novel they have read and turn their map into a mobile using key words to describe character, setting, theme, and their personal evaluation of a book. These mobiles hang around the room where other students can "read" them; students may also use their mobiles to illustrate brief oral reports. These activities encourage students to share their books with others and to learn what others are reading. Students may also use large butcher paper or poster paper to make maps for the same purpose.

Once students can map stories, the teacher may want to keep a "map mobile" with hooks so that items can be added or removed. The teacher may add articles to the mobile to stimulate new speaking or writing assignments. Students may want to get into the act and should be allowed

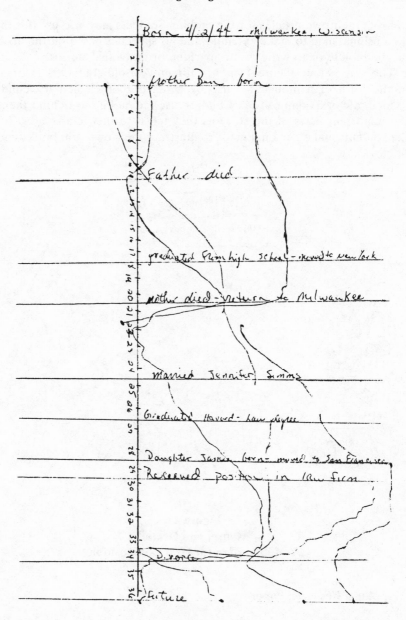

Born 4/2/44 - Milwaukee, Wisconsin

Brother Ben born

Father died

graduated from high school - moved to New York

mother died - return to Milwaukee

Married Jennifer Simms

Graduated Harvard - law degree

Daughter Jessica born - moved to San Francisco

Received position in law firm

Divorce

Future

Figure 10
Mapping a Short Story

This map, by a twelfth-grade student, is the "lifeline" of the projected main character for a short story. After constructing the lifeline, the student focused on a crisis as the primary element of the story, using the other incidents as background information for the author. (By Kathy Sabo, Alameda High School, Alameda, California.)

to bring their own articles for the mobile. Students may also use this three
dimensional map to make extemporaneous speeches based on the articles
on the mobile or to write group, partner, or individual stories.

The map below (Figure 11), by a fifteen-year-old student, was created
in the form of a mobile for use by a teacher of elementary children
to facilitate oral composition. Children use the mobile to remind them of
the important parts of the story as they tell it to their classmates. Later
the students make personal maps to illustrate their own oral book reports
or stories.

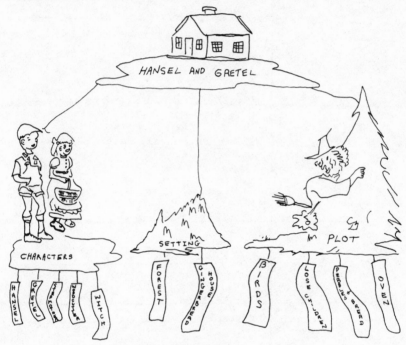

Figure 11
"Hansel and Gretel"
A Mobile Map for Oral Composition

Mapping a Research Paper

Many students merely copy information from encyclopedia articles
for research papers because they don't know how to paraphrase or get
the main idea of an article. Mapping can help students overcome these
deficiencies by forcing them to read for key words and ideas.

Students first brainstorm to generate words about a subject, categorize
their words, and begin to arrange them in a map. Following this exercise
they go to the library to get more information on the subject, or the teacher may distribute an article to the entire class. Students map this article

and rely only on their maps to recall information they want to use for their papers. After practicing with this article, students should have a good idea of how to cull information from primary and secondary sources.

The following paper by a nine-year-old girl is a good example of what can happen when a map is used to do a research paper, and of what can happen when a map is not used. The girl mapped the first parts of her paper, but neglected to map the last part. The result is original writing in the first part of the paper, followed by copied polysyllabic words which were incomprehensible to the girl. The mapped part of her essay is clear and original and the unmapped part is simply copied.

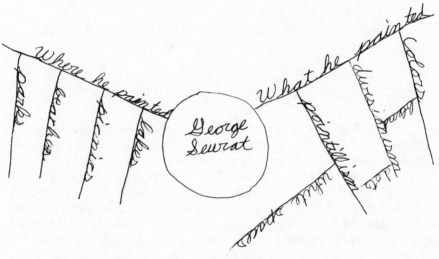

Figure 12

This part of Jenny's paper was mapped first:

> George Seurat did not paint pointillism, he called his painting divisionism and it often got mixed up with pointillism. Pointillism leaves white sections on the canvas. And George Seurat painted with out leaving spaces.
>
> In his pictures he uses very many colors. Especially in his sky, here are the colors he uses: green, blue, light blue, white, gray. But all the different colors blend together to make one color.
>
> He paints of outdoor places and at the places the people are having fun. Here are the places he paints, parks, beaches, picnics and lakes. You see in his pictures people sailing, people strolling, children bouncing balls and holding their mother's hand, and people with their pets, people in shade under their umbrellas, people fishing and canoeing.

This is the part of the paper which Jenny did not map:

> Impressionist art is natural and direct. Seurat's paintings are stiff, and figures seem immovable.
>
> In the painting Courbevore Bridge the striking power of colors based on the contrast of tones is sustained by a pattern of aspiring verticals broken only by the hazy, distant horizontal of the bridge and the dark diagonal of the riverbank.

The last paragraph above was copied directly out of the encyclopedia and is incomprehensible to the girl who wrote it. Fortunately, she ended in her own words:

> I think Georges Seurat's paintings are good because of the colors he uses and the way he uses them.
>
> George Seurat died of diptheria at the age of 31. George Seurat knew a lot about dots and now so do you.

> —Jenny, Age 9

Silent Brainstorming, Mapping, and Writing

This entire exercise is done silently. As students come into class and settle down, the teacher says nothing. He begins by writing a word or phrase on the board such as "I love to write, I just can't stand the paperwork," then hands the piece of chalk to a student who writes a comment on the board and hands the chalk to another student. If the teacher is not sure the students will catch on, he may want to tell one or two students before class so they can help get things started. The class spends the whole period filling the blackboard with comments; the teacher may want several pieces of chalk for this so more than one person can write at a time. Some students may get into silent dialogues.

The sayings and words are left on the board for the next day when students will brainstorm, map, and write short stories, dramas, or essays based on their selections. Students then share these with the class.

Other Possibilities

- Provide groups with a map with the spaces for who, what, when, where, and why filled in with key words for a published story or essay. Groups write a story based on the map, compare the group stories, and finally, read the original published version. Because mapping uses only key words or phrases, groups have great latitude when creating their stories or essays. This activity shows students how to map for their stories as well as how to map to comprehend another's story.

- Show students a mounted picture or a picture on a transparency and tell them to map a story based on the picture. Students then tell their stories orally or in writing.

- An activity for group composition is to have small groups responsible for each part of a short story: who, what, when, where, and why. When each group has mapped and written its part of the story, the sections are combined and read to the entire class. These stories are fun and can be repeated so each group has a chance to write each of the five aspects of a story.

- A map can illustrate the form of a short story or novel before students read or write. Use a large map to illustrate the elements of a tall tale, legend, or myth, for instance, before assigning students to write one.

- Using a map filled in with pictures rather than words, students write a story or essay basing the primary and secondary ideas on the pictures. These pictures help students to create short stories, essays, or poems.

- Students can write a biography or autobiography by using the map form, hanging pictures on a mobile or glueing them to butcher paper. The central picture illustrates their controlling idea, the extensions illustrate secondary and tertiary ideas. They can use pictures of themselves to write an autobiography, pictures of historical figures for a biography, or randomly selected interesting pictures to create a fictional character or mythological figure. In each case students share their stories.

- Have students map a television program or film in preparation for an oral or written report. It is nearly impossible to illustrate the relationships of characters in an outline but relatively simple with a map.

- Orally or in writing, have students compare and contrast a film such as "An Occurrence at Owl Creek Bridge" with the original short story by having students map both. While it is inappropriate to ask students to outline a film because they would miss much in this visual medium, they can map without fear of missing key images because mapping requires so little writing or concentrating on the paper.

- With half the class blindfolded and half with cotton in their ears, take the class for a walk. Those with cotton help the blindfolded ones follow the teacher. After the walk the class is divided into "blind" students and "deaf" students; each group brainstorms about their experiences on the group walk, maps these experiences, and writes a sensory monologue to be shared and compared in small groups and with the entire class. This process gives students a chance to learn about experiential differences and points of view in writing.

Maps for Composing by Professional Authors and Teachers

Figures 13, 14, and 15 below are examples of the use of mapping as an aid to composing by adult professionals. Tony Buzan, writing in *Use Both Sides Of Your Brain* about the use of mapping as a tool for notetaking and reading comprehension, mapped each chapter of his book to illustrate the process for his readers. Douglas Hofstadter apparently mapped the structure of his immensely complex *Gödel, Escher, Bach.* The map (his term is "semantic network") in Figure 14 is "a tiny portion" of his map for the book. The map in Figure 15 was created by fifth grade teacher Mark Stephenson to aid his composing of an integrated thematic unit for his class.

Mapping and Notetaking

Though some teachers give students lectures on notetaking coupled with a few practical experiences, it is an area overlooked by many. On many college campuses private companies sell students notes on teachers' lectures, notes which will be of little help to most students. Research indicates that students who take their own notes in outline form remember more than students who have the lecturer's own notes. More importantly, research shows that students who map lectures remember fifty percent more than students who outline lectures (Russell, 1979). In their college

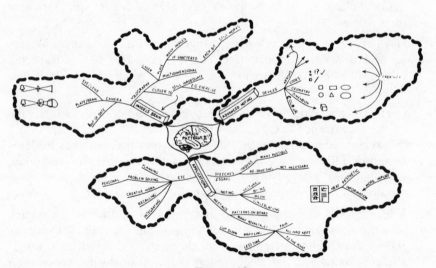

Figure 13
"Brain Patterns II"
Map for a Chapter of *Use Both Sides of Your Brain* by Tony Buzan.
(Reprinted with the permission of the publisher, E. P. Dutton & Co., Inc.)

Figure 14

"A tiny portion of the author's 'semantic network'" used by Douglas
Hofstadter to plan his Pulitzer Prize winning book *Gödel, Escher, Bach.*
(Reprinted by permission of the publisher, Basic Books, Inc.)

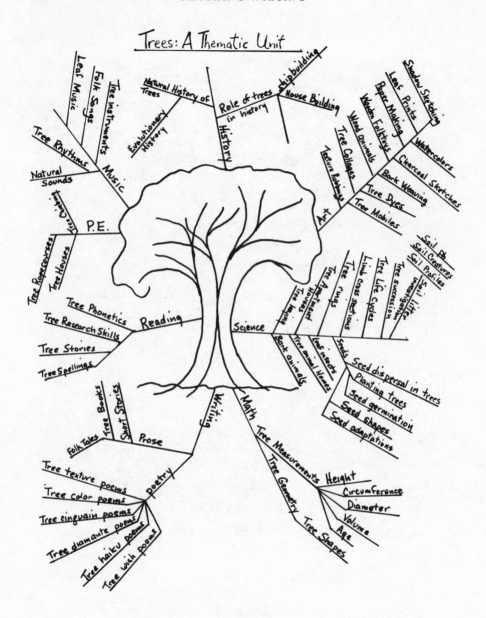

Figure 15

This map, by Mark Stephenson, fifth grade teacher at Mary Farmer
Elementary School, Benicia, California, was prepared as a part of the
planning for a thematic unit integrating all school subjects.

careers most students probably do more writing in connection with lectures than with anything else; because of the research we now have on mapping, it is extremely important for teachers to teach this skill. Of course, using mapping to take notes also means that every time a student maps a lecture he is also getting a lesson in composition.

To teach mapping as a notetaking skill, teachers may begin by providing students with blank map forms or maps with some key words filled in based on a lecture or short talk they will give. Following the lecture, students may compare maps. Students then move on to creating the form of the map themselves as they listen to lectures.

The following map (Figure 16) illustrates the way a fifteen-year-old girl organized a lecture on phrases, clauses, and sentence types. Note that the map not only organizes the lecture for the student, but also allows the teacher to check the student's comprehension with a quick glance.

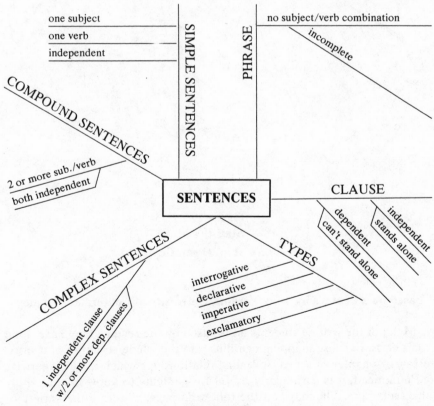

Figure 16

I made the map below during a three hour lecture in a graduate course in statistics. Because the map required a reconstruction of the lecture, the details are easy to remember.

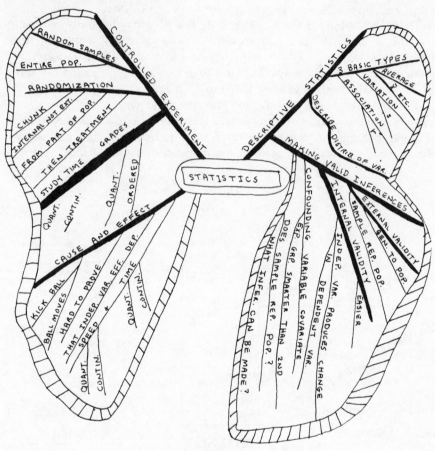

Figure 17
"Statistics"
Lecture Map, Owen Boyle

Based on a Lecture by Tony Vernon, University of California, Berkeley

Much of the writing students do is based on the reading they have done for a class. Because mapping can illustrate the whole structure of a story, essay, or chapter of a text, revealing relationships which might otherwise go unnoticed, it is particularly useful for students to know how to apply this technique. The maps on the following pages illustrate the variety of forms such maps may take.

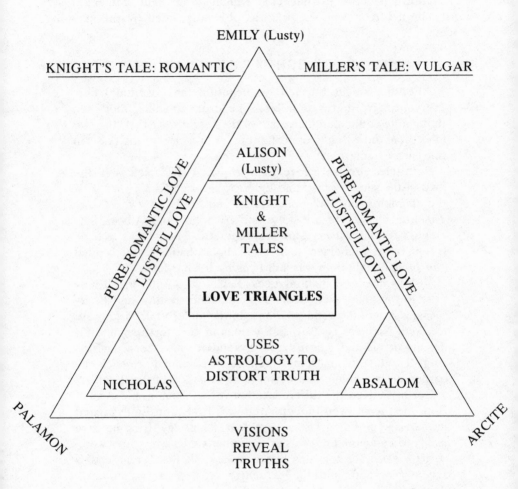

Figure 18
Map comparing Chaucer's "Knight's Tale" and "Miller's Tale"

Figure 18 is the first attempt by a student who had been given a twenty minute introduction to mapping. This student's essay follows, showing the effect of mapping on form and content. This sophisticated paper on the relationship between Chaucer's "Knight's Tale" and "Miller's Tale," written by a fifteen-year-old girl, was obviously aided by the mapping process.

COMPARISON OF KNIGHT'S TALE AND MILLER'S TALE

After the knight finished his beautiful (and overlong) tale, everyone agreed it was noble. The drunken miller, however, thought he could match any tale of the knight's. At first, the two tales seem to be totally opposite; but, after a closer look one can find many similarities.

Both tales involve a love triangle, where two men seek the love of the same woman and fight for her. In *The Knight's Tale* the characters are Palamon, Arcite, and Emily. In *The Miller's Tale* the characters are Absalom, Nicholas, and Alison. The knight's triangle is very pure and romantic. The miller's triangle is somewhat raunchier, such as Nicholas had already bedded Alison while Absalom was still begging for her love.

Visions are used in both tales. Palamon, Arcite, and Emily pray to the gods in an effort to guide their destiny, and Emily sees a vision of the goddess Diana. In the miller's tale visions are mocked. Nicholas is also using visions in an effort to guide his destiny or his and Alison's. He pretends to have seen a vision from the gods, telling him a great flood is coming, to trick 'the carpenter into hiding in a barrel in anticipation of the flood.

Destiny solved the differences between Palamon and Arcite. Both men won, even though Arcite died; he won Emily's hand in marriage and then had an accident. As he lay dying he gave Emily to Palamon. So it was in the miller's tale; everyone "won," so to speak. Absalom has kissed an ass, Nicholas' rear end is severely burned, and the carpenter receives a broken arm. Alison and Emily just sort of stood by and got the best of both deals.

The miller took almost every detail of the knight's tale and twisted them into something vulgar so that they seem to be very dissimilar. However, after careful scrutiny, many likenesses can be found. As a matter of fact, both stories parallel each other.

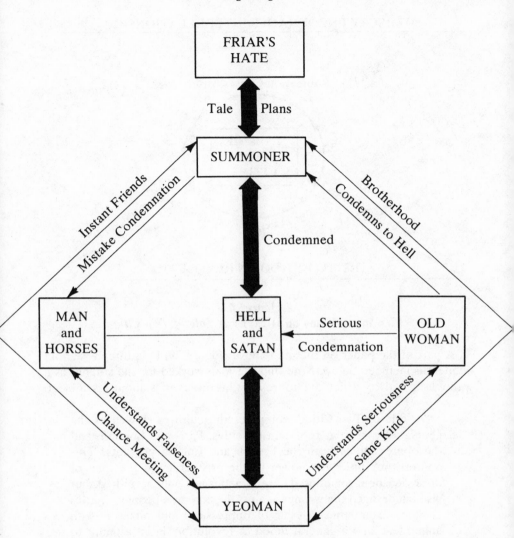

Figure 19
Map Based on Chaucer's "The Summoner's Tale"

A fifteen-year-old student made the map above (Figure 19) in preparation for an essay on "The Summoner's Tale." Mapping the story made it possible for him to visualize the relationships and discover a thesis for his essay.

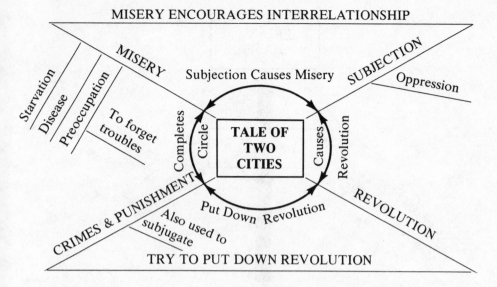

Figure 20
Map for an Essay on Dickens' *A Tale of Two Cities*

A part of the paper on the map above (Figure 20) by a fifteen-year-old student is included below. Note that the map worked for the student as a prewriting activity which did not restrict his discoveries about his subject.

"A Tale of Two Cities" compares the cultures as well as the people, of two great 16th century cities, Paris and London, and the oppression of both the French and English peasants. This oppression typifies the power of the aristocracy at the time of these decadent societies. These societies not only permitted, but also encouraged the wrongs against the common people. Charles Dickens exemplifies this air of oppression, and mixes it with anger, fear, and a general mood of revolution, in an attempt to recreate the attitudes of the 16th century cities.

In the opening half of the book the constant fears of travelers for highwaymen, and the general distrust among fellow travelers typifies the unrest among the people, and the hatred and fear of those belonging to the ruling class. The English were also oppressed by the aristocracy along with being heavily taxed. Although the peoples starved, suffered, and died, the cities continued to thrive for the aristocracy.

The fears in the two cities were also widespread throughout the country of which they were part. The fear of being falsely accused of a national felony and the gruesome punishment was a real fear, however, it did not outweight the fear of starvation and disease.

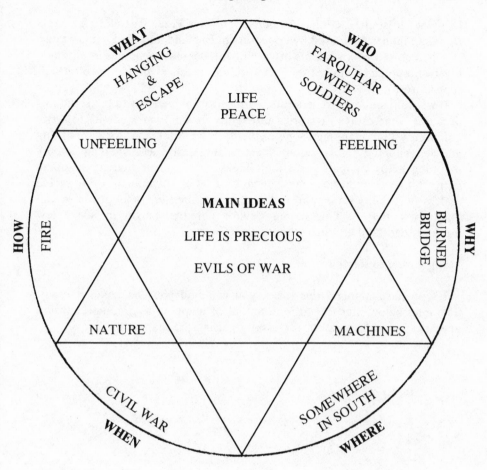

Figure 24
Mandala Map of "An Occurrence at Owl Creek Bridge"
by Ambrose Bierce

The mandala above (Figure 24) illustrates how a student used this pattern to help her understand a complicated short story. The more creative students become in determining the pattern they will use to illustrate a story, the more likely will they be able to comprehend and write about the story.

CONCLUSION

Mapping is a powerful new tool used in writing, reading, listening, and speaking. In the last few years mapping has been used by professional writers such as Robert Pirsig, *Zen and the Art of Motorcycle Maintenance,*

Douglas Hofstadter, *Gödel, Escher, Bach,* and Peter Russell, *The Brain Book,* and it has been used by educators in England and the United States. It is being used with students of varying intellectual capacities in all grade levels. Mapping is one of the tools which all teachers should have in their repertoires.

If we want students to generate words easily, if we want to help students organize their essays or stories efficiently, if we want students to write coherently, then mapping is one of the tools we will teach. As a prewriting activity mapping helps students start writing easily, as a shaping activity mapping helps students form their ideas, as a holistic activity mapping helps thinkers synthesize ideas. Because it takes advantage of our verbal and visual abilities, mapping adds a new dimension and power to all language activities. This simple visual technique, taught in just a few minutes, can help all our students write better.

Using a Map to Review

If you have mapped this essay, you will find you can recall it easily. The map below illustrates the potential of mapping as a comprehension activity. Test your recall of the essay by using the map below.

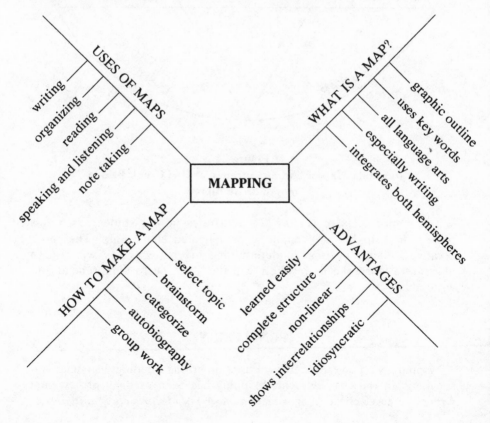

4. Drafting

Writing from Given Information

Stephanie Gray
Foothills High School, Pleasanton

THE RATIONALE

Training Students for Writing In School and On the Job

If we were to survey the kinds of writing assignments given in all curriculum areas throughout the secondary and college years, we would surely find that straightforward exposition—a setting forth of facts, listing of qualities, summarizing of events, citing of reasons, describing of processes— is the type of writing which is most often required of students. Mastery of this mode is therefore essential to their academic success. When a history teacher asks students to "cite some of the major causes of the Civil War," or a science teacher asks them to "explain the difference between ionic and molecular bonding," the instructor will expect an expository reply, not a personal essay in which the writer (however vividly) describes some of his feelings about living in the South or his excitement at having created salt from hydrochloric acid. That the writing of such "personal" responses may be a valuable educational experience is beside the point; a student who is unable to express required information with some ease in clear prose is, and will continue to be, severely handicapped within the present school curriculum and in most professional and many semi-professional vocations.

The job-related writings which our students will be asked to perform after graduation will probably be almost exclusively "informational" in quality. In addition to those careers which traditionally require factual report writing—police officer, civil servant, journalist, lawyer, military officer, and so on—teachers ought to be aware of the increasing number of other professions in which a demand for informational writing plays a key role. Recently, for example, a speaker at a conference on minorities in engineering estimated that engineers in supervisory positions spend more than 60 per cent of their work day writing reports. He added that the single factor which prevents most engineers from achieving supervisory rank is their inability to write clear prose.

Giving students practice in conveying information clearly can be of considerable help to them both in the future and during the key secondary years. My program is designed to give students such practice by providing them with what can best be described as "given information"—collections of data which I have gathered from many sources, including such curriculum areas as science and social studies. This information has been transformed into charts, lists, maps, illustrations and so on. Students are asked to convey the given information in clear prose—in effect to re-transform the information from the non-verbal mode in which they see it, such as a map, to a verbal one, such as a paragraph. The data is presented to students in packets, each of which deals with a different type of information (general information, information on processes, information about events. and so on). Sample assignments are described and analyzed below (pp. 222-227).

Because the approach draws so heavily on information from fields outside of English, it provides opportunities for across-the-curriculum projects, with perhaps several teachers from various course areas getting together to select and create data packages, using them not just to reinforce writing instruction but to teach some of the specific content of their courses.

Diagnosing and Attacking General Composition Problems

A Diagnostic Tool

Many student essays are flawed by a severe lack of coherence. It is sometimes difficult to judge whether this coherence results from a student's failure to think through his topic or from actual lack of skill in expression. In more instances than we suppose, it may be that the student's thoughts *are* clear to him, but he lacks the rhetorical resources or verbal control which would allow him to present these ideas coherently. Providing the student with a concrete content for his writing can allow us to determine very quickly whether the student's control of language and structures is at fault. If the student cannot present such "given" information clearly, it is doubtful that he will be able to perform more complex writing tasks successfully. Therefore, before moving on to such tasks, we can concentrate on the kinds of practice we have determined are most needed. We might determine, for example, that most students in our class under-use transitional signals and that concentrated practice with these devices would improve coherence in their writing.

A Spur to More Fully Developed Writing

Student writing is often much thinner than we would like. Assertions are weakly documented, details but lightly sketched in, ideas only slightly developed. Such poor development, normally signalled by production of extremely brief paragraphs, results in writing that may appear to be only a series of vague generalizations. It may be that if students practice expressing a dense collection of given information about a topic they will recognize the advantages of using information of this kind as documentation in their other writings where appropriate. For example, the longer paragraphs which generally result when students express given information may give them a better instinctive sense of the amount of material needed to document a single point. More important, the habit of working continually with very specific material may encourage greater specificity in general—whether that specific material takes the form of information, examples, or descriptive detail.

A Motivational Tool

To those who write fluently and find pleasure in exploring their own ideas through writing, it may seem unlikely that very structured assignments to express already given content (the "given" information) could motivate writing. However, for students who have had little success with writing or who feel intimidated by the whole process of selecting a topic and an individual approach to it in an essay, a predetermined subject and content can provide a sense of security which leads to greater willingness to write. Such assignments seem manageable to a less able student. And while some of the more able prefer assignments which allow imaginative scope, others find creative pleasure in devising logical, even elegant, arrangements of given data.

The data itself may also serve as motivation. One of the groups in the experimental study specifically commented to their teacher that they were interested in the information *as information*—they found the data generally intriguing and relevant—and this interest encouraged them to write.

THE METHOD

There are other teaching approaches which rely on giving information to students. The "case-book" approach, in which students are given capsule accounts of critics' interpretations or other summarized material, is an obvious example; less obviously the sentence-combining techniques of such teachers as O'Hare and Strong (see References) depend on giving students complex information that has been broken into simpler "bits." But all of these present the information in strongly verbal form: the material from which students are to write is generally given in whole sentences or even whole paragraphs. I have taken a different tack, presenting the information, insofar as possible, in non-verbal form—through the use of charts, graphs, maps, and other pictorial representations. I chose this method for two reasons. First, I wished to encourage students to discover for themselves the language and structures that would best convey the information. Second, in most cases I did not wish to restrict the kinds of relationships students might discover between various parts of a single data package, and I feared that a wholly verbal presentation of the information would imply my own sense of these relationships.

A sample assignment will help clarify these distinctions and indicate the unique focus of the approach (see Figure 1).

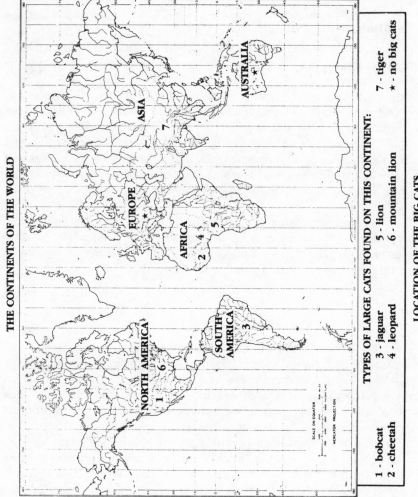

Figure 1

Assignment

Express clearly in writing the information about the locations of the big cats given in the map above.

The format of this assignment—the presentation of concrete information about a topic of general interest presented by way of a map and legend accompanied by directions to express the given information clearly in writing—is typical of most of the assignments in my materials. The following assumptions underlie such assignments:

1. Charts, maps, graphs imply, through spatial arrangements, that logical relationships exist between separate bits of information; students, recognizing these implied relationships, will be forced to produce verbal methods for expressing them—methods which will later aid them in expressing relationships between *other* ideas or data.

2. Given specific content, students can shift their attention from "what to say" to "how to say it"; there is automatically more emphasis on the importance of word choice, sentence structure, and arrangement in such assignments. (Students themselves acknowledge this difference in emphasis. While working on such assignments, their questions usually focus on problems of craftsmanship: "Can I combine these two phrases?" "Can I put this list in the middle of the sentence?" etc.)

3. While the content of the sample assignment is factual, it will suggest a variety of emphases around which the facts can be organized. Some students, for example, may choose to emphasize the large number of big cat species which exist, others the wide territorial range of the cat, others the comparative richness or paucity of big cats on the various continents, and so on. Given several similar assignments, almost all students will discover the advantage of having such an emphasis (from another perspective, an emphasis we might label a "main idea statement") when they try to express information coherently.

4. Students who have difficulty writing will benefit from a technique that allows them to visualize what is to be said. While these students may have trouble perceiving the logic of a traditional outline—a device often suggested as an aid to poor writers—they seem able to assimilate fairly easily content that is spatially or visually arranged.

The variety of information which can be presented by way of data packages is greater than one might at first suppose. Some of the possible range is indicated by the two additional sample assignments below, the first (Figure 2) from a packet on explaining events and the second (Figure 3) from a packet on explaining processes:

Figure 2

Assignment

Using the information given below, write a brief account of the life of the comic-strip character Superman.

Superman

Born:
Where: Krypton (planet in another solar system)
To Whom: Jor-El and Kal-El (Krypton scientists)

Sent to Earth:
When: as infant
Why: Krypton doomed to explode
How: in rocket ship

Found:
By Whom: elderly American couple (Eben and Sarah Kent)

Became:
What: the Kents' adopted child
Who: Cla⌐k Kent

Discovered to have:
What: unusual powers (ability to leap tall buildings, enormous strength, x-ray vision)
When: as he grew up

Employed:
When: when adopted parents died
Where: Daily Planet (large newspaper)
As What: reporter
By Whom: Perry White (editor of paper)

Kept identity hidden:
From Whom: fellow workers (Lois Lane, reporter, and Jimmy Olsen, cub reporter
How: by assuming disguise (glasses, business suit, and meek manner)

Assumed true identity when needed:
How: *by removing disguise to reveal Superman costume (blue tights and red cape)*
To Do What: fight crime and rescue people

Figure 3

How to Make Popcorn

Write a clear explanation of how to make popcorn based on the information given in the illustration above.

Because visualizing relationships seems so helpful in writing about information, I encourage students to create visual/spatial arrangements of their *own* information (information gathered from lecture notes, reading, films) from which they might write more easily. To provide practice in organizing information, I include a few exercises in each packet in which information is given in various stages of disorganization. Students are asked to arrange the relevant facts in a chart or diagram. Sometimes, as in Figure 4 below, specific organizational clues are given:

Figure 4

ORGANIZING INFORMATION

Assignment

Below is a chart which as yet contains no information. All the information that belongs in the chart is given in the sentences below it. Copy the blank chart onto your paper. Then, using the headings on the chart as a guide, fill in all necessary information to complete the chart.

SOURCES OF ESSENTIAL VITAMINS

Vitamin	Food Group Which Supplies this Vitamin	Specific Foods in this Food Group

1. Vitamin A is found in corn and carrots.
2. Leafy green vegetables include spinach, kale, and mustard greens.
3. Vitamin D is supplied by dairy products.
4. Citrus fruits provide Vitamin C.
5. Milk and butter are dairy products.
6. Whole grain cereals and bread both belong to the food group called "cereal products."
7. Corn and carrots are yellow vegetables.
8. Vitamin C is found in oranges, lemons, limes, and grapefruit.
9. Spinach and kale are good sources of Vitamin K.
10. Cereal products provide vitamin B.

In other exercises, such as Figure 5 below, students are asked to create their own organizational design:

Figure 5

Assignment

Below are some sentences giving information about the relationship between body type and personality. Create a chart that conveys this information in a simple and logical form.

INFORMATION:

1. Some psychologists say that a person's personality is keyed to his body type.
2. A person who is medium-sized or muscular is said to have a *mesomorph* body type.
3. *Ectomorphs* enjoy quiet activities.
4. *Mesomorphs* are outgoing: they are not bothered by loud noises or large groups.
5. *Endomorphs* are people who tend to be plump.
6. *Ectomorphs* dislike crowds.
7. People who are thin or slightly built are called *ectomorphs*.
8. *Mesomorphs* are usually athletic and enjoy activity.
9. *Endomorphs* are cheerful and sociable.

STYLISTIC STRATEGIES

Writing assignments and organizing exercises at first formed the entire teaching approach. But a phenomenon which repeatedly occurred as I experimented with the materials in class led me to extend the method to include the teaching of specific rhetorical/syntactical strategies as well. Again and again as students read aloud their responses to a writing assignment from the packets, other students would comment on how "good" certain papers were. Since the content in all papers was virtually the same, students were obviously reacting to the *way* certain writers were conveying that information. What was especially intriguing was my perception that almost all these particularly successful writers were relying on a particular set of rhetorical devices, and that some of these devices were frequently associated with certain kinds of information.

For example, the not-so-successful writers relied heavily on the word "then" in giving their directions on making popcorn:

Put in one-fourth cup oil in a corn popper. *Then* add one-fourth cup
kernels.

But almost every writer who had done an outstanding job made heavy use of
adverbial clauses or participial phrases:

After you have put one-fourth cup oil in the corn popper, add one-
fourth cup kernels.

After pouring one-fourth cup oil into the corn popper, add one-
fourth cup kernels.

Similarly, virtually all the successful papers on explaining events made heavy
use of appositives, while the less successful struggled with constant
repetitions and over-use of the verb *to be:*

Superman worked as a reporter on the Daily Planet. *The Daily
Planet was* a large newspaper.

Versus:

Superman worked as a reporter on *The Daily Planet,* a large
newspaper.

or:

Superman worked as a reporter on a large newspaper, *The Daily
Planet.*

Therefore, it seemed reasonable to provide, with each information packet,
instruction and practice in the technique which had proved most effective in
presenting that type of information.

The following list of stylistic devices taught with the various packets was
derived from analysis of papers by average tenth-grade students. Other
students at other grade levels might benefit from using other devices to
express these kinds of information, depending on their particular degree of
writing competence.

Packet One: "General Information" - DEVICE TAUGHT: Methods
               of incorporating a list of examples within a more
               general sentence

Packet Two: "Information about a Process" - DEVICE TAUGHT:
               Use of adverbial clauses to indicate time or sequence.

Packet Three: "Explaining Events" - DEVICE TAUGHT: Appositives

Packet Four: "Making Comparisons" - DEVICE TAUGHT: Use of transitional words or phrases that indicate similarity or difference

The first step in training students to use the particular stylistic device was to help them recognize it in their own and others' writings. Following the first writing assignment in the packet are some questions that help students analyze what they have just written to see to what extent they are already using the desired technique. For example, to determine whether they need to make greater use of adverbial clauses, the packet asks them to examine their first writing and count how many times they relied on the word *then*. They are also asked to determine their average sentence length. The packet then briefly explains the stylistic device to be emphasized and shows two student samples like those below, the first not using the desired technique, the second making heavy use of it, to demonstrate the device in action. The following student samples from the packet "Making Comparisons" demonstrate the use of words which signal similarities and differences:

Writing #1

The movie *Jaws* was based on the novel *Jaws* by Peter Benchley. In the novel the wife of police chief Brody becomes involved with Hooper, the young scientist. The movie ignores this romantic subplot. The novel portrays the fisherman Quint as motivated primarily by greed. The film shows him obsessed by a hatred of sharks. In the book Hooper does not survive the final shark attack. In the movie version, he and Brody both make it to shore safely.

Writing #2

Peter Benchley's novel *Jaws* and the movie based on the book are different in several important ways. In the novel the wife of police chief Brody becomes involved with Hooper, the young scientist. The movie, however, ignores this romantic subplot. The novel portrays the fisherman Quint as motivated primarily by greed, while the film shows him obsessed by a hatred of sharks. In the book Hooper does not survive the final shark attack. In the movie version, on the other hand, he and Brody both make it to shore safely.

This method of teaching the required device proved insufficient for some students. Both teachers in the experimental study found it necessary to provide supplementary instruction at this point for most packets. One asked students to do additional grammar exercises to reinforce their understanding of some of the devices.

The packets themselves include some special practice in using the technique, such as these sentence-combining exercises on the adverbial clause:

Example: A. First you add the flour to the liquid mixture.

B. Then beat until all the lumps disappear.
After you have added the flour to the liquid mixture, beat until all the lumps disappear.

1. a. Do not try to replace the fuse yet.

   b. First you should be sure that the main switch is turned off.

2. a. The clouds darken and a sudden silence descends.

   b. At the same time the wind starts to drop.

3. a. The baby alligator escapes from the egg.

   b. Then it instinctively races for the water.

4. a. The surgeon makes the incision.

   b. But first his assistant swabs the area with antiseptic.

5. a. A smart businessperson thoroughly reads an important contract first.

   b. Then he or she signs it.

6. a. First food is chewed by the teeth.

   b. Then glands within the mouth secret saliva containing enzymes which digest food starch.

7. a. One must first remove all paint and surface finish from the wooden boards.

   b. One can then steam-treat the boards in a steam box to remove warps.

8. a. Berries from the coffee tree are washed in running water.

   b. They are washed to the point where all the good berries sink to the bottom.

9. a. Make a plan on paper of where the furniture will go first.

   b. Then you can actually move it.

   c. You will save yourself work.

(SUGGESTION: use two adverbial clauses—one beginning with "if" and one with "before.")

10. a. The knights would put on their heavy armor.

    b. Then a crane would hoist them into the air.

    c. Then the crane would lower them onto the backs of their horses.

Teachers working with the materials commented that more exercises of this kind would be useful.

One final note about such exercises, whether they come from the packet or from a grammar text: for most students, this "grammar practice" will have greater than usual impact because it is directly keyed to particular writing problems students are trying to solve. There is little resistance to learning the stylistic techniques because students can see immediately that the devices aid them in presenting information effectively. This letter from a student in that ninth grade class at Northgate High School, at which the materials were originally tested, expresses a typical reaction:

> Dear Mrs. Gray,
>
> My english class has been using your composition workbook for the last quarter and my hand has nearly fallen off from all the writing we've been doing. However I found it very worthwhile to me because I have wanted to learn how to write better. All of my previous english teachers have told me, "I want to see you write excellent compositions, not kindergarten stories." Well how do they expect us to be able to do that if no one wants to teach us what were doing wrong and how to correct it? Thanks to your pain in the neck workshop I now have the knowledge to do so, except for the paragraphing. I still am not sure how and when to make a new paragraph. Maybe you could include something on paragraphing next time?

Following the intensive practice with a stylistic device, each packet concludes with an exercise asking students to employ the desired technique in revising a given paragraph. The paragraph lacks coherence or contains other flaws which could be removed by using the new device. The sample "faulty paragraph " that follows is from the packet on comparisons:

> The paragraph below is confusing because the similarity/difference relationships between the statements is not made clear. The sentences are also rather choppy. Rewrite the paragraph, adding words that signal comparison or contrast as needed. Combine any pairs of short, choppy sentences that show contrast with the word "while."

> It can be difficult to distinguish between a cold and a hay fever attack. Their causes are quite different. A cold is caused by a virus. Hay fever is a reaction to pollens or other irritating substances in the air. The person with a cold will sneeze or cough; his eyes may feel watery and his throat raw. The hay fever victim may suffer sneezing or coughing spells, reddened eyes, and a scratchy throat. A cold sufferer will usually run a slight fever. The allergy victim will not. And a cold usually disappears within a week or two. The allergy may hang on for several weeks or even months.

To summarize, each packet contains the following materials:

1. Writing assignment number one: writing from a given data package.
2. Self-analysis of style used in writing assignment number one.
3. Samples of two student writings—one using a special stylistic device, one not—and discussion of the device.
4. Exercises on use of this device.
5. Faulty paragraph to revise.
6. Additional writing assignments similar to number one above.
7. Exercises in transforming disorganized written data into charts, diagrams, etc.

CLASSROOM USE

The materials that I designed and that we tested for this experiment were aimed especially at average tenth grade students. However, in determining whether the materials are "too hard" or "too easy" for a particular group, much seems to depend on the level of perfection the teacher demands in the completed assignments. Teachers who tried the materials with their ninth grade classes—classes which represented a very wide range of ability—reported few serious problems. One teacher did comment that many of her students began to create run-on sentences when they first began to incorporate specific lists into general statements, but she drew little attention to this problem, assuming that the problem would eventually solve itself, as in fact it did. Another teacher, however, might view this development with alarm and thus perceive the materials as being too difficult. The teachers in the experimental study had complex reactions to the difficulty of the materials but generally found the ninth grade class struggling at times and the eleventh grade finding some portions too easy.

Another factor which undoubtedly affects perception of the materials' degree of difficulty is the manner in which they are integrated into the on-going curriculum. One teacher in the experimental study felt that though the materials were themselves not too difficult, they often placed an unfair burden on her students because they were added to an already crammed eleventh grade curriculum. Often her students were asked to do this work at home since class time was spent primarily in discussions of required literature.

Because this teacher's students were well-motivated and perceptive, they were generally successful working on their own. However, for most classes I would strongly recommend allotting class time for the materials. Students frequently desire assistance with the problems of craftsmanship; this offers excellent opportunities for one-to-one teaching—by the teacher or by a more advanced student. Moreover, as soon as students have finished a writing assignment, it can be shared with either a small group or with the whole class with good effect.

The sharing of responses to a particular assignment is almost essential. It is through such sharing that students perceive the variety of approaches which can be taken to a given problem and begin to evaluate which are most successful. Because the content of all student writings to an assignment will be similar, however, it is important that the teacher devise some means of avoiding the monotony of having every paper shared with the whole class. The teacher can read randomly selected papers aloud; small groups can read each other's papers and select "best" papers for sharing; sample papers can be written on the board—or any combination of these techniques can be tried. However the sharing is done, the emphasis should be on discovering methods that work especially well with the material. Teachers should allow sufficient analysis of these methods so that other students can use them in their next writing.

It is less important that the exercises on particular stylistic devices be done during class time, although the two ninth grade teachers who used the materials had their students do all the work in class, concentrating the materials into the final six weeks of the second semester. Such concentrated focus has much to recommend it if student interest can be maintained during the necessary block of time. A careful integrating of the program with other instruction also seems appropriate as long as the material is not merely "added on" but truly integrated.

An excellent means of supplementing the materials while integrating them with other curriculum is to select prose passages for analysis which can also serve as models for the kinds of exposition covered in the packets. The reading of a passage by Gerald Durrell on ways to smoke animals out of a tree, for example, can provide an excellent example of explaining processes, while also providing practice in reading for main ideas and details. One of the teachers in the experimental study made a special effort to include such models in her instruction and reported a very favorable response from her students.

I had suggested that after the experimental groups finished each packet, they should be given a major writing assignment keyed to the kind of writing emphasized in that packet. After the packet on explaining information, for example, students were asked to write an article for a newcomer's handbook that gave information about some special place or event of interest in their community. These major assignments give teachers the opportunity to judge the degree of carry-over from the packets and to spot any confusion students may reveal in attempting to use the new stylistic techniques.

CREATING YOUR OWN PACKETS

Teachers who would like to try this approach but are unsure how to create packets which will be appropriate for their particular students may find the following suggestions helpful:

1. Determine what types of information are of special interest to students at your grade level by noting the kinds of books they select on their

own, the kinds of subjects they most like to discuss, or by actually polling the class. Start a search for material in these subject areas that can be represented visually/spatially—information that can be charted, mapped, graphed. Particularly good sources are series like the *Time/Life* books, illustrated instruction manuals, *The People's Almanac, The Book of Lists,* atlases.

2. Alternately, you can make up generalized chart outlines like the "Comparison of Two Similar Retail/Food Items" chart which follows.

Figure 6
Comparison of Two Similar Retail Food Items
(sample)
Items to compared: *deluxe cheeseburgers*

STORES:	#1 *McDonald's*	#2 *Burger King*
COSTS:	#1 *$1.19*	#1 *$1.29*
MATERIALS/ INGREDIENTS:	#1 *2 meat patties,* *3 buns, chopped* *lettuce, onions,* *sauce, pickles*	#2 *1 large meat* *patty, 2 buns* *lettuce, tomato,* *pickles, mayonnaise*
APPEARANCE:	#1 *tall, somewhat* *narrow, sesame* *seeds on a bun,* *sauce oozing down* *side*	#2 *wide, flat, bun* *dull brown in* *color, somewhat* *squashed*
PERFORMANCE/ TASTE;	#1 *lettuce very crisp,* *meat rather dry,* *hard to fit into* *mouth because so tall*	#2 *lettuce soggy,* *meat juicy, drips* *as one eats it*
COMMENTS:	#1 *very fast service*	#2

ITEM PREFERRED AND WHY: _____

_____

_____

Have your *students* do the research, either by having them do comparison shopping, looking up facts in reference books, or tapping the texts they are currently using in another course area. I particularly suggest the use of charts to convey information when students are first assembling information because they create less confusion than graphs and take much less time than pictorial representations. However, if you have some artists in class, you should certainly take advantage of their talent and encourage the production of illustrations of data as well as charts. Carrying this process one step further, once your students have had some experience in working with data packages or filling out charts, you can have them do *both* the research and the creation of a data package that will present their information in clear and logical form.

3. Decide what kind of exposition each data package you have seems to call for (describing a process? giving general information? making comparisons? citing reasons?). Gather into a large packet several data packages that call for the same kind of writing assignment. Each packet will stress a particular kind of informational writing. Tentatively arrange the assignments within each packet from least to most difficult.

4. Try out each packet on a small group of students and carefully analyze the resulting writing. What features did the more successful writings share? What stylistic or rhetorical devices in conveying the information emerged in your samples? Begin to determine—even if tentatively—the devices which most need to be learned by students if they are to deal with the material in the packet.

5. Determine ways to teach these devices to your class as a whole while they are working through each particular packet. You may, of course, wish to create your own exercises or instructional materials to teach these devices, but if you have standard usage or grammar materials on hand, chances are you can use them very satisfactorily for this purpose as long as you stress to students that these exercises are intended to help them solve the immediate writing problems they will be encountering as they work through your materials and are not just busy work.

The teacher in the experimental study who was teaching a literature-centered curriculum asked students to apply the whole "data package" approach to their reading. For example, she had them make charts about the various characters in Arthur Miller's *All My Sons* and then use these charts both to devise a thesis and as outlines for a paper about the play. She noted that while the resulting essays were extremely well organized, they tended to be somewhat thin, indicating that a single chart seldom provides enough material for a full-length essay. She used a second kind of charting to help students generate more detailed support for their central theses. Her experiment was a provocative one and demonstrates how successfully the approach can be integrated even with a strongly pre-set curriculum.

"The Freshman Handbook" from The Write Occasion

Patrick Woodworth
Tomales High School

For the past six years in the small rural high school where I teach, sophomore English classes have begun the year with a project we call *The Freshman Handbook.* It is a sequence of activities and assignments designed to help the students to consider their roles as students by encouraging them to reflect on their previous school year and then to make statements in a variety of forms about their reflections. The final product of this three to five week unit is a number of handbooks written and designed in small groups to be given to entering ninth graders for their use, enjoyment, and response.

In developing the sequence of assignments for this unit, I have attempted to synthesize the best of what I have learned from using Moffett's *Interaction* materials with the techniques and attitudes I have absorbed during the four years of my work with teacher/consultants in the Bay Area Writing Project. Originally I conceived the project as a preparation for students who had never used Moffett's *Interaction* assignments. I wanted students to learn how to do focused, disciplined work in small groups. The opportunity to write for a real audience helped impose a certain seriousness on this endeavor that carried over into the small group work all year.

The project has become a tradition. Once the ninth grade students read the handbooks composed for them, they look forward to the time when they, as sophomores, will be able to create their handbooks for the naive ninth graders. They realize that they will be able to recount their own experiences for an audience other than the teacher. They know that their readers will respond and will benefit from their writing. For these reasons the project has an authenticity about it that most other assignments lack. Moreover, during their work on the project, students form personal relationships both through thinking, talking, and writing about the task (small group and class processes) and through talking and writing brought about by the accomplishment of the task (interchanges between tenth and ninth grade classes).

From almost the first year onward, I noticed that the writing produced during this period was out of the ordinary for most students. I often found it hard to stimulate such eager and successful performance again during the remainder of the school year. Not only were students willing to revise and edit their writing, but even early drafts were longer, richer in detail and voice than any other classroom writing. Clearly this was an inspiring writing occasion.

What follows is a description of the series of assignments, much as I present them to teachers in Bay Area Writing Project in-service programs.

CONTEXT

Most of the 250 students of Tomales High School, situated in northern Marin County, come from families engaged in farming and fishing. A few come from professional families. Ten to twenty percent go on to college; the rest return to family businesses or go on to secretarial schools and into skilled labor of various kinds. The entering ninth graders will stay with one of the two English teachers for two years before they enter the junior-senior elective program. During that time they are heterogeneously grouped, with the exception of those reading several years below grade level, who are enrolled in special reading classes. Our English department capitalizes on the diversity of language abilities and attitudes by having students work in pairs and small groups. Classes are small enough (15-25) so that such work can be managed productively by one instructor. Since students may live as much as fifty miles from one another, the school is a primary social environment in the community. The students are quite willing to work in small groups. The teacher's task is to provide a focus which will sufficiently distract them from their need to talk with friends about what happened last night, a focus or problem of sufficient intensity to engage their thoughts and energies and enable them to practice and develop their language skills. Since *The Freshman Handbook* asks that each person observe his social environment, everyone has equal access to and interest in the "subject matter" of the problem. Even the student who does not like school has an opportunity to express the point of view.

SEQUENCE: LETTER TO A FRESHMAN

Pre-Write

Sophomores begin the year by reflecting on their previous year—first as a class, then individually. While someone takes notes on a large piece of butcher paper tacked to the wall (these notes are preserved and seen by other sophomore classes), I ask them to list events, classes, people, scenes that are memorable. As responses range from things everyone remembers to those recalled by one person only, the resulting list reflects both collective and individual memories. Questions are raised about the accuracy of memory and about differences in how people experience their ninth grade year. A variety of attitudes surfaces so that the crucial question of point of view arises in a natural way. I do not insist on it, but point to the variety both within the individual class and, later, when all three class lists are on display, among the different sophomore classes. To stimulate reluctant memories, I may conduct a guided memory "tour" of the year from June back to September, pointing out certain events which held attention for a time.

Working alone, each student makes a personal list, using what he can from the work on display and adding anything new he may think of or may not have wished to share with the whole group. At this point it is helpful to introduce "clustering" as a way of exploring a generalized memory in greater detail. Several clusters of details or events around significant memories can form the nuclei for a like number of paragraphs in the first writing assignment—the letter to a ninth grader. It is usually sufficient to demonstrate clustering once at the chalkboard for students to see its value as a way of elaborating an idea. For instance, a student may want to tell the freshman about his experience with school lunches. His cluster might look like this:

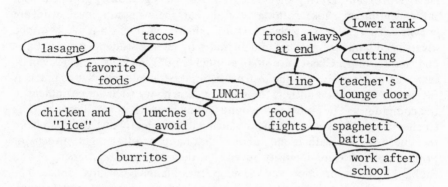

The paragraph which evolves from this cluster might begin:

> While standing in the lunch line you will inevitably taste the teacher's lounge door. I ate it quite a few times last year: an excellent appetizer before a school lunch. As a freshman you're sure to notice how the line grows longer in front of you and shorter in back. Since the door is at the end of the line you'll meet that tasty door again and again. Because of your lower rank you can't cut. Upperclassmen don't cut; they "place" themselves in front of you.

It might go on to describe food fights, good and bad lunches, and other aspects of school lunch which the student recalls as he writes. The cluster does not restrict the scope of elaboration; it gives the student a "center" around which the paragraph may coalesce.*

When each student has recorded a number of memories, we have a class discussion of the dominant attitude(s) in their lists and clusters. Is there a prevailing emotion or mood? How, I ask them, do you feel about your memories of last year? It is this dominant tone around which I ask them to organize their letters. Which incidents they choose to relate will depend on the mood they want to convey.

---

*The passage can be found in *How We Write* by Hans Guth (see References).

Write

Each student writes a letter to a particular ninth grader, telling him or her what to expect of the ninth grade year. Although this assignment is merely a preliminary step and will not actually be delivered, each writer is instructed to address his letter to a specific student, either someone known to the writer or a name drawn from the ninth grade roster. The letter writers are urged to illustrate their assertions or judgments with examples and specific incidents from their experiences as ninth graders and to maintain a consistent tone throughout. Teams of two students edit the rough drafts, focusing on the need for additional examples, for specificity and concreteness and pointing out lapses in consistency of tone.

Post-Write

The revised letters are shared with other members of the class. Listeners identify tone, comment on the point of view, and discuss the impressions a ninth grader might get from reading the letter.

Grouping

Now that each student has chosen and revealed a particular stance from which he will describe his ninth grade year, I ask those who share a common attitude to form a group. (There will be four to six groups in a class.) I try to generate a sense of collaboration, particularly among those students who are "outsiders" or who usually don't participate in class activities. The new groups will each produce a handbook, with up to eighteen books created by the entire sophomore class to be distributed among the ninth graders.

The groups know that they are to make informative and entertaining booklets to serve as guides for the perplexed ninth graders. At this point the students recall the handbooks read the previous year, and although I do not bring out last year's handbooks to serve as models, many remember them well enough to want to create more forceful and effective booklets.

Focusing the Group

In the course of grouping themselves, students have read a good portion of the class letters. By the time they have chosen their groups they know the attitudes they share. At this point I ask them to decide on a "frame" that reflects the tone of their letters and leads naturally to a concept or form for the handbook. Last year I gave them a list of suggestions:

1. Tomales High School is a new colony on another planet. Freshmen have just landed. You observe their behavior.

2. You are an explorer meeting this unique culture for the first time. You describe it to the settlers who will follow.

3. THS is enemy territory. You are a spy who must report back to control (freshman).

4. You are an inspector of schools reporting to your superiors on the quality of life at THS.

5. THS is a disaster area. You have to determine whether it qualifies for relief.

6. You are on assignments from a TV studio to make a documentary on THS.

7. You are an interviewer trying to catch the essence of life at THS through students' talk. Bring pictures and interview statements together in interesting and unusual ways.

8. You want to help freshmen survive their first year at THS. Tell them how to get good grades, enjoy themselves, participate in activities, avoid trouble, etc.

9. THS is a place of great evil and destruction. You must prepare a manual on how to avoid the terrors and dangers of THS for all those who might enter.

10. THS is a model high school. You must prepare a report for principals and teachers everywhere on how to make a perfect high school.

11. You are a systems analyst whose assignment is to report on THS efficiency. Where is effort wasted? Where is it applied well?

Although all but one, two, eight and nine were ignored, students could see the kind of unity I was aiming for, and, as a result, the handbooks were more integrated than they had been in the past when I left selection of point of view up to them.

The adoption of a group frame or theme injects new energy into the project just when students are wondering whether what they have to say is all that interesting after all. The school is small, experience not that varied. And they have been immersed in their memories to the extent that everything seems all too familiar. It becomes apparent to them that their frame is central in this communication to the ninth grade, and they begin to ask how much exaggeration is allowed. I remind them that their purpose is to be both informative and entertaining and that their work actually will be read by ninth graders whose imaginations they must capture.

SEQUENCE OF WRITINGS FOR HANDBOOK

In the course of designing and composing the handbooks, every student completes four writing assignments:

1. Description of behavior in or around school
2. Recording of a conversation in or around school

3. Interview of another student

4. Observation of an adult who works at the school

Students need not write these with the group point of view in mind. If they choose not to, they may revise the pieces later for inclusion in the handbook. Only those that fit will be included. Others I simply credit students for having completed. Students are thus allowed to use their editorial judgment, and they learn selection: not everything they write need appear in the published handbook.

I suggest other writings that might be included:

1. "That was then, this is now." Poetry or prose showing how things have changed.

2. Useful data. Tricks, short cuts, how-to, inside tips, etc.

3. A-Z in Tomales High. Less imaginative students like this alphabetization of experience. Some have organized an entire handbook this way.

4. Real or imaginary notes passed in class.

5. Stories, poems, fantasies.

As often as possible we begin class with a short writing exercise designed to get the class as a whole thinking about the handbook project before they begin working in groups or writing on their own. The exercises are designed to increase awareness of point of view or to induce a fresh perspective on what might be done with the materials at hand.

1. I show topical photos from Arthur Tress's *Dream Collector,* a book of children's dreams translated into photographs. Students write from the point of view of the child in the picture (for instance, a boy in a dunce cap).

2. We rewrite news articles taken from local newspapers from various points of view.

3. We make lists of everything the school is not.

4. If the school were destroyed suddenly (we're directly over the San Andreas fault) and we were asked to design a commemorative plaque, how would it look?

5. We draw a picture of the student "body" on a large piece of butcher paper and label its parts. Just what or who is the brain? the armpit? the navel?

6. We walk away from the school and observe it from a distance during class. What's going on in there right now? How much do we know? What do we imagine?

Editing, Proofreading

Do all the pieces a group wants to use in its handbook reflect the chosen frame or point of view? This question provides a focus for small group evaluation and subsequent revision of the complete book. In this sense each group member is an editor responsible for the overall character of the handbook. With my help or on their own they make suggestions for revision or decide not to include a piece. If it is to be included, it receives a particularly close proofreading before being drafted in final form. Other work is kept in individual folders.

Handbook Format

Each student is given these instructions:

> In preparing *The Freshman Handbook* you will take a look at your environment from a fresh (naturally) point of view. Having just completed your first year, you have an intimate knowledge of your audience and what it takes to inform, entertain and persuade them. The choices you make in writing and laying out the book should reflect your experience of last year and your understanding of what it is to be a ninth grader in Tomales High School.

Each handbook must have:

1. a cover with legible title and attractive design suggestive of contents
2. a table of contents
3. writing from each member of the group
4. consideration of page layout
5. space for feedback at end with specific questions:
   > Was this book helpful?
   > What do you expect from your freshman year based on this book?
   > What grade would you assign this book?
   > What parts did you enjoy?
6. Title page with credits: editors, writers, correspondents, artwork
7. a definite point of view sustained throughout

For this paper, the work is done on 8½ × 11 inch construction paper. I encourage the use of photos, cartoons, drawings, comics, graffiti, jokes, captions and marginalia as ways of unifying and reinforcing point of view, creating continuity, and counterpointing or complementing text. A natural division of labor usually occurs, as those more visually oriented take charge of layout and design, while those with greater verbal facility devote their efforts to preparing text.

Since the finished handbooks integrate writing, drawing and photography, and marginalia, each is a unique production with a character all its own. Only color reproductions of pages could convey this variety of presentation. The total composition is but the "artifact" of the process of talk and decision, expression and selection, composition and editing that is *The Freshman Handbook*.

Teaching Expository Writing

Richard Murphy
Radford University, Virginia

Introduction

By "expository writing" or "exposition" I mean writing about ideas, discursive writing of description or analysis governed by an idea, what James Britton has called "transactional" writing, the kind of writing which in school includes fourth grade book reports and seminar papers for graduate courses.

Teaching such writing is sometimes a dispiriting task. Student essays are frequently insubstantial and incoherent, perfunctory and heartless. Every writing teacher I know gets such essays, and the consequent temptation for teachers is to assume that exposition is by nature "dull" and "boring." This is a widespread, if hidden, assumption. It is manifested in the back-to-basics principle that we all ought to grin and bear it in the teaching of writing. ("Sure, the essays are dull," the principle seems to say, "but this essay writing isn't supposed to be fun; it's work.") One high school teacher, I am told of (he must be somebody's caricature; he must not be real) reportedly tells his students that when it comes to writing essays they should try *not* to be creative, try *not* to be interesting. "I want to be BORED," he says to them year after grueling year.

After one of my colleagues at the University of Santa Clara had shared a research paper assignment with other faculty, she conceded with a shrug of her shoulders that it was probably no better than any other because the essays she got in response to it were dull. "Dull...dull... dull," she insisted, looking around at all of us, taking for granted that we all knew what she meant.

This attitude can be seen too, I think, in the fact that teachers tell their students to make their essays "interesting." Every semester I ask my new students to list the qualities of a "good" essay; always, at the top of the list, is "interesting." "You've got to grab your reader's interest," they say, and fairly enough. But what they mean by "interesting" is "clever," "unexpected," "decorated," and these reveal a lack of confidence in the intrinsic value of what they have to say. "Your introduction should be catchy," they say, echoing someone's prescription, because an introduction that simply declares its subject and aims is too "dull." Better to cast around for some gimmick, to go miles out to left field (or years back in history) to find some detail related to your subject by which to lure your readers, to trick them, into listening to what you have to say.

Thus the following, the first sentences of an introduction to a student essay about why cigarette smoking should not be permitted in public places:

> Since its introduction to the thirteen colonies, tobacco has been a chief American crop. For the last three and a half centuries, most of the tobacco was used for one main and popular habit—smoking. Once considered chic during the roaring twenties, smoking has drawn much opposition....

Here he is, after all the stuff about the chief American crop and the roaring twenties, finally getting to the point about the propriety of smoking in public. But as much of an achievement as it represents—simply getting down to the point after such a tangential opening—this introduction was written under a false and disabling assumption. The writer did not believe that what he had to say was of any genuine value, that his essay was anything more than an exercise in the "stuffy" skills of exposition. He did not really believe that his readers wanted to know about public smoking; and he did not believe it, I think, because the teacher who told him to catch the reader's interest did not believe it either.

Our task in teaching exposition, then, is to persuade our students to believe in what they are doing, to take themselves and their ideas seriously in writing essays. Eudora Welty in two fine sentences has set the problem for us: "The trouble with bad student writing is the trouble with all bad writing. It is not serious and it does not tell the truth." Two of my students' essays may help to illustrate briefly how expository writing can be serious and truthful. In imitation of an assignment Josephine Miles gave to her 1948 freshman composition class,[1] I asked my students to write a twenty-minute essay in class about their home town. Here are two of those essays:

1.

> My hometown is Watsonville, California. Watsonville is a small town of about 20,000, which originated around the year 1860.
>
> The main source of business in Watsonville is agriculture. Located in the fertile Pajaro Valley between Monterey and Santa Cruz on the Pacific Coast, Watsonville's climate is ideal for growing lettuce, strawberries, artichokes, and especially apples. Watsonville is now the official apple capitol of the world.
>
> The people in Watsonville are like those of any small town, very conscious of what goes on and how things look to the public. In a small town, news travels very fast—especially bad news.

Such is the case in Watsonville. We have our socially prominent families giving elegant dinners every Christmas Eve—you know— the ones in which everybody who's anybody is invited. We have the mayor who used to own a photography shop on Main Street. We have the old section of town, with our small town department stores and grocery stores. Very few chain stores come to Watsonville.

Watsonville is small now, but it used to be a very important railway stop, so what town there is grew fast. We even had a "Chinatown" section where the laborers lived. But the agriculture had to stay, so the city had to stop growing.

We still have the city plaza, which is as old as the city, and we still have the migrant workers. We have the tradition, the social exposure, and the problems of any small town. It's typical, but I could write volumes.

2.

My home town is San Jose, California. San Jose used to be a fairly decent place to live. It was not a hick town, but yet it didn't have the clutter or sprawl of San Francisco or L.A. Being such a nice place to live, however, had disadvantages in that many people who feel the same way, but who are not residents decide to become residents. The result is, that over the past fifteen years or so, San Jose has gained about 500,000 new inhabitants. Now I don't know about you, but I have a hard time getting along with 500,000 people strangers—especially when necessitates a complete change in the face of the city. Examples; Capitol Ave., a nice little two-lane road winding from a little beyond my old house to Milpitas, is now Capitol Expressway, a four to six lane monstrosity. Or take that huge field that used to be down the street from my old house; my friends and I used to chase squirrels up an down it's breadth on our way to school—and during the winter rains, ducks would migrate to wallow in the makeshift ponds. Now that piece of land has an apartment complex, a gas station, a Banco de San Jose, and a McDonald's, as well as an assorted housing tract here or there. I could name further examples, but it seems pointless to try to "go home again"—even in my mind. I regret that being so young I could not more fully appreciate those fields and orchards and little two lane roads. My memories are vague and it is often hard for me to picture San Jose as being any other way. This, to me, is the saddest fact of all.

The first student is a more technically skillful writer. In this timed exercise he wrote fluently and correctly, his syntax and punctuation sure, his paragraphs grouped reasonably. The second student left syntactic slips uncorrected ("people strangers," "when necessitates"), he punctuated erratically ("Examples;" "it's"), and he chose diction somewhat uncertainly ("up an down it's breadth"). But I think the second writing, not an essay, only a paragraph, is much better than the first for several reasons.

It has an idea, first of all, a *main* idea which governs its statements, giving them coherent organization. The first is a hodge-podge. When the twenty minutes were up, I asked my students to write down the main idea each essay expressed. The first student wrote: "Watsonville is a small, typical, yet unique town." Leaving aside the contradiction between "typical" and "unique," this is not the idea which governs his essay; *no* idea governs his essay. What he wrote is a list of uncoordinated thoughts about his town: the first thing he thought about (population and date), then the next (agriculture), then the next, a series of topics that even he realized might have gone on indefinitely ("but I could write volumes").

The second student wrote: "the awful changes growth can make on a once nice town." Characteristically, his idea is not grammatically a statement, only a fragment, only a subject without a predicate to make it whole. But he knew intuitively and exactly what his idea was; when we have read his paragraph, we know too ("Growth has made awful changes on my once nice town") because this idea governs everything in his paragraph. From the assertion that San Jose "used to be" a nice place to live everything follows and converges handsomely in his sparely stated sadness at the loss.

The second is more forceful writing, too, because it is more personal, not confessional, but exploiting the experience of the writer in the service of his idea. The first student was standing back from his subject (his lack of an idea was partly responsible for this), outlining Watsonville as a silhouette with no scars, with no color. We have shops with no names and "we" with no "I." The second, however, names the sprawl ("a Banco de San Jose, and a McDonald's") and the streets ("Capitol Expressway"), and points us rhetorically to things we can see (the road winding "from a little beyond my old house," and "*that* huge field that used to be down the street").

As a result of both its idea and its personal focus, I think, the second is finally more substantial than the first, even though both writers had virtually unlimited information about their subject. The first writer happened to remember the date of founding, the kinds of crops, and several disparate facts about the history of Watsonville. These *are* facts, and presumably reported accurately. But they are finally thin, because they lack any relationship to each other, and unconvincing, because their writer seems to have had no commitment to them. We learn fewer facts about San Jose, but what we learn is denser, richer. It does not matter, we feel, whether the writer is accurate about the number of new people who have flocked to San Jose; he perceives and reports their awful effect on the city clearly—in the number of lanes and in the variety of new buildings needed to accommodate them. And he knows that the change is awful because he measures it against his memories (even only "vague" ones—a masterful rhetorical stroke) of the squirrels and ducks of the city's past. The writer of the first is a pretender; the writer of the second an expert.

In fact the achievement of the second writer—in twenty minutes, from a cold start—is astonishing, the more so because the assignment was so general and artificial. But I do not mean to evaluate the *writers* of these two pieces. I mean to use their writing, instead, to define the problems we ought to address in teaching exposition. Students need to learn to organize what they have to say; they need to integrate their experience with their ideas so they can write both precisely and honestly; and they need to become expert about their subject so they can write with power and conviction. In other words, we must try to teach our students to write expository essays that are serious and that tell the truth.

The suggestions I have to offer aim at both.

I

The first suggestion is that we teach our students how to organize their ideas. I do not want to start qualifying what I have to say immediately, but it is not always the case that they need to know how to *put* organization *on* their material; sometimes, more often than not, they have to *discover* the organization that is implicit *in* their idea. But in either case, they need to know what organization *is,* so they can generate or recognize it.

First of all, we need not apologize about teaching organization. We are not cramping anybody's style; we are not prescribing artificial, unreal writing. We are teaching our students one of the most important things they can learn about their writing or their thought: that ideas are *statements* of *relationships.* When the five-paragraph essay is mistaught, it is taught as a formula (state the three things you're going to talk about, then write a paragraph about each, then a conclusion—presto!) What the formula neglects to make clear is that those "three things" are *related* to each other; that they are all constituents of some larger, govern'ng idea; and that they are there in the essay at all only because of their relationship to each other.

Here is what I ask my students to do:

1. *Ask a question that requires a plural answer.*[2]
   - What were the results of the technological revolution?
   - Why (this question asks for reasons) should Gary Gilmore not have been executed?
   - What qualities make Volvo the car for people who think?

Such questions explicitly or implicitly require a plural answer with parallel parts that can provide organization for an essay.

2. *Answer the question in one sentence, specifying the parts.*
   - Some of the results of the technological revolution were an increase in production, a decrease in the need for manpower, and a concentration of wealth in the hands of those who owned the new machines.
   - Gary Gilmore should not have been executed because there is no evidence that the death penalty deters crime and because other criminals who have committed similar crimes have been given far less severe punishment.
   - Volvo is the car for people who think because it is comfortable, efficient, and safe.

Such plural answers provide an essay with its "main idea," what is often called its "thesis statement." But what is usually not noticed or taught is the fact that it is the relationship between parts of the statement that provides the essay with its content and direction.

The thesis statement is often criticized for its length, criticized unjustly, as if length were an aesthetic defect. But it is not, as two long thesis statements will show; the first is long and clear, the second long and obscure.

> The six-year old affirmative action program at U.C. Davis should not have been ruled unconstitutional for the following reasons: the program could have contributed to the amelioration of the effects of hundreds of years of racial injustice in this country; other equally selective admissions policies have never been challenged; and the court decisions of recent years have established a legal precedent for the constitutionality of affirmative action programs.

This sentence might have stopped at "reasons," but it does not confuse the reader by going on to specify at length what those reasons are. Each of the reasons is announced clearly, and arranged clearly in a parallel list (first the "program," then the "policies," then the "decisions"). The writer has committed himself here to a specific idea and articulated that idea with precision for his reader.

The second example, however, shows how even a shorter statement may be confusing, not simply because its syntax is more complex, but because the writer was unsure of his idea.

> Although I don't smoke, I think it should be legal, because people should be able to enjoy smoking as long as they have concern for non-smokers, who in turn should not depend on bureaucratic laws, which would be ridiculously ineffective anyway, to handle such a simple everyday problem.

This is much more difficult to follow than the first thesis because each of its parts pulls the writer further away from his reasons for thinking that smoking should be legal. Here length is a liability to him and to his reader because it allows him to slip from the reasons to a requirement that he wants to place on non-smokers and then to a description of the futility of bureaucratic regulation. But length in itself is no disadvantage, so I encourage my students to elaborate the parts of their thesis statements, specifying as exactly as they can the relationship between them.

Such a thesis statement, such a "plural answer," is the blueprint for an essay: an idea whose parts are each specified, arranged in a rhetorical order, and unified by a single stem which relates them to each other in a coherent whole. When students ask if they *have* to have *three* parts, they have misunderstood. The answer is no. They have to have more than one part to have an essay; otherwise, they can have no more than a paragraph. But the number of parts depends on their idea.

3. *Structure the essay, following the thesis statement exactly.*

Once they have the thesis statement formulated, it goes as the last sentence of the introduction, followed by one paragraph for each of the parts in the order in which they occur in the thesis.

But now I have to qualify again because this is not a formula for writing; it is instead a strategy for teaching organization. I have found all of these requirements helpful to students beginning to write essays of exposition, but none of them is absolute. The thesis statement may be formulated not first, but last, as in most cases it probably will be (just as the most accurate outlines and abstracts are usually written last) after the idea has been discovered in the writing of early drafts. It may go anywhere in the essay; it may even be left out. And its parts may be developed in any order and with any emphasis that fits the writer's rhetorical purpose. The persistent challenge of exposition for almost all of my students, however, lies in *sticking to* their idea, in governing what they say by that idea, in subordinating all their discussion to that point. It is to help them do this—to help them see that it can in fact be done—that I require them at first to follow their thesis statement exactly in the organization of their essay.

This plural-part thesis statement is a powerful teaching device; it provides students quickly with a simple paradigm for organization. Once they understand it, it can be varied: the parts do not need to be explicitly stated, the parts do not need to be parallel, the parts may be themselves multi-faceted. When we teach our students such variations (and there are others), we are making clear to them that they are not to "pre-fab" their essays. We are teaching them the principle of organization: that if an essay about an idea is to be understandable to us, then it must have a *point* and that point must be complex enough to establish and sustain relationships among subordinate ideas.

My students regularly report that this is the most valuable thing they learn in my writing classes. They have heard of "thesis statements" and "main ideas," some of them report, but they generally do not know what these things really are. Although some of them have even been taught the "five-paragraph essay," they have just learned to follow the formula; they usually do not understand what they are doing. The plural part thesis statement, however, helps them understand what they are doing, and it may be used at many grade levels. Instead of asking elementary school children to write a "report" on Peru or on dolphins or on the California missions, we should ask them to answer a question that will help them focus all their material. Most teachers do not ask such a question or help their students generate one: they say "discuss" or "report" and then give detailed instructions on handwriting and footnote form. My ten-year old son, for example, wrote an essay on Santa Clara according to such instructions. One of his chapters, however, illustrates in its order and coherence the possibility and value of teaching this kind of organization much earlier in the curriculum than we have thought appropriate.

> When Father Fray Thomas de la Pena arrived in the Santa Clara Valley he met some Indians that were part of the Costanoan tribe. They were friendly and skillful.
>
> One thing that they were good at was making arrowheads. They would make long skinny ones and stubby ones out of obsidian. Their arrowheads were all different colors like brown and black.
>
> Two more things they were skillful at were woodworking and making baskets, they could make bows and axes and spears and they could make these things very smooth. The baskets they made were pretty and they were so tight that they could hold water.
>
> Not only were they skillful but they were friendly and when Fr. Thomas had founded it the Indians used their skill to help build the mission.

Thesis statement, a paragraph on each part, and a conclusion in which the parts are deftly integrated (because they were friendly they used their skill to help).

The most persuasive testimony for me, however, comes from already accomplished student writers like the following woman. She came to Freshman Composition with wit, with an already highly developed sense of language, with the power to integrate her fresh perceptions with her thought. But she wrote in her journal that before this course she did not know how to write; that before we worked on the thesis statement, she did not realize either the value or the possibilities or order; and that then, suddenly, she understood. Here is the opening section of one of the essays she wrote:

> My parents' house is very formal, and my brother Tim and I were expected to behave accordingly. We were taught to be neat and clean and, more important, to be sweet and gracious. We could never be wild. Although our house was big, everything was breakable, and we had very little room to play in. We lived in starched and pressed calm. Understandably, we adored any place that was different from our home.

We loved going to the Tuschons' house because it was such a mess. Their dogs lived inside and their cat had kittens in a closet. We could eat potato chips and Oreos without being seated at the table, and there were piles of unfolded clothes in the laundry room that we could crawl around in. The best part of their house, though, was the lower level, which belonged to their daughter Elizabeth. Elizabeth was between Tim and me in age, and she could do anything she wanted down there. Her mom never even came down. Down there, we could run in and out of the house without having to wash our hands and take off our shoes each time. We could even throw food at each other. We left the T.V. on and the doll things out. Not having to worry about anyone taking it apart, we could build a covered wagon out of patio furniture and blankets. When we played hide-and-seek, Tim and I loved to hide in Elizabeth's fireplace. The messier the game, the more fun it was. My mother always looked like she was going to faint when we came home. She would put us in the bathtub immediately, while we were already planning the next visit.

My Aunt Nellie's little apartment in San Francisco was not messy, but we loved it because it was modest and informal....

I did not teach her to write such a wonderful phrase as "starched and pressed calm"; that came from her years of reading good writing and from an intuitive grasp of the power of figurative language. I did not teach her that in a single detail (such as their wearing shoes in the Tuschon house) she could capture the habits and spirits of both homes for us. But the thesis statement gave her an order. She compressed the multiple parts into "any place," each of the paragraphs of her essay describing a different place, and all of them unified by her childhood love of them. The organization is not the most remarkable virtue of her essay. It is a simple device. But it provided her, she said, with an elegant and lucid frame for her memories.

II

My second suggestion is that in teaching exposition we not isolate it from the personal experience of our students. We should not quarantine it in Advanced Placement classes (or even, for that matter, in English classes, as opposed to classes in art or biology). Neither should we set up for ourselves or for our students some false distinction between the "stuffy" essays of exposition and the "fun" narratives of personal experience. If we do, we will conceal a signal from ourselves, but not from our students, that exposition is "harder" than personal narrative, or that it is by nature "dull."

We should encourage our students, instead, to *use* their personal experience, to deploy it wherever it is relevant and rhetorically helpful, whatever their subject, whatever its form. They will not be accustomed to this suggestion. They will ask, puzzled: "Do you mean I can say 'I' in my essay?" Yes. Probably not in a paragraph explaining the physics of lava, but perhaps in an adjacent paragraph that describes the time you were dangerously close enough to *see* what boiling lava looks like.

Our students' resistance to this instruction should not be surprising. Wasn't everyone in America taught at some time or other to *not* use "I"? We all had the same teacher who, in order to help us broaden our focus beyond ourselves, to objectify—a good end—gave us a bad rule. I now have a graduate student still so handicapped by the rule that all the verbs she uses to write about her own thoughts or actions are in the passive voice, and when she cannot avoid referring to herself, she does so with a phrase like "this researcher." Another of my current students, back from two years of anthropological field work, reports that graduate professors in her department publicly abuse students for referring to themselves in their essays: "I don't want to know what YOU think!"

The inhibition is so strong that it is often hard to see where using our personal experience might be both relevant and rhetorically powerful in an expository essay. A recent group of remedial writing students at the University of California provides a nice example. Because their college entrance tests seemed to warrant it, they were required to take a three-hour diagnostic writing exam (the Subject-A exam). They were asked to read a passage from an essay by W. H. Auden and write an essay answer to one of four questions about the passage. The Auden selection was challenging and the questions probably sounded terrifyingly "stuffy"— especially to a captive audience of cold, unsure freshmen who were at the additional disadvantage of being there only because their writing skill was in question. Not an ideal situation, but their responses were illuminating.

What Auden had to say in essence was this: "labor" is what you do because you have to, to get money, to live; "work" is what you do because you love it, what you would do even if you were not lucky enough to be paid for it. The last three of the four questions asked for definitions of culture, analyses of the relationship between social classes, speculations about the direction of western civilization—all three questions drawn more or less from Auden's essay. The first question, however, was approximately this: "Based on your own experiences, or the experiences of your family or friends, to what extent do you agree with Auden's distinction between work and labor?" Of the ten examination essays I was asked to read, nine were about the last three questions, and all nine were unsatisfactory. Only one passed, and it was the only one to answer the first question: "I agree with Auden's distinction between 'work' and 'labor' because while I was growing up I saw that my father was sometimes a worker and sometimes a laborer."

I understand that failure on this exam was due to a variety of causes, and that the single success was due to more than that one student's choice of questions. But when I showed the passing essay to my students in the remedial course that followed the exam, they were unanimously surprised because they had all been taught that they were not permitted to write about themselves or their experience. The question had asked them explicitly for their opinion based on their experience, but they were not able to believe that it meant what it said because they were supposed to be writing, they knew, an "essay."

Even when the idea is general, a reference to ourselves may give it clarity and force. Loren Eiseley writes about the secret of life—as abstract a subject, perhaps, as one could find—by describing himself rummaging around in the autumnal refuse of an empty field near his home. George Orwell indicts colonialism for its debilitating effect on the colonizers themselves by telling the story of how he was shamed into shooting an elephant. In fact, it is *only* in reference to ourselves—to the extent that we have been able to grasp the meaning of an idea in our world, to integrate it with what we already know or feel—that we can know or learn anything. But we have isolated experience from thought for our students (if not for ourselves) in the way we teach writing, making it very difficult for them to write about their ideas as if (even if) they really care about them.

In a Subject A class, for example, I asked my students to write an essay evaluating James Degnan's argument that schools encourage "babble"— inflated, vapid gobbledygook—by assigning textbooks written in it and by rewarding students adept in it with A's.[3] Here are the conclusions to two of my students' essays:

> Professors assign books that more than seldom contain babble. More important than learning new words is understanding root words because language is mostly general until people start talking about different meanings. For example the word "throw" can mean to project, to cause to go, i.e. "to throw a bridge across a river, to throw a man into prison," to connect, to engage, to permit an opponent to win a race, to cause to fall off, i.e. "thrown by a horse," and "throw" has twenty more definitions. The texts are needed for students to learn the professional jargon necessary for their careers. All students working towards their career goals have a special language to learn that can be loaded with babble. Many people think that many words have the same meanings, which is not true. Usually there is a more appropriate word they can learn if they take the time to look.

(That is it. End essay. When the students had read this, one of them blurted out with acute directness, "That sounds like it has a lot of 'babble' in it." Here is the concluding paragraph to the second:)

Writing babble is unconsciously taught by instructors because they demand lengthy essays and encourage inappropriate diction. I can profess this to be true, since I am the product of such teachers. Until my Subject A class, I got A's and B's for unclear, verbose writing. I wrote such phrases as "due to the fact that" instead of "because" and "formulates" when I meant "creates." I believe that I would have made an "art" out of it, if I had not been told to stop and look at whether I was really saying anything clearly and succinctly.

The writer of the second essay had clearly discovered something the writer of the first had not, that her experience was relevant and rhetorically valuable. In an essay on whether schools encourage "babble" the writer of the first went off on a formless and inconclusive tangent about the multiple meanings of words. The second, however, realized that the best evidence of the effect of academic jargon (Macrorie's "Engfish") on student writing was her own writing, which she then illustrated with pointed detail.

So we must not isolate our students' feelings from their thoughts. We must broaden their perspectives on the world, yes, but in such a way that they are able to integrate themselves with it. Robert Hogan's poem "After Sending Freshmen to Describe a Tree" ends with the line: "For God's sake and mine, look *outside* your heart and write."[4] And in one sense he is right, as all our teachers were. But our students need also to be taught that they can only find conviction for their ideas in their experience, and that the moment of their experience, however personal and limited, can lend their essays matchless force.

As a complement to this emphasis on their *use* of experience, we should also assign our students writing *about* their personal experience. Valuable in itself, such writing also helps students learn to write more exactly and directly. One of the causes of the inflated gobbledygook of expository essays (as Orwell has explained in "Politics and the English Language") is that the words tend to lose specific reference, tend to float free of any concrete ground by which their accuracy or logic or even honesty can be measured. If a writer, however, describes his first visit to the beach in Hawaii with this sentence, "When my eyes first caught the azure blue, my walk turned into a run," you can ask him, "Really?" The question is easily answerable here (as it tends not to be about abstract sentences) because the student can refer to the concrete experience which his words purport to describe. When I asked "really?" about this Hawaii sentence, the writer was able to say, "Well, no...not exactly." At that moment he was confronting directly the meaning of what he had written.

It is a frustrating, embarrassing, ultimately liberating experience to focus sharply on the meanings of our words. I often find that like my student I do not mean exactly what I have said. This dismaying discovery, though, also reminds me that words *can* operate precisely and that it is my job, as a writer, to use them so. Our students need this discovery, too, and I have found that they can make it most readily when they are writing about their personal experience.

A freshman writer at the University of Santa Clara turned in the following sentences as the introduction to her first college essay:

> A major problem that is posed to young individuals and their personal identities is that of conformity. The world is full of pressures trying to merge many different personalities and values into one person with acceptable traits....

Really? She had an inchoate idea about conformity beneath these sentences, but it is not literally true that "the world is full of pressure trying to merge many different personalities and values into one person." She could not recognize this because, at the level of abstraction which she assumed college requires, she thought the sentence was perfectly accurate. (This was college, after all, she said later; wasn't this the kind of writing that was expected?) What freed her writing from this kind of pretense, or at least allowed her to begin to assess the precision of her words and sentences, was her next essay. There she wrote about being lost as a little girl at a terrifying pistol shooting demonstration, and then found; and there she was able to write exactly, testing her words as she went against her vividly remembered fear.

We should recognize in her explanation, however, how responsible *we* are for the academic pretense in our students' writing. We tell them they are in high school now and should write more complexly than they did in elementary school; or that when they get to college, or graduate school, they are going to have to be able to write with more sophistication. We build up their word-power and teach them to use a thesaurus (wrongly) for the basest of reasons—so they will sound "smart." At least that is *their* impression. At all four of the colleges where I have taught writing, my students have eventually volunteered that *that* is the reason for their consciously artificial language: when you write an essay, they say, you don't want to sound "dumb" or "like you're still in high school." (A former student of mine, even then an administrator in the middle of a successful academic career, was secretly terrified that his writing made him sound "too simple" because it was relatively free of the jargon that decorated the essays of his fellow graduate students.) And we make them read, without apology or apparently any notice, mountains of muck.

The following paragraph illustrates the enormous liability our students labor under. Written as part of an essay about a book assigned for a religion course, it was submitted to me as a piece of self-explanatory expository prose. (The bracketed comments are mine.)

> According to what Dulles [the author of the book in question] calls "the principle of incarnation" the gospel demands to be realized in distinctive ways in different social contexts. These

> differences are based somewhat on differing emphasis on one or
> another secondary authority. Furthermore [?], pluriformity [unde-
> fined] is necessary to Christianity because: 1) the Christian
> revelation should be thematized [?] in terms of the expressive
> materials offered by any given culture, 2) faith should adapt its
> forms of thought and expression to the successive situations
> where it finds itself, 3) pluriformity [still undefined] is encouraged,
> furthermore [the second sign of the writer's misplaced confi-
> dence in the compelling logic of his paragraph], by the diversity
> of secondary authorities emphasized [by whom?]....

(But we can only fully understand the causes of this impenetrable writing
if we read Dulles, the author my student was trying to understand and
explain; the next and last sentence of the paragraph gives us a taste:)

> ...As Dulles puts it "by holding a multitude of irreducibly dis-
> tinct articulations in balance one can best position oneself to hear
> what God may be saying here and now."

"What does this *mean*?" I asked as neutrally as I could. Pause—and the
pause is as vivid for me still as his answer—"I don't know."

I am not arguing that we should encourage our students to trivialize
complex ideas, to thin them for "the man on the street." Expository essays,
like all writing, should be written for as particular an audience as possible;
that audience is hardly ever the man on the street. But even for an expert
audience our language should be exact. Some years ago, I am told, Monroe
Hirsch, the Dean of the University of California School of Optometry,
publicly chastised his colleagues for obscuring their ideas with jargon
and convoluted sentences which even professional optometrists could not
decipher. There is a measurable distinction, he was arguing, between exact
and obscure technical writing.

This distinction is usefully illustrated for me by two paragraphs, both
about the same subject, both written at the same time under the same
conditions—during a midterm examination in an upper division Geology
course at U.C. Berkeley.[5] I do not know what "magma" is; if you don't, so
much the better. The difference between these two paragraphs is apparent
even to an in-expert audience.

> Viscosity of magma affects the texture of a rock by its ability
> to change position in the respect of raising to a higher level allow-
> ing the magma to cool faster giving glossy texture. In lavas the
> same hold but the environment differs in that it may be exposed
> allowing even faster cooling. The moving magma due to low vis-
> cosity may pick up rock particles will alter texture.

This paragraph was written in exam conditions, at speed and under duress,
so ignore the syntactic slips. They are not, in any event, what makes this
paragraph hard to read, nor is the vocabulary, nor even is the subject.

This paragraph is opaque because it does not express precisely the *relationship* between the viscosity of magma and the crystalline texture of rock. But this relationship *can* be expressed precisely and (if it is) can be at least provisionally understood, even by readers who do not understand geology. Witness the second paragraph, written during the same exam:

> If the viscosity of magma is high, the movement of ions toward centers of crystallization is impeded. Therefore more and smaller crystals tend to form. On the other hand, if the magma is very slightly viscous, there is rapid movement of ions toward centers of crystallization which attract the ions, and fewer and larger crystals form.

This student, from the first crucial word "if," was writing exactly, deploying technical terms economically and in a sequence whose logic is both manifest and sure: *If* X, then A and *therefore* B; *on the other hand, if* Y, then C and D. Complex, technical, but perfectly lucid.

Geology is a long way from personal experience, but the writing about both operates on the same principle, and it is the principle finally that we should try to teach our students: that the language is capable of powerful precision and that if we demand such precision of our own words and of each other's, our thought will become more accurate, more logical, even more honest.

One of my current students, a teacher with years of experience in the classroom, wrote the following sentence as part of an essay advocating curriculum reform: "This philosophical framework will provide the tools to extract appropriate environmental and human resource descriptions." What she meant, we worked out together, was approximately this:

If my assumptions about the nature of learning and the purpose of education are correct,	*This philosophical framework*
we ought, as teachers,	*will provide the tools to extract*
to organize our classrooms and approach our students in certain ways which I will now outline.	*environmental and human resource appropriate descriptions*

Why did she write the sentence the way she did? I have been describing some of the reasons here—her fear of being personal, the powerful spell of abstract academic gobbledygook, the desire to sound intelligent, and a hazy conception of just what her idea was. But if in all these ways her sentence illustrates the weaknesses to which expository writing is vulnerable, it is still very much like the Hawaii sentence: "When my eyes caught the azure blue, my walk turned into a run." Really? No.

So we assign personal experience writing to our students to teach them to imagine concretely what they mean—what they saw and did and felt and thought—and to show them how to ask of their own sentences "really?" We are helping them discover that they do not have to fake their writing, that they can simply admit their thrill at the sight of that splendid ocean. And that they can say simply "classrooms" instead of "environmental resource" and "students" instead of "human resource." We are helping them take *both* themselves and their ideas seriously and to write, finally caring most for the truth.

III

One of the reasons that students tend not to take their ideas seriously is that they do not believe they *have* any ideas. There are other reasons. Like all of us, they are less interested in some subjects, less committed to some ideas than to others. And essay assignments are notoriously awful: "discuss the rise of the Greek city-states" gives *no* writer enthusiasm, or even direction. But a crucial reason derives from their sense of themselves as *student* writers, as *pretending* to write, as not having anything genuine to say. William Irmscher has described this experience in terms of their attitude toward their audience, an attitude reflecting as well their attitude toward themselves.[6] Writers may have various relationships with their audiences, Irmscher explains, depending on the degree to which one or the other of them is expert. An expert to an expert, an expert to an amateur, an amateur to an amateur—all of these relations between writer and audience permit the writer to take himself and his idea seriously. Most students assume, however, and perhaps unwittingly we encourage their assuming, the relationship that makes writing most difficult—amateur to expert, student writing to teacher, student pretending to know a little to teacher who knows it all.

My third suggestion, therefore, is that we help our students get so involved with their subject that they become expert, that they develop a genuine intention to write, and that they consequently care for the truth of what they say.

One way to accomplish this goal is to have them share their material. If we have them read and write about the same text—not because it is the only text for which we have enough copies; not because it is on The Syllabus for American Lit.—they can all then measure their interpretations and assertions against a common standard, available to them all. It is my experience that discussions deteriorate at a speed directly proportional to the secrecy of the crucial information; I can not argue with someone who has private access to the facts. So we should get the facts out in the center of the room—in this case, a common text, *Macbeth* or *Patterns in Culture. When someone speculates about the motives of Lady Macbeth,* then, everyone can assess that speculation; when someone argues that the serenity of Zuni culture was really enervation, the evidence of the text is there to challenge him. The search for truth is collaborative. The more we encourage this collaboration among our students, the more they will become involved with their subject.

I suggest that *we immerse* them in the subject if possible, using not only a common text, but a common body of material—all the stuff we can gather about the damming of rivers for hydroelectric power, about the history of whorehouses in our town, about desert flowers or marine mammals or race cars, about the concentration camps in eastern Europe. I put together such a body of material about the Bakke case while it was being argued before the Supreme Court, a stapled-together, xeroxed compilation of almost "raw" data: newspaper clippings, abstracts of lower court decisions, transcripts of correspondence among the principals, letters to the editor. The first of a series of assignments was to sift through this material (everyone had a copy of everything) and to report on a particular aspect of it: what happened, who the principal figures were, what the essential arguments of the lawyers were, and so on. Everyone was limited to the material in the xeroxed packet; if the students knew about relevant information that had been omitted, they could use it only if they brought a copy for everyone to add to the packet (no secret data). The final assignment was to argue in an essay, based on the information in which they had become expert, whether the affirmative action program which had excluded Bakke was or ought to have been found unconstitutional. (Such an idea, I now realize, is not new. For a few years in the late 1950's "casebooks" in a variety of different fields were quite popular as texts for writing classes. Unfortunately, the fad passed, and all the books are out of print. There ought to be a new series.)

I made up the packets for the Bakke unit myself, but one might also organize a unit in which the *students* collect the data about a subject they have selected. Or one might dispense with the packet altogether. I gave my students a deliberately general essay assignment in which I specified only the broad subject—Northern Ireland. Their initial job was to start looking for information about Northern Ireland and to bring back to class whatever they found. Their information came in haltingly, some of it redundant, some of it fragmented, some of it vivid and terrible. But it was a collaboration in the making: when one student ran out of sources on the peace movement, another came up with a fascinating article about it that she had just read while looking for something else. The essays were finally on different aspects of the large subject of Northern Ireland, but in the process the students had immersed themselves, together, in the subject.

What I am describing here is research, not as a separate activity with note cards and bibliography cards and formal outlines and hours of wandering aimlessly among library shelves, but as an activity integral with writing about ideas. And not as an activity which one performs alone but in the midst of a conversation with others involved in the same or a similar search—a conversation by means of which one's questions are clarified, direction focused, knowledge enriched, a conversation by means of which one becomes expert.

For increasing students' immersion in the subjects of their essays, Ken Macrorie has developed as assignment which he calls the "I-Search" paper.[7] The premise of the assignment is sound—that students need to care about their ideas to write purposeful expository essays, and that one way to foster that care is to have them write about their own searches, to make the search the subject of the essay. I think this is a good assignment, but I think we should do more. Macrorie's assignment has students focus on themselves; I think they should be able to focus, too, on their ideas, to believe that they know enough to think and write something significant, to believe that their ideas have inherent value. Only when they do will they be able to write expository essays of clarity and power.

Besides needing confidence in their expertise, however, students need also the *intention* to write, and this requires that they have an audience, a real, demanding, attentive audience. Traditionally, in school, their teachers are their audience. This is frequently the source of the paralyzing intimidation I have described. But if we are to help them feel more confident about themselves, we must also *listen* to them when they address us in their essays; we must take them seriously. Students do not think we do. They think we are interested in how long their essays are or in how neat their handwriting is, in how many library sources they cite or in how close they can come to *our* idea about *their* subject. During a conference about an essay on *The Sound and the Fury,* a student told me that I was the first person who ever really wanted to know what she meant in her writing. I doubt that, but imagine how hard it must have been for her to *intend* to write, during all those years in school, for an audience that she thought was indifferent.

We can also create other audiences for our students, the most available being other students in the classroom. Small peer groups organized to read and respond to writing in progress are enormously helpful in improving expository writing.[8] (And they add wonderfully to the community spirit, to the workshop spirit, of the class.) An extension of the collaborative exploration of the subject, these groups make the writer accountable for what he says. They help eliminate the most blatant pretension. Few students are willing to read out loud to their peers the pure tripe they might submit silently and privately to a teacher. The groups also provide invaluable feedback for the writer, letting him know where his idea needs elaboration or revision, suggesting more relevant illustration (and offering specific alternatives), challenging or praising the thoroughness and perception of his argument. The other members of the group do not have to be astute readers or experienced writers; and the writer does not have to heed their suggestions. What is most important is that they are a real audience trying to grasp the sense of the writing; they make possible, therefore, quite beyond whatever specific reactions they have, the student's intention to write.

We should encourage our students also to write to a particular audience where possible. At Alameda Community College my students wrote essays (but finally chose not to send them; I should have encouraged it more insistently) to the Army Corps of Engineers, arguing whether the dam in Maine should be completed or the endangered furbish lousewort saved. The more particular their audience—their draft board, the Lions Club Scholarship Committee, the incoming class of freshmen —the easier it is for them to take seriously what they have to say.

We should, whenever possible, publish their writing. However it is done, and there are lots of ways, publishing makes writers careful and proud. The simplest way is to just collect their essays, xerox them (or ditto them), and staple them together. (I do this only if my students want to pay for the duplicating; they have always wanted to.) A more ambitious project was suggested to me by Taz Takahashi, who makes books with her sixth grade class in San Mateo, California: my freshman students at Santa Clara decided to make a book of essays about different aspects of the Depression. Collaborating throughout the project, they each developed a different essay idea, read and revised their essays in subject-related groups, made or found illustrations for each other's work, compiled an annotated bibliography, revised, typed, and xeroxed the whole (91 pages, only about $1.50 per book, because someone in the class got us a special break on the duplicating costs). This is the sort of expository writing they produced for their book:

> In Oakland they endured the night in giant, unsold construction pipes. In New York they made do with subways, and in Chicago they resorted to the parks. They existed in makeshift towns called "jungles" when they weren't being arrested for vagrancy. They came from all walks of life and had no real future. They were cold too often. They were hungry too often. They died too often.
>
> "They" seems a fitting pronoun for the young vagabonds of the Depression because it captures the uncertainty and anonymity of their lives. These homeless wanderers were a phenomenon which grew out of the hopelessness of the times. "Things had to be better someplace else" they kidded themselves. Fortune Magazine compared these vagabonds to the disgruntled bezprizorni of Russia who took to the road after the overthrow of their monarchy in 1917. Our wanderers never became violent like the bezprizorni, perhaps because they were too intent on the search for better times. The search for the estimated 200,000 boys my age was a difficult one. In my easy, secure life it is hard for me even to imagine the problems these vagabonds faced in finding adequate food and clothing and in traveling from town to town.

Lynda Chittenden and the fourth and fifth grade "Kids in Room 14" at Old Mill School in Mill Valley, California, went further (and it is good to end with them, to emphasize again how possible, how valuable, exposition can be even in the early grades). I hope they describe in detail some time *how* they did it, but their book is beautiful. Called *Our Friends in the Waters,* it is full of fascinating expository writing about various classes of marine animals, all of this bordered by brilliant drawings and graphs and poems, printed, bound, copyrighted and for sale.[9]   Its organization is careful and consistent, the parts all unified by a common question about the adaptability of different mammals to the sea. It is unabashedly personal, its exposition framed by excerpts like these:

> I wish I could see one breach. Any whale. Any WILD whale. I never thought anything about whales until this year. I just thought of them as one huge thing—cold blooded, like a shark. But now I think of them as one of us. My mom asks me now about the whales—she says I'm her source of information.
>
> I wish I was rich so I could go on a boat and go right by one and touch it. Then get in some scuba gear and swim with one. That's what I would like to do. I wish that I could go and hear what they are saying. I want to know what they think. I want to be a whale.

Amy Crosby, Jill Nickerson, Laura Stopes, and Whitney Wright wrote the introductory chapter to the book from which the following excerpt is taken:

> Where Did Marine Mammals Come From?
> Of all of today's marine mammals, the first ones whose ancestors returned to the sea are called Cetaceans (whales and dolphins). Some say they are the most perfectly adapted to their environment of all the mammals on earth. The adaptation or change was so well done that their body shape today resembles a fish. In fact, some people still think that whales are fish.
> Cetaceans were followed to the sea by the ancestors of Sirenians (manatees and dugongs). Then the ancestors of the Pinnipeds (seals and sea lions), and most recently the ancestors of the Sea Otter returned to the sea.
> Many body adaptations or changes over many millions of years were necessary for terrestrial (land) mammals to evolve into these marine (sea) mammals.

Such exposition is direct and unpretentious, accurate because it is the product of these children's long and intensive study of the sea, and committed because it reflects their love of what they studied. It is a splendid achievement, a proud book. Its writing, like all good writing, is serious and true.

NOTES

[1]Josephine Miles, "Freshman at Composition," *College Composition and Communication* II, 1 (February, 1951), pp. 7-9; reprinted in *Working Out Ideas: Predication and Other Uses of Language* (Berkeley: University of California, Berkeley/Bay Area Writing Project Curriculum Publication No. 5, 1979), pp. 5-9.

[2]I was taught this series of steps by Brother John Perron, c.s.c.

[3]"Masters of Babble: Turning Language Into Stone," *Harper's Magazine*, September, 1976, p. 27; reprinted in *Speaking of Words*, ed. James MacKillop and Donna Woolfolk Cross (New York: Holt, Rinehart and Winston, 1978), pp. 149-152.

[4]"After Sending Freshmen to Describe a Tree," *American Association of University Professors Bulletin* (Winter, 1957); reprinted in *College English: The First Year*, ed. Alton C. Morris *et al.* (7th ed.; New York: Harcourt Brace Jovanovich, 1978), p. 558.

[5]These paragraphs were included in the "Report of the Committee on Prose Improvement" written by Josephine Miles at the University of California, Berkeley, in 1952. This report has been published as "The College at Composition" in Miles' *Working Out Ideas*, pp. 10-13.

[6]*The Holt Guide to English* (New York: Holt, Rinehart and Winston, 1972), pp. 20-23.

[7]See *Searching Writing* (Rochelle Park, New Jersey: Hayden Book Co., 1980).

[8]See Thom Hawkins, *Group Inquiry Techniques for Teaching Writing* (Urbana: ERIC and NCTE, 1976); Mary K. Healy, *Using Student Writing Response Groups in the Classroom* (Berkeley: University of California, Berkeley/Bay Area Writing Project Curriculum Publication No. 12, 1980).

[9]*Our Friends in the Waters* may be purchased by sending $5.00, plus $1.00 to cover postage and handling, to Lynda Chittenden, Old Mill School, 352 Throckmorton, Mill Valley, CA 94941.

5. Responding and Revising

Using Student Writing Response Groups in the Classroom

Mary K. Healy
University of California, Berkeley

Teachers of any subject have an implicit or explicit picture of students who are successful in their area. Below is my description of successful writing students:

1. They begin writing without debilitating trepidation and anxiety.

2. They realize that they will make discoveries about the subject through the act of writing.

3. They take into account the purpose and audience for the writing.

4. They realize from past experience that the development of the paper will progress through drafts.

5. They have the confidence to use personal anecdote or experience to illuminate arguments.

6. If circumstances allow, they try out the paper on others; if not, they try to imagine the intended audience.

7. They know that the writing will be difficult, frustrating work but proceed anyway.

I believe that involving students in small writing response groups between drafts of writing in the classroom—any classroom whether English, science, social studies, etc.—provides the context for developing the characteristics listed above. The basic premise behind this use of small groups is that, to provide a student writer with a sense of audience, he must receive audience reactions *while engaged* in the process of writing, not at the end when the paper has been handed in, days have gone by, and the piece is handed back, minutely evaluated by the teacher. In order for the writer to develop that automatic awareness of a reader's needs which is characteristic of most professional writers, the student needs frequently to try out works in progress on other members of the class for some kind of clarifying response. This essay outlines a process for developing student ability to work effectively in response groups.

I use the term "response group" rather than "editing," "proofreading," or "writing" group to place emphasis on the active involvement of group members—giving reactions, asking questions, making suggestions. The words "proofreading" or "editing" imply making corrections near the end of the composing process. *To respond* is more immediate; it occurs earlier in the writing process—usually after a first draft has been completed.

The use of student response groups in the classroom is an effective means both to enable students to help each other with their writing and to lessen the paper load for the conscientious teacher who believes students learn to write by writing. By encouraging students to listen and respond to each other's written work, the teacher achieves a variety of useful purposes: students develop a sense of a responsive, questioning audience; students are helped with their writing while it is *in progress;* students develop a sense of writing as a process which involves revising based on reclarification of their ideas and purposes; and students help each other eliminate many of the errors which block the reader's comprehension.

Students of any age bring a wealth of knowledge about language to the classroom. Whatever their previous school experience, students have been using and learning language for years. In addition, many of them are out-of-school readers with sensitivity to language often not acknowledged in the classroom. Just living a life requires language awareness and comprehension skills rarely mentioned in textbooks. All of these language skills are brought into play when students respond to each other's writing in small groups.

From systematically using small response groups in the classroom, I have noted the following evolving characteristics in student writing: more specificity of detail, more supporting examples, more transitional and introductory phrases directed at the reader, and, as a consequence of a combination of the above, more fluent and complete pieces of writing. After a year's work with response groups in the classroom, students generally *request* time for group work when they are between drafts of a particular piece of writing. Slowly, over the course of the year, they begin to regard response groups as useful to them in a variety of ways. They can read their papers aloud to an attentive audience; they discover that in the act of reading aloud, they themselves hear omissions in their papers, awkward word choices, run-on sentences, sentence fragments, ambiguous sections, etc. It becomes common for a student reading a paper out loud to stop, reread a phrase, and make a change before moving on to the next line. "That doesn't sound right" is a frequent reaction of the writer upon a first reading aloud. "I forgot to tell you about the part when..." or "There's something missing here" are other common reactions by writers to their own work. These *writer* reactions occur even before the small group begins to respond to the piece.

Preparation for Small Group Response Sessions

THE CLASSROOM CONTEXT

Students' attitudes toward writing shape the type of comments they make about each other's writing in small groups. In large part, those attitudes were formed by past experiences with writing, both at home and in school. And, since writing is generally considered a school-related activity, it is probable that the attitudes and values students have developed toward both the writing process and its eventual product were shaped by their *school* experience. The experiences each student has had depend upon decisions made by previous teachers.

- What have these teachers valued in the student's writing?
- How did these teachers respond to the writing—with letter grades alone? With mechanical corrections? With comments? With a combination of these?
- What model of the writing process did the teacher work from?
  a. That a piece of writing has stages of development—a gradual movement from first draft to last, with plenty of time to try out the draft on others in between?
  b. That a piece of writing should be evaluated and corrected first and *then* the student begins to revise and rewrite?
- What types of comments did the teachers make about completed pieces of writing?
  a. Did they focus on the weaknesses in the writing and discuss plans for remediation?
  b. Did they read some strong selections aloud for the enjoyment of the class and make brief comments on why the examples were strong?
- Did the teachers seem to *enjoy* the writing of their students?
- Did the teachers themselves write and share some of this writing with their students?
- How much "play" with language went on in class?

The attitudes of student writers in our classes now are the sum of all that has happened to their writing in the past. The teacher who wants small groups to function successfully in the classroom will spend some time before starting group work both ferreting out the origins of present attitudes and taking actions to shape new ones if existing attitudes are constricting or counter-productive. I use the following activity for that purpose:

Practice

Early in the year or the semester, I assign students the topic "Writing in School." In a pre-writing discussion, I ask about their earliest memories of writing in school—how they learned to form letters and words, what early topics they remember writing about, how they felt at the time about the writing they did, how teachers responded to their writing, what specific lessons they remember being taught, and, finally, how they go about writing something. Then they are asked to write about these individual experiences.

When this initial assignment has been handed in, I generally read and write responses to it—commenting on the content, asking questions when they occur naturally. I ignore mechanical or structural flaws because the purpose here is to elicit from students a description of their current stance toward writing along with information about how that attitude developed over time.

After reading and responding to the papers, I usually comment to the class about various attitudes the writing revealed, and then I read several selections aloud.

Following an activity such as this, I describe what I value in my students' writing and how classroom activities for the rest of the year will reflect that attitude. Specifically, I describe writing as a process made up of *stages* so that it is not necessary for all writing done in class to be polished into final draft form. I talk briefly about the importance of trying out writing on an *audience* before preparing a final draft, to learn how readers hear the words. I refer to my written comments on their papers as an example of the *reactions* of a reader rather than the *corrections* of an evaluator. Then I stop talking, knowing, as always, that my actions in the classroom rather than my talk about the process will be the ultimate persuasion.

For the next two weeks or so, we do many short "originals" or first draft writings on a variety of topics—reactions to the literature we read, reactions to TV and books, memory pieces about the students' childhoods, descriptions of scenes around the school or specific school situations. I read all of these, write comments or ask questions, and the papers are filed in the students' individual writing folders along with the rest of their writing. These folders remain in the classroom, either in boxes or file cabinets.

THE STUDENTS' SENSE OF LANGUAGE

If students have had no previous work in response groups, I find it necessary to encourage them to become conscious of how they respond to language they hear and read. What do they like or dislike? Often, they have never been asked that question in school before, so at first they have no immediate answer. Unless they *can* respond, they cannot function effectively in a small group because they have nothing concrete to offer a writer.

One way of making students aware of effective writing is frequently to reproduce selections from student journals or other first draft writing, have students read these anonymous selections aloud, in turn, and then have each student underline any word, phrase, sentence, or passage which she particularly likes, for whatever reason. Each person in the class, including the teacher, selects something to read aloud. Repeating the same words someone else has read is encouraged because the purpose of the lesson is to call attention to effective use of language, and repetition emphasizes the most effective language in each piece. Below are some examples from eighth grade student journals. The underlinings were made by other students in the class and the adjacent numbers indicate how many students in the room read that particular line.

My mind, as stupid as it is, is just right for me. If it wasn't it wouldn't be on my head. My mind seems to have a short memory, but is quite good at figuring things out. That is why I am the worlds worst speller and a semi-good mathematician. The only things that stay on my mind are girls, soccer and work, not that I like work, but just that I am so far behind in it I can't get it off my mind. (5) At night my mind is still at work keeping me awake.

* * * * * * * * * *

When I think of my mind I think of a room filled with little gears, motors, wires and tubes. The gears and motors make my body function and the wires and tubes absorb information and knowledge. When I hit my head a tube gets broken or a gear gets jammed and I get a headache, but it always repairs itself. When someone dies from a head injury, I think of it as if they broke all the motors and tubes in their head. I think of skin as a gooey substance that is poured on and dries and then provides a little protection for the insides. (4)

* * * * * * * * * *

On cold rainy mornings, I am so cold. I can't even get out of bed. I'm like a cold and stiff nail stuck in a block of ice. (4) Then I wait until someone turns on the heat, then when my room gets warm I begin to defrost and slowly get out of bed.

* * * * * * * * * *

Today all I have done is rush. When I got up in the morning I had to rush. To get my work done in class I had to rush and immediately when I got home I started to rush and now I am rushing to do this original. When I was told to do an original on a rambling thought I tried and tried to ramble but I couldn't so I thought.

I thought and thought but I couldn't ramble. (3) Then I had to rush so I never ended up rambling.

This activity, repeated once or twice a week, accustoms the students to listen for effective use of language and to individually choose their own preferences. They grow in confidence about their ability to recognize strong writing; they no longer feel they must wait for the teacher's final judgment. When they are at ease with this activity, I usually begin the first stages of small group work.

THE WHOLE CLASS AS A RESPONSE GROUP

Deciding just when to begin response groups is crucial. Beginning too early in the year or the semester is counter-productive because it takes time for students to become more fluent writers. I usually wait until after students have been writing original drafts for about one month and then introduce the idea of working in small response groups before they write their final drafts. Over the years, I have accumulated audio and video tapes of group work by my previous classes. I play several excerpts to introduce the process, asking students to comment afterwards on what they hear and see.

Via Overhead Projector Transparency

Next I plan a whole class writing assignment, usually a childhood memory piece. When the first drafts are completed, I choose several papers to reproduce on transparencies for class response. Before working with the transparencies, however, I emphasize to the students the difference between *evaluation* and *response:*

Evaluation: The final assessment of a finished piece of written work which has already gone through drafts. Final evaluation will be the teacher's responsibility.

Response: The initial reaction to a piece of first draft writing, usually in the form of questions to the writer about the content or form of the piece. Response will be the responsibility of the students and the teacher.

After reading the piece aloud, I have the students respond to the writing on the transparency by asking questions about the writing. Then I write the students' questions on the transparency next to the appropriate line, repeating the procedure with each of the transparencies. The session ends with students exchanging their own papers with a partner and writing questions which occur to them about each other's papers.

Via Ditto

Within several days of the overhead transparency response lesson, I plan another whole-class writing assignment, again a personal narrative piece—perhaps based on the memory of a childhood fear or a frightening experience. Then I choose several of the original drafts and run off dittoed copies of them exactly as written, after asking the writers' permission. I ask the students to write responses, either questions or comments, directly on the dittoed sheets and hand them in to me so that I see how they are responding to each other's work. I comment on the type of response each student is offering and try to indicate whether it would be helpful to the writer. The written responses are a useful indication of the students' understanding of the process, and they alert me to students who will need further encouragement and direction.

THE MODEL SMALL GROUP

After completing the overhead transparency and ditto response sessions, I find it helpful to have one or two "live" sessions with a group of students or teachers responding to one another's writing in front of the rest of the class. For example, my team teaching partner and I often role play different types of response to our writing, attempting to illustrate the spectrum of response possibilities:

1. Useless: "Oh, your story is O.K." (No specific help for the writer)
2. Marginally useful: "I thought the part about your brother throwing spinach was funny." (Encouragement for the writer)
3. Useful: "How old was your brother when that happened?" (The writer learns what information the reader needs.)
4. Very useful: "I was confused when you said your aunt came in. I thought you said earlier that you were alone in the house." (Again, the writer hears from someone who *wasn't* there when it happened, someone who needs more information.)

Establishing Response Groups

DETERMINING GROUP MEMBERSHIP

There are many ways of arranging small groups in the classroom. Some teachers arrange groups by "ability" levels, believing that students of similar writing ability can respond more helpfully to one another's work. Other teachers attempt to include students of varying abilities in a group in order to provide written pieces of varying quality for response. Finally, some teachers use a "psychological" method, attempting to secure a harmonious balance of personalities in the group. I have tried all of these and abandoned them one by one. Now I just say, "Please get into groups of between two and five" and wait to see what happens. What usually happens is that students sit with their friends. In my experience, this arrangement allows for maximum participation by group members and maximum involvement with one another's writing.

However, using this friendship method of grouping is messy at first. One group is too large—the students huddle in a protective bunch of seven to nine or so. Individual students wander around the room, groupless. A group in the corner, ostensibly arranging furniture in a circle, shoves their chairs into one another's and the noise is growing. A typical beginning. At this point, I simply split the large group in two and quiet the noisy ones by joining their group. Dealing with students who have no group is more delicate, and what I do depends on the individual, the day, and the amount of tact and sensitivity I can muster. Usually, I request one of the groups to accept a student. If that doesn't seem feasible, then I arrange to work individually with the student until an appropriate group can be found.

PHYSICALLY ARRANGING THE ROOM

To control noise, I try to arrange the groups so they are physically as far apart as possible. I use corners of the room, the area around my desk, the outside corridor—whatever space is available. Movable furniture is, of course, a great advantage. But whatever the arrangement, the room will be noticeably noisy; this is natural. To control the noise, I discuss appropriate noise levels with students and ask members of a group to raise their hands when their concentration is disturbed. When hands go up, I usually ask for general quiet and point out the disturbance. If a particular group is consistently louder than others, I might join that group to settle it down, disband it if it is simply not functioning, or find an isolated spot for it (perhaps a corridor, a stair landing near the room, or an adjoining empty classroom).

Just before the end of the first small group session, I usually call the whole class back together and we discuss the procedure. Examples of helpful response from partners are quoted, writers mention things they noticed about their own pieces, and any problems are discussed. If the small groups are scheduled to continue the next day, I review this discussion before they begin again.

USING CHECKLISTS AS GUIDES TO THE PROCESS

At each stage of the small group process, I find using short checklists quite helpful for guiding student progress. The following list of small group procedures is either written on the board before each session or dittoed and stapled to the students' writing folders:

Working in Small Groups

1. Keep the groups small—two to five at first.
2. Sit as far away as possible from other groups for noise control.
3. Write the names of your response partners on the top of your original draft.
4. After hearing a paper read, ask the writer any questions which occur to you. The writer will note those questions on the paper.
5. Encourage the writer to ask for help with difficult sections of his/her paper.
6. Make all revisions on your original draft before doing the final. Staple both copies together.

Then, during the first few months of work in small response groups, I usually ditto a checklist for each assignment that is to be revised into final draft form. The students find these checklists to be helpful reminders of the steps in the process, and I find that they eliminate much correction time for me. I am not constantly writing reminder notes on student papers and can concentrate my comments on the content of each paper. Two sample checklists follow:

1. **I Remember Assignment (English Class):**

| **I Remember** | Name _____ |
| | Date _____ |

I. Original Draft	Excellent	Satisfactory	Needs improvement
A. Partner's names appear on top.			
B. Response suggestions noted on paper.			
C. Writer shows revision on paper.			
II. Final Draft			
A. Correct heading on on paper.			
B. Written in ink, skipping lines.			
C. Used specific detail to make memory clear to reader.			
D. Correct use of spelling and punctuation.			

Teacher's Comment:

2. Middle Ages Role Play Assignment (Social Studies):

Name _____

Section _____

Date _____

Response partners _____

Social Studies
Written Role Play

	Partners	*Teacher*
I. Content		
A. Writer included factual details about		
1. Geographical location of housing	_____	_____
2. Family members and friends	_____	_____
3. Job and position in society	_____	_____
4. Favorite activities and possessions	_____	_____
5. Effects of religion on life	_____	_____
II. Presentation		
A. Successfully assumed the role of a Middle Ages person	_____	_____
B. Uses Middle Ages terms correctly	_____	_____
C. Successfully proof read paper (eliminated any spelling and punctuation errors)	_____	_____

Comments:

MONITORING RESPONSE GROUP PROGRESS

Keeping track of seven or eight small groups operating simultaneously in a classroom can be a frustrating experience, especially when the students are new to the process and seem to need the teacher's attention continually. However, over the years my team teaching partners and I have evolved several methods for remaining in touch with the groups' progress.

Sitting in on Response Groups

Once the groups are functioning and individual problems have been dealt with, I try to sit in on as many groups as possible during a 45 minute class period, staying with a group for at least the reading of one paper

and the subsequent discussion of it. This participation allows me to contribute to the response and to note the responses others are making.
As soon as possible after the class period, I make brief notes in an anecdotal record book about my observations in the groups. Reviewing these
notes periodically also helps me balance my time between groups, an
important detail when one has five or six different classes per day.

Audio or Video Taping of Response Groups

In addition to sitting in on groups, I try to have three or four tape
recorders distributed around the room to tape the proceedings. Generally,
I use small, inexpensive cassette recorders, either the school's or borrowed
from students. I request that the students keep the recorders on during
their entire session, including inevitable digressions from the writing at
hand. Then, in whatever spare time is available—usually in the car driving
back and forth to school—I listen briefly to each tape, running it ahead
until I find something of particular interest to play back to the class. I
listen especially for extremes—excellent, sustained response to a particular piece, or inattentive, non-helpful comments. The next day I play
sections back to the class, asking for their reactions and giving my own.
And I also enter my comments and evaluation of the tapes in my anecdotal
record book.

From time to time, I arrange to have response groups video-taped,
and then the whole class participates in playback discussion sessions.
The key point here is only to videotape volunteer groups; otherwise,
self-consciousness and resentment get in the way of the group process.
As mentioned earlier, I often use videotapes of past group sessions to
introduce the small group response process to new classes.

Noting Revision from Original to Final Draft

Another method of monitoring the progress of individual response
groups is to examine closely the revisions made from original to final
draft. Students are required to hand in all drafts of papers with the final
draft on top. I urge them to skip lines on their papers and make visible as
many of their revisions as possible, as well as writing down the questions
or comments made by their response partners. I find it takes very little
time to scan the first draft, noting the suggestions and revisions, before
closely reading the final draft. And the contrast (or lack of contrast)
between the drafts serves as the basis of my comments to the student.
As I worked with groups over the years, it became clear to me that if I
wanted students to take responsibility for responding to other writers'
papers and for revising their own, I must make both response and revision
the focus of my continual evaluation of student progress. If I find no
revision apparent between drafts of a paper which clearly needs it, then
I immediately return the paper to the student before evaluating it *and*

call over the student's response partners for a conference about their responsibility to the writer.

Another method of monitoring which has been suggested to me, although I have not tried it, is to ask members of a response group periodically to write comments to the teacher about the strong and weak aspects of their group's work.

Using Examples of Small Group Response

From time to time, when a particularly interesting exchange takes place, I transcribe a tape or section of a tape to share with students or other teachers as an illustration of the benefits of small group work. The two excerpts and one full transcript which follow are typical of those that I have duplicated in the past. They reveal students who are intent on clarifying what the writer was attempting to say. All are unedited, reproduced just as they occurred. I include them here as examples of response groups in action.

Excerpt from Transcript I

In the following excerpt, three eighth grade girls discuss a paper. The response partners (B and C) not only ask the writer (A) for clarification of terminology, but also suggest the form for revision.

A. (Eighth grade student who is reading her paper about a Russian gymnast)

"...she is the only woman gymnast that can do a round-off double back somersault."

B. Well, wait a minute, wait. What's that?

A. You know how you do a round-off back semi?

B. No.

A. Well, a back flip in the air. A back flip in the air.

B. Oh, is that when you're on the small one, and you go back...

A. She can do, she can do: OK, you know what a round-off is, right?

B. Yeah.

A. You know how you do...you know how I do a back-hand spring? And I try and do it with no hands?

B. Yeah.

A. Well that's....

B. You mean you're doing, she's doing, she can do two flips in the air without touching the ground?

A. Right, back, up....

B. One thing you might do, cause like, some people don't really know, like us...so like try to explain, just say "doing two back flips without touching the ground," or something like that.

   C. No, just write that down and then put in parentheses or dash, and then put it down, and after you write what it is, just put another dash.

Excerpt from Transcript II

This excerpt, also from a discussion by eighth grade girls, illustrates the involvement and concentration possible when partners are working well together. It is clear that the responder (A) has many questions about the situation (an elementary school drama production) her partner is describing, all of them forcing the writer toward more specificity of detail.

   A. ...and write the rest of the word down here. It's hard to read it, and you could, you could explain here, when it says, "If I could face all the kids who were in my drama class, why couldn't I face anybody else?" You could say, were they, were they laughing at you?

   B. No. Well, I don't know. I didn't want to hear any laughing, I was too embarassed to find out.

   A. Well, where, I mean did you just stand there? Forever?

   B. No, not forever. They didn't wait for me to say my lines. They just went on and said theirs. I couldn't blame them either.

   A. Or did they just stop a second...

   B. I just stood there like this, and about two, three seconds later they waited for me to say my lines, and then, they knew I wouldn't say them, and they, um, I just, I froze and then they said theirs. The two people behind me.

   A. But did they say, like (in a whisper) "Michelle, this is your line," you know?

   B. No.

   A. (whisper) "Say this."

   B. No, we weren't required to study any lines, like...we just had to make up our own. Because we didn't have many lines. The people who were standing, the eleven people...

   A. So what do you mean? I mean, like, we could be doing a play right now, or something, and I could just...make up my own lines?

   B. Yeah, that's right, as long as it has to do with the subject.

Transcript III

As an example of the entire process from first to final draft, I have included the following complete transcript of two seventh grade boys discussing a legend one has written. The session took place in late February; the boys had begun response group work the previous October. The transcript illustrates several important points about the benefits of small group work:

- The responder (J) asks many specific questions of the writer (T) who, in turn, increases the specificity of his final draft.
- Both boys become quite involved in the development of the legend. There is little extraneous talk and much concentration on the task at hand.
- By this time in the school year, the *process* of working in small groups has become natural to the students; they both exhibit great tact with each other and it is clear that they value each other's comments.

T. O.K. Let's do mine now.

J. O.K. Now start yours off...now read it then I'll...

T. You want me to read it...do you want to read it?

J. No, first you read it to me and then I'll look at it.

T. The wind howled over the topmast and the ship rocked and crashed. The Pacific...

J. Wait. What's the...title? Do you have a title for it?

T. Oh, well. Oh, I'll get that later...The Pacific Queen humbled along ever so slowly in a hurricane off Australia. The captain, Taylor Hobson, barked his orders over the rushing wind, trying to dodge the Great Barrier Reef. Looming over the ship, a twenty foot wave swept over the ship. It rocked and creaked and scattered supplies all over the ship. The crew weren't worried where they were going because of the supplies thrown on the ship. While they were cleaning the mess, the ship snuck toward the reef. A jarring noise ripped the ship and put a huge hole in the ship. Taylor had a lifeboat lowered in the rough sea. The men scurried about the doomed ship for provisions to supply the long journey of the lifeboat. The men scampered down the side of the ship. The lifeboat swayed away from her berth. While the men jumped ...while the men jumped. The men jumped but most...but most never made the lifeboat. Yells of "Help" filled the air as the Pacific Queen went under. Left on her were two dozen men, a few provisions, and twenty-one people were lost—one of them Captain Taylor Hobson. Forty-one people survived. The lifeboats floated around the ship's last stand. Dazed, injured, surprised and scared, the men didn't know what to do. The lifeboats were battered and the big waves didn't help much. Three men were injured but they had no first aid. The first mate, Samuel Gold, took charge. He tried to lash the three boats together with rope. Two boats got lashed, but the winds kept the lines from reaching the third boat. Night fell so fast that the men didn't notice until it was pitch black. The men couldn't sleep and the injured men groaned the night through. In the morning, Gold and the rest of the crew woke up to a terrible sight. Two of the three injured men had died in the middle of the night. Worst of all, the third boat was out of sight. Where was it? They couldn't follow it because they didn't know where it was...went. Morale was low; they thought they were going to die. Gold told the men that they wouldn't die and they would make it. Days passed. The morale grew because of Gold and his talks. The crew sang songs and took swims. The 23rd day...on the...23rd day... The 23rd day after the wreck they saw land. By night they landed. And it's not...I don't like my ending...Samuel Gold became a legend. See, I've got to write about the legend...a man...

J. Just say...um...Samuel Gold became famous for...well, after ...ok...after the...

T. Or I could just go...

J. ...after the story got out about the 23 men...

T. Yeah...

J. ...About the 23 men...

T. No, it's 40...oh, well...

J. The 45...whatever...After the story got out about how many men made it back and how Gold kinda led them back...

T. Yeah...

J. And kept their morale up and everything, you could say he became...

T. In the newspaper, how they...

J. famous in the country for...um...

T. his...

J. his achievement in getting...not losing...not losing his confidence...

T. Yeah...

J. And keeping up courage and...um...just knowing how to... do it...

T. Or I could say later he went back and put buoys or something, you know, to mark off...probably help the ship people, masters or whatever...

J. O.K.

T. O.K. Is it clear?

J. Yeah...

T. Could you understand it?

J. Yeah...it...like...it's just these...it was pretty...yeah...it wasn't boring. It was clear. I could understand it easily.

T. Yeah...but here I have the Pacific Queen, I got to say...

J. It was just...uh...

T. ...The Pacific Queen, a...like banana ship or a...

J. What kind of ship was it?

T. Yeah...

J. Like you got to say...

T. Yeah...

J. What was it doing? Like where was it going?

T. What...yeah...kind...

J. What was it...was it...a...uh...

T. Where...

J. Was it a tour ship? Was it a...

T. Yeah...

J. You know...like...

T. Yeah...

J. Did it have just men...or like...kind of like was it navy, army, or what?

T. Yeah...O.K....

J. Or was it a passenger ship?

T. But I think I should say more how they're...when they're in the lifeboats...I got to say more...

J. Yeah, say more...like you just...

T. Yeah, I know...

J. Talk about...like...um...what did they do? Did they have to eat anybody...like in *Survive*...

T. ...Yeah...

J. Did they have to do any...

T. Yeah, rationing...

J. ...super drastic things...like...where was their water... where did they get their water?

T. Yeah, well that was off the ship...O.K....um...all right...

J. What were they...like, were they...they were in the ocean, right?

T. Oh, yeah...O.K....here it starts...any more about them in the ocean...in...the...ocean...and...Yeah, and I got to describe more how their morale got higher and higher...

J. Tell them how he got the morale higher...how did he get

them going? Did he tell nice stories...Did they...you know
...did he...

T. Yeah...

J. Or did he...like did they catch fish at all. Did they have anything to catch fish with? Were there any attacks by sharks?
or did they...

T. ...yeah...

J. Were they scared? Were they really super scared about the
whales or anything?

T. ...Yeah...There are a lot of big...killer whales down there...

J. Yeah...there's a lot of sharks, I know that...

T. Yeah...

J. Like, were they rubber rafts or what?

T. Well, I got to say the date because the clipper ships. O.K.
what kind of ship...clipper...You know, it's back in 18
something or other. 18...

J. O.K. Um...

T. Um...date...1881...

J. O.K. yeah, well, that's what I was wondering...did they have
modern provisions...?

T. ...Yeah...

J. Did they have modern anything that was...

T. Or should I say that their lifeboats and all that were old stuff...

J. Ah huh...like they didn't have a motor on the boat...it was
pure rowing and manpower and...

T. Yeah...ok...old...what kind of...how should I say that...
Oh, were...Was equipment old? Was it...

J. Like was it modern to them? Did they think it was...for them
was it pretty good stuff or was it old...

T. Oh, yeah...

J. ...you know, kind of medium or...old...and...um...

T. ...old...old material or old...

J. ...like did they have to...did they do any rationing?

T. ...yeah...

J. Where did they get supplies? Did they bring food from the
ship or what?

T. Yeah...well, they got it off the ship before it sank...old supplies...did they ration...

J. Was the food O.K.?...or do you think it got...soggy or...?

T. Yeah, old food...yeah, all right...let's see, what's another of my questions...is it boring? I mean, should I add any more exciting...

J. No. ...Yeah, like the...like I'm not saying it's boring because it's not, it's pretty exciting...

T. Yeah...

J. ...but add...like if you can add something about...

T. ...the sharks...

J. Yeah, sharks...and did the guys fight amongst each other...

T. Yeah, I was going to...mutiny or something like that...

J. Yeah, did any of them...like, want to just die or...

T. Yeah...want to swim off...

J. Yeah, try to make it by himself...

T. O.K. let's see...what needs improvement?

J. Improvement...it was pretty...we've been kind of covering...

T. Yeah...

J. So I guess maybe...

T. Yeah, I guess we got everything...

J. O.K.

The Teacher's Response

Because this monograph is particularly about small group response sessions themselves, I will not describe in detail what happens to a paper after it has been revised. I will, however, briefly outline the subsequent steps to set the whole process in context.

1. If I have not been part of the response group, the writer may choose to have a brief conference with me before writing the final draft.

2. The student staples the final draft, typed and double-spaced or in ink and written on every other line, to the original draft and hands it in.

3. I read the final draft after skimming the original and then I:

- underline (without identifying) any mechanical, spelling, or structural errors. (I use discretion, of course, with individual students by choosing *which* errors it would be most helpful to point out.)

- write comments on the content of the paper at one side of the text or at the end. I attempt to make these comments specific and explanatory, not simply laudatory ("good!") or judgmental ("weak point").

The emphasis in my comments is on being understandable to the student so that a particular way of writing can be either eliminated or repeated in future papers. Here are some examples of helpful and non-helpful comments:

a. Not "good comparison," but "this comparison helps me imagine the size of that dog."

b. Not "weak point," but "you haven't given me enough background about what specifically happened at the party to let me understand why you felt this way."

c. Not "unclear," but "what *is* the connection you see between inflation and automobile production?"

This method of commenting might seem to take more time, but because response groups have eliminated many of the more obvious problems in student papers, it actually does not. And in the long run, the more I make specific the comments, the *fewer* times I have to repeat them over the course of a semester or a school year. Also, because the final papers end up in the students' writing folders, I can ask them to refer back to previous papers before completing current ones.

4. Before making any entry into a record or grade book, I hand back the papers and the students do the following:

- In the spaces between the lines, they correct any errors under-lined. If a word is misspelled, that word is written on the student's personal spelling list in the writing folder.

- Also, in the spaces between the lines, the students rewrite individual sentences for clarification.

When these changes have been completed, the student again hands in the paper and I check it over. *Now* the paper is finished and can be entered in the record book. I find that this way of handling papers eliminates the discouraging reaction where, in the past, after I handed back papers, students briefly glanced at the comments or the grade and then tossed them away.

EVALUATING RESPONSE GROUP WORK

If students have never experienced writing response groups before, it takes a while, probably one to two months, before they can be weaned from dependence upon immediate teacher evaluation of their writing and are comfortable with the longer process of response and revision. I find it imperative to remind students consistently of the value I place on this process. And, besides my daily attitude in class, my method of grading each quarter's work further emphasizes the importance I place on response and revision.

REPORT CARD EVALUATION

Below is a supplemental report card form I attach to the regulation one-sheet affair where all the different subject grades are paraded next to each other.

Language Arts / Literature / Personal Reading　　　**Grade Report**

SECOND QUARTER　　Name: _____
EIGHTH GRADE　　　Teacher: _____
　　　　　　　　　　　Section: _____

Student/Teacher Evaluation Form

I. *Language Arts:* One class period per day this quarter has been devoted to composition and literature. All writing is kept in the student's own folder—along with a record of the books he/she has read.

	Excellent		Satisfactory		Needs improvement	
	Stu.	Tea.	Stu.	Tea.	Stu.	Tea.
A. *Composition* 1. Original Drafts completed on time.						
2. Thoughtful response given to writing partner(s)						
3. Revisions made on original draft.						
4. Correction of underlined errors on final draft						
5. Misspelled words added to Personal Spelling Chart						

6. *Spelling*

　a. Record of weekly lists and study methods

　_____ _____ _____ _____ _____

　b. Record of test scores

　_____ _____ _____ _____ _____

　c. Personal spelling chart up to date:
　　　Yes: _____　No: _____

7. *Mechanical Skills to Work On*
   _____ eliminating run-on sentences
   _____ eliminating unnecessary sentence fragments
   _____ improving capitalization
   _____ improving punctuation, particularly _____

B. *Literature*

	Excellent		Satisfactory		Needs improvement	
	Stu.	Tea.	Stu.	Tea.	Stu.	Tea.
1. Understanding of stories read						
2. Participation in seminar discussions						
3. Quality of written work for seminar discussions						

FINAL LANGUAGE ARTS GRADE _____

II. *Personal Reading:* One class period each day this quarter has been devoted to personal reading, except for the students attending art class. All students have been expected to read at home as well.

A. My goal for the second quarter was to read _____ books.

B. I read _____ books during the second quarter.

C. Personal Reading Record completed thoroughly and up to date.
   Excellent: ____   Satisfactory: ____   Needs Improvement: ____
   Comments:

Student Signature: _____

Teacher Signature: _____

Parent Signature: _____

This form is eventually signed by the student, the teacher, and a parent, so it makes clear to all parties what is expected of students in the class. And, since all writing completed during a quarter is kept in a folder in the classroom, there is tangible evidence of involvement and progress over nine weeks' time. After this evaluation form is completed, it is stapled inside the student's writing folder as a reference for describing progress in the next quarter.

STUDENT-TEACHER EVALUATION SESSIONS

The appropriate columns of the report card form described above are completed by the student before I see it. I usually spend the last week of each quarter having a brief conference with each student in the class. We discuss the areas listed on the form, and I fill in the teacher's column by referring to the student's writing folder, my grade book, and my anecdotal record book, all three of which are before us as we talk.

This system makes the unreasonable task of assigning a single letter grade to an entire quarter's work less disturbing, primarily because the grade, required by the school administration and parents, is adequately documented and discussed, and is ultimately arrived at through agreement between the student and myself.

Coping with Problems

Often, when talking with other teachers who use response groups in the classroom, I've found that certain problems frequently surface. These are *real* problems and, like most aspects of classroom life, cannot be eliminated quickly. However, steps can be taken to help, so do not be discouraged if:

1. *Some students do not want to share their papers with other students.* This may be an indication of a student's lack of confidence in her writing ability. Initially, arrange for frequent opportunities for the whole class to respond to papers so that students become accustomed to the process. Then, if some students are still reluctant, work alone with them or in a small group with other reluctant students until they feel more comfortable with this process.

On the other hand, some student writers do not need small group response because they have evolved their own revision strategies. Accepting this, I usually ask the students to give response to others, even if they do not always ask for it themselves.

2. *Some students make superficial or non-helpful comments.* As in the suggestion above, whole-class response to papers helps underline the importance of specific, thoughtful comments. Also, it is helpful to tape groups in progress, and, after listening to the tapes, play back to the class

examples of particularly useful responses. Class discussion of the characteristics of a helpful response partner helps focus attention on what is
expected in groups. If all else fails, speak individually with students about
what is lacking in their response to writing partners.

3. *Some students do not feel they are helped by their writing groups.*
Examine the drafts of such student papers, looking especially for suggestions which have been made by the group and consequent revisions made
by the writer. If necessary, speak to the writer's response group about the
nature of their suggestions. Make your own suggestions to the writer and
perhaps recommend that the writer try joining another group.

4. *Some students fool around in the group and ignore the work at hand.*
Be particularly alert to a lack of revision in their papers and specifically
comment on it. Also, sit with troublesome groups and model response
behavior for them. If these methods fail, either disband the troublesome
group or LOWER THE BOOM in whatever way fits your particular style
as a teacher.

5. *Some students have well-written sections eliminated by their response
group.* While checking drafts you may come across lines or sections which
you think excellent but which disappear in the final version. Talk with the
student about this situation, explaining why you think the eliminated
writing is strong and why you would not eliminate it. However, always
leave the final choice up to the writer.

Summary

Students will, of course, develop differently in their abilities to respond
helpfully to each other's work. However, I believe that one of the most
important factors in determining how deeply students get involved with
the revision process is the value they place on response group interaction.

I can remember when I first used response groups in my classes how
impatient I became with the students' initial superficial comments, the
rapidity with which they raced through each other's papers, and the final
inevitable question: "Should we copy it over now?" And my reply: "You're
not copying it over, you're *revising* it. If there aren't any changes you want
to make, then just hand it in." Then the questioning student would turn to
another and say: "She said we didn't have to copy it over if we didn't want
to." In those days I probably called the whole class to attention and gave
(yet again) an earnest explication of the differences between recopying
and revision. Predictably, nothing would change on the basis of that talk.

I have since learned to ignore all but the most blatant misunderstandings
of the word *revision* and to wait. To wait until I can tape a notable exchange within a response group, play it back to the class, and ask them
what they hear happening. We discuss what they hear and then, if it is

available, look at the first draft of the paper in question and at the subsequent revision. I ask the class which they like better and why. Then we go on to other things, but I repeat the same process every time I tape a session. And, at the same time, I emphasize in my written comments instances of thoughtful revision I see in the papers I collect from the students. Slowly, as their perception of the differences between their first and second drafts grows, their involvement in the revision process deepens. But it takes time and continual nurturing, an effort sustained by my belief in the evolutionary development of an individual's writing ability.

To emphasize to your students your commitment to this writing process, it is helpful to take the following steps:

1. At the beginning of the school year or semester, be a response "group" of one for your students. Before students can offer their work for response in a small group, they must have a sense of themselves as students who *can* write. Consequently using small groups in a class of "remedial" writers is difficult. First, the *teacher* must be the *encouraging* responder who points out, again and again, what the students *can* do, at the same time designing lessons to help with the areas of major difficulty.

2. Don't be a strict critic of students' first efforts at small group response; instead, find areas to praise, to hold up as models, to encourage. Initially, talk generally to the whole class about areas for improvement rather than singling out a group for specific criticism. Some students learn best from seeing what other students do rather than from listening to the teacher.

3. Allow your actions to serve always as a model of responsive behavior. Question, comment, then question again. As all successful teachers know, the art of asking the right question at the right time is crucial. The "right" question is usually one which provokes thought and further action on the part of the person questioned.

4. Be a group member yourself and contribute a piece of writing which needs response. If your classroom situation will not permit you to join a student group, then try to join a writing group comprised of other teachers or friends. A writing teacher should be engaged in the writing process, somehow, somewhere.

5. Help the students to monitor their own writing development through a periodic review of their papers. Ask them to tell you the changes they notice over a period of time and then discuss your own observations.

6. At least once every two weeks, if not more often, read two versions of the same piece to the class and ask them to comment on the differences. This procedure helps students develop touchstones for making their own choices.

7. Finally, and most important, read to the students as often as possible. Have students in the class volunteer to read intriguing pieces they have found. By filling your classroom with a rich diversity of language, you are actively building the store of resources the students will bring to their writing.

Writing Class: Teacher and Students Writing Together

Dick Friss
Northgate High School, Walnut Creek

I wont out of this class, Becouse it is An A.B class AnD I Belong in An C,B class, I Am not planing on going to Callage Becouse it takes money AnD Im not rich I might learn some thing in this class But Id rather ReAD more than I would wrisht in An english class.

This was my first introduction to Ken. I was teaching a new writing class for tenth graders who had done poorly in ninth grade English. I was not exactly warmed by Ken's first written statement but wrote on his paper, "If that is what you want, see your counselor and present the reasons you have written here. I'm sure something can be worked out." Little did I know that in the ensuing months, Ken and I would be working together with mutual eagerness, and that he would be a source, not only of challenge, but of inspiration that would last long after the semester course had ended.

Most of the students enrolled in "Writing Clinic AB" (or "Writing Class," the title I gave the course) had been recommended by their ninth grade English teachers the year before but, given the realities of our high school, there were also eleventh and twelfth graders in the class. Some of these had signed up to resolve schedule conflicts. They had needed an English class, and the period mine was offered had fit easily into their schedules. A few had wanted to have me for their teacher. Others had been left stranded without an English class at the end of registration and had been placed in my class by their counselor. The result of this "selection process" was a group of rather mixed abilities rather than a remedial class.

The modest goal for the course, set by the English department, was to help students having difficulty at the sentence level and, by the end of the semester course, to move them to proficiency at the paragraph level, so that they might more easily succeed in the elective program for tenth through twelfth grades. These goals were also chosen to "protect" the integrity of the "Composition" classes where more ambitious objectives were entertained.

By the time the course began in the fall, it had taken on a new identity and new goals in my mind. These changes had come about largely because of my participation in the Open Program of the Bay Area Writing Project during the summer, an experience that caused me to have greater faith in what I felt to be valid about writing and the teaching of that process; and a teachers' strike with long hours on the picket line in which to sort out what really mattered in my life, particularly in the teaching of writing. It would further change as a result of my encounter with Ken and his classmates once the course had begun, expanding and crystallizing many of the practices I now take for granted in the teaching of writing in *all* classes.

As the course opened, my goal was to help students develop their own writing styles rather than imitate someone else's—their teacher's, Twain's, James's, etc. This did not mean total permissiveness or lack of guidance. To me, guidance means *drawing forth* rather than putting in. Another related goal was to help students say what *they* wanted to say for an audience beyond the teacher. The framework for the class became personal experience writing: students writing about themselves, their experiences, feelings, and *ideas.* I hoped that through this type of writing experience each student would come to see the value of his own personal experience and how it had contributed to making him who he was, and to see that the writing process, by taking subjective experience and objectifying it, would intensify this understanding. I also wanted them to arrive at answers to two important questions: What is writing? Why do we do it? I shakily promised myself to abandon anything that did not work and to be open to new ideas wherever they came from. The latter decision led to one of the most valuable experiences of my teaching career: using the teacher's writing process as a tool for teaching writing to students. The suggestion came from my students and grew out of our mutual frustrations along the way.

The school in which I taught, though located in what is loosely called "suburbia," was in reality much like an inner city school: downtown;

working class, primarily, with the last remnants of solid middle class; a smattering of foreign students (Asian, Persian) and a few blacks. Total enrollment—about 2,000. My own classroom was often described as "weird" by students, for all available wall space was covered with posters; hand written quotes from literature, the arts, "Peanuts"; poems, including those of my students; objects created in the varied elective courses I taught—anything to stimulate thought and feeling and to celebrate the human condition. My favorite and most often quoted proverb was, "If you give a man a fish, he will have a single meal; if you teach him how to fish, he will eat forever."

Into this setting drifted Ken, a tall, lanky seventeen-year old, and his twenty-four classmates. After I had explained the course and its objectives, we began our first day, as we did every day thereafter, with journal entries. I asked the class to "fill up a page or two with whatever is on your mind today. Do not be concerned about form, spelling, etc., but be clear." Once this writing had been done, I asked the class to "select one idea out of what you have written and write about it in more detail." This was their first assignment. It was in response to these directions that Ken wrote his "I want out of this class" paper. As days passed, we brainstormed for ideas, childhood memories, specific topics; played with sentence combining; indulged in word associations and games that led to the generation of sentences and paragraphs; wrote daily journal entries: sometimes free-writing, sometimes on topics I suggested. Occasionally this writing was shared in groups of four students each. Sometimes what the group considered best was shared with the whole class.

We began our second major writing assignment by reading and discussing the material I had prepared on SHOWING AND NOT TELLING* in writing. Then the students started the written assignment.

Showing and not Telling in Writing

Telling:

> Each morning I ride the bus to school. I wait at the corner along with the other people who ride my bus. Sometimes the bus is late and we get angry. Some guys start fights and stuff just to have something to do. I'm always glad when the bus finally comes.

> —Seventh Grader

Showing:

> A bus arrived. It discharged its passengers, closed its doors with a hiss, and disappeared over the crest of a hill. Not

---

*This assignment was suggested by a presentation by Rebekah Caplan in the Bay Area Writing Project Open Program, summer, 1977.

TEACHING WRITING

one of the people waiting at the bus stop had attempted to board. One woman wore a sweater that was too small, a long loose skirt, white sweat socks, and house slippers. One man was in his undershirt. Another man wore shoes with the toes cut out, a soiled blue serge jacket and brown pants. There was something wrong with these people. They made faces. A mouth smiled at nothing, and unsmiled, smiled and unsmiled. A head shook in vehement denial. Most of them carried brown paper bags rolled tight against their stomachs.

from *The Book of Daniel*
by E. L. Doctorow

Re: showing

1. What is the subject of each paragraph?
2. What words show something about the bus in paragraph two?
3. What do we learn about the people at the bus stop in the order they are presented?
4. What does "showing" do that "telling" does not?
5. What is the writer's attitude toward the people at the bus stop? How do you know? Cite evidence.

After discussing ditto on the above, write a paragraph that *shows* rather than one that merely tells. Begin with a simple statement you can expand through use of details and descriptive words. Develop it like the model from *The Book of Daniel.*

Suggested "openers" like "A bus arrived":

1. The bell rang. (a school situation)
2. The car came to a stop.
3. The teacher began to speak.
4. The cheerleaders exploded onto the field.
5. The door opened.
6. My dad began to frown.
7. The news came an hour ago.
8. I opened the letter.

During the beginning of the writing, I circulated about the room asking questions in response to those of the students, drawing them out, responding to "what do you think of this?" I found Ken stuck but smiling. In talking to him I discovered he had a wealth of ideas but couldn't get started. I later came to realize he felt he couldn't write (by which he meant spelling, grammar, syntax) and thus felt he *had* no ideas. By encouraging him to focus on what he wanted to say, supplying sufficient details so the reader could see and feel the experience as he did and forgetting about spelling, grammar, etc., I finally got him to try the assignment. A crucial part of this process, not only for Ken but all students, is the climate of mutual respect developed in the interchange.

The following is the process we used weekly for all major writing assignments:

Process Used in Writing Groups

A. Students write first draft of a given assignment.

B. Students proofread paper and copy onto ditto.

C. Papers are then run, a copy for each writing group member (4).

D. Students meet in writing group and, *one at a time,*
   1. hand out copies of their paper
   2. read paper to group
   3. receive comments and help from group members who:
      a. tell writer what they *liked* about the paper
      b. tell writer what he could do to make his writing clearer, more effective, more interesting.

   This process continues until all papers are read and commented upon.

E. Students rewrite papers, handing in dittoed draft with suggested changes and finished paper.

F. Teacher reads finished paper, comments and returns to student.

G. Student reads comments from teacher, shares with writing group and returns paper to teacher.* Papers are kept in student's file in classroom.

On the following pages is Ken's attempt at the previously described assignment developing the lead line: "The car came to a stop." The first version is his rough draft with changes and my comments. The second is his revision after meeting with his group and reading my comments.

---

*This step was not part of the original process but was added as a model for students' comments on papers being read.

The car came to a stop The inside of the car was Filled with white smoke that had come from the Tires when the driver locked the Brakes up and sent the car sliding and skidding down the steep Hill untill it came to rest At Bottom. Then I noticed the man who was Driving, seemed to have a half smile on his Face, As if he had Just head A funny Joke And Didn't laugh Just smiled. I started to get out when he started up the Hill As fast or Faster than we came Down, you could hear the car straning As it went up the Hill, when we got to the top he Didn't say A word he just Drove on Just like nothing ever happend

Ken:

I think your group should have given you some help with punctuation. Sentences begin with capital letters and end with periods.

The car came to a stop. The inside of the car was filled with white smoke that had come from the tires when the driver locked the Brakes up and sent the car sliding and skidding down the steep Hill untill it came to rest at the Bottom. Then I noticed the man who was Driving, it seemed to have a half smile on his face, As if he had just heard A Funny Joke and didnt laugh just smiled I Started to get out when he started up the hill as Fast or Faster than we came Down, you could hear the car straining as it went up the hill, when we got to the top he didnt say a word he just drove on just like nothing ever happend

Were you in the car? From your writing you didn't seem to be

Use handwriting and observe rules for capitalization and punctuation.

What you have written about—a deranged driver—is interesting. You maintain a cool aloofness throughout the paragraph in spite of the wild scene. How you write it—punctuation?—is confusing.

After our first writing group discussions, I had students write in their journals what this experience was like for them. Here is such an entry from a girl who also had been a student of mine the previous year in ninth grade English:

> I survived the first week in your class. I must confess, I really feel I can be myself in here cause I love writing like this. Even though it might not be so hot "yet". Talking to everyone, as we did in our groups today, was really a feeling that's hard to describe. It made you feel as though you were the teacher. Helping everyone, and receiving advice that you need to help you do better. Everyone was honest towards each other. The working in groups, telling the stories we've composed and getting the advice from people our own age, helped me get over my problem of reading my works out loud (not entirely but it helped.) I hope when this semester is over, I will be doing my work the way you have wanted me to for over a year. Thank you for recommending me to this class. I felt at first, I was sorta dumb, cause I didn't get to choose the Eng. class I wanted (I was free to do so but I chose your recommendation because you have more knowledge on what's right for me.) But when I saw M. G---- and M. M---- (maybe others) I felt I was lucky. Thank you again, you don't know how I appreciate this.

Because of what I learned from reading the students' journals (each had an assigned day of the week to hand it in) and because of my new observations about the class, I made my first major departure from what had initially been outlined. First I requested students hand in their very first drafts in addition to the dittoed second draft and final draft. I wanted to get a larger picture of whatever changes occurred from first to last writing. Secondly, and I held my breath on this one, I told the class I would like to stop putting grades on their papers. Originally, each weekly writing assignment was to be graded. Quarter and semester grades were to be based on improvement and the number of completed assignments. We discussed my proposal. I wanted us to be free of grades. *I* wanted to be free of my anxiety in trying to assign an appropriate grade for improvement when the same paper in another class would earn a lower grade. I wanted my students to be free of anxiety about grades so they could concentrate on the writing process. The class agreed, and no paper ever received a grade again. As a result of the students' difficulty with our next assignment —write a short paper telling how you began doing something you customarily do—I introduced a third change. I did the assignment myself. In so doing, I saw where the difficulties were and thus prepared better directions. Little did I know this was to become a regular feature of the course. My paper and the new directions follow.

The Purple Pen

Some years ago, an enormous Huck Finn appeared in one of my Freshmen English classes. Despite his seeming attentiveness to everything other than what was going on in our class, he could verbally recount everything that had been discussed, responses to the topic and what the speaker was wearing. But when it came to writing, Chuck was a Mo-Ped in the Indianapolis 500.

We discussed this reluctance to deal with writing on many occasions. We even began writing back and forth in the margins of his "papers," sometimes leaving them looking like they had been removed from the flesh of the "illustrated man." This dialogue was long in getting started and came about by pure chance.

Apparently, on a series of papers, at a time when my comments were really being read, I had used a purple pen. Since our class wrote almost daily, there was much purple flowing forth until the day arrived when the pen dried up and I picked up whatever was handy.

The next day, when I returned the papers, Chuck, who made a great show of never reading my comments, said "Where's the purple pen? Why'd you switch?" I was stunned. He'd been reading my comments all along, perhaps even looking forward to them. That day after school I bought several purple pens and I have never used any other kind with student papers since.

J. R. Friss

Assignment: Write a short paper telling how you began doing something you customarily do.

Give some thought to something you do and how this practice originated.

Begin writing about how this activity or attitude originated. (See paragraphs one and two above.)

Then tell what the activity is and how you came to continue it. (See paragraphs three and four above.)

Choose some simple activity that has become a part of your life, something you are experienced with and have knowledge of. It need not be some earth-shaking activity that changed the world.

For some reason, Ken did not do what came to be known as the "Purple Pen" assignment, so his entry is not included here. There followed a two week period wherein I felt I was spinning my wheels and getting nowhere or, at least, the class and I were not travelling with the momentum and enthusiasm previously established. I attributed this "stall" to a well motivated but poor decision on my part. I attempted to introduce literature into our writing class: Maya Angelou's *I Know Why the Caged Bird Sings*. The class enjoyed my reading to them and our discussions, particularly about how Angelou wrote vividly of place and memories. Yet we seemed to get farther away from the quality of experience we had previously enjoyed. We had turned away from our lives and were now looking at that of another who seemed remote. I was unable to make the needed connections. With a sense of guilt, partly induced by the old admonition that literature and composition must be integrated and never taught separately, something I came to disagree with, I dropped the biography as part of our class work. Students continued to read on their own. I attempted to get us back on the road we had veered from: students writing from their own experience.

Since first quarter grades were on the horizon and because I wanted to know how *I* was doing, I had students begin writing what came to be known as the "letter to J.R." The directions follow. Before writing, we reviewed the course objectives, talked about my goals as well as any they may have set for themselves, and discussed the class procedures being used. I tried to get across the idea that this letter was not "just an assignment," but that I was really interested in what they had to say. I asked them to be very specific and, while they were writing this to me, also to keep in mind a larger audience of English teachers everywhere. Those instructions launched them into heated discussion that continued until the bell rang. As they walked out, I wondered how many would really write when the heat of the moment had died down.

> Given the goals listed for this class in the front of your folder, write me a letter—in your best writing form—telling me the following:
>
> 1. how am I doing as your writing teacher (include reasons why you feel this way);
> 2. what kind of assistance would you like that you are not getting;
> 3. what has been helpful so far in making you a better and/or more confident writer;
> 4. how do you now feel about your writing groups as a source of help
>   a) strengths
>   b) weaknesses
>   c) would you like to continue with the same group for the second quarter;

5. anything else you'd care to share at this time.

I would like your sincere comments in your best writing.

Ken chose to respond to this challenge. His letter signaled some departures from his earlier writing. It was more formal. He wrote to specific points relevant to himself. He ventured criticism of some of our practices but did so with a sense of humor. He was able to recognize the connection between frequent writing and improvement. He asserted himself, something new for him. Above all, he stated his ideas clearly. He had become involved.

Dear Mr Friss

you have stated in a ditto you handed out earlier this year that this class will help me improve my hand writing, vocabulary, spelling and so on. So far in my opinion, I have gotten better in all the Feilds that you listed on the ditto and I think this shows how you are doing as my writing teacher.

I think I need some assistance in punctuation). I should be getting in in my writing group but Im not, I think its because we are all afraid to say some thing and there are no girls in my group and they almost always have some thing to say.

I think I am getting better and more comfident in my writing because I am writing more so I get more practice.

As a source of help my writing group is dead. I think I would rather be in another group next quarter.

I am have some trouble in this

Class and it is making me work harder but
I think I will (profit) for this experince
as I get older

Yours truly

Kenneth

I read the letters with great enthusiasm and, because of them, made some changes in our class. The first was a modification of the writing group process (see pp. 293). After papers were read by me, they were returned to individual student writers who read them with my comments as before. But now these teacher evaluated papers were read by each member of the group. My reason for introducing this step was to permit students to see my response to their group members' papers and thus get a clearer idea of how they might have been helpful to each other at the revision and editing stages. The second change was in restructuring the writing groups. From the letters, I learned most students did not want to work in a group in which participation was low or non-existent. While I felt and stated to the class that even without a paper a student could learn from the process, they felt they, the writers, were being short-changed by not seeing writing from everyone and not getting as much help as possible. I decided to let them handle the problem as they chose. This meant that, generally, groups were formed on the basis of who had a paper. Ironically, this procedure got the non-writers writing more regularly. Ken moved to a group of better writers, another boy and two girls who "almost always (had) something to say." The third change in class procedure proved to be the most valuable of all and came from the students themselves. I was to do each assignment and join a writing group each week, handing out dittoed copies, reading my paper, receiving suggestions (they *did* come), and helping each member with revision. My participation included help with the thorny problem of how to give constructive criticism on a piece of writing while leaving the writer's dignity intact. I was also to move about from group to group each week. At this point, I became more involved in the writing process because I, too, now had a "real" audience: my students. The first week I joined a group, I noticed a definite lowering of the noise level around the room when I read my paper. Everyone wanted to hear what the teacher had written. To get around this disruption in the other groups' process, I promised I would read my paper to the class after group meetings but before the students' final editing. With this promise the room returned to its usual productive noise level and we were off once again.

The first assignment in which we all participated follows:

> The purpose of this piece of writing is to describe a room or place that is very familiar to you, one that is vivid in your memory.
>
> Your writing should *show* the reader, create a vivid picture in his mind by the clear way you use words. Your choice of words should not only cause your readers to *see* the room or place, but also they should feel what it is like to be there. You may also wish to use dialogue and typical action to bring the place into your readers' minds. Try to use some of the sentence combining skills we have been practicing on worksheets. These skills should enable you to create sharp, vivid images.
>
> Your audience is your writing group who has not seen the room or place you are writing about.
>
> Try to write *at least* one highly descriptive paragraph of six to ten sentences. The number of sentences is not as important as is the clear, vivid picture you create.

To prepare for the assignment we brainstormed to discover various ways we might view the room and came up with this list:

room or place, ways to view

contents	changes in people
architecture	tempo of activities
effect of light and temperature	who shares room
activities	compare room to person, object
time of day	effect of time and activities
people there (doing what?)	compare full to empty
changes during day	conversations therein
purpose of room	general vs. detailed appearance
feelings generated	

While students had been *hearing* my writing before—I had read my responses to various short assignments—with the exception of the "Purple Pen" paper, they had never seen it before. Below is my entry. I am writing from this room now.

My Study

Sunlight filters into the quiet room through a window overlooking a terraced garden in which tall trees stand guard at the highest point, providing privacy to the room within. Perpendicular to the window, a wall of books reaches from floor to ceiling, inviting one who stops here to explore the recorded endless journeys of the mind while sinking into the rust colored cushions of an an-

cient, friendly sofa, across the room, that has nourished young and old for almost a hundred years. Above this, on the wall, framed drawings mirror memories of forty years: a young man whose aristocratic head held high welcomes all challenges, confidently; a Miami debutante—clear eyed, full mouthed, regal; a large nude woman whose soft, brown, supple body caresses and envelopes the chair of which her body has taken possession; an abstract, elongated line drawing of two opposing groups, each accusing the other; a smaller frame almost exploding from the tension of the struggling figures locked within. Dominating the room by its enormous size and central position, stands an elegantly carved, massive, walnut desk whose endless papers, books and organized clutter await the occupant's return from school. Near the door, on a small rush seated chair from Mexico, sits a papier mache, pig-tailed, little girl with freckles scattered across her face and flowing hands that dance stories only fathers of little girls are blessed to know and understand.

　　　　　　　　　　　　　　　　　　　　　　　J. R. Friss

With this assignment, Ken began a series of papers written with sensitivity and vitality, and vivid in imagery. He was more open in class, actively seeking my help and that of other students. He became a respected member of the class and engaged in heated discussion, anxiously wrestling with the frustrations of writing which, I feel, he began to see as part of the writing process all writers engage in. He saw that those he had placed far above him as writers—his teacher, other students—also struggled. Included here are the dittoed paper he took to his writing group and his finished paper. Note the changes he has made in his "final" draft, changes made *after* I had read and evaluated his writing. This revision showed his degree of involvement and his recognition that a piece of writing is never really finished.

It was early morning. In the boat everybody seemed to be tense, afraid to relax, as the boat cuts through the water. Approaching the beach, something about it reminds me of a movie of people going to a deserted island ~~looking for gold~~ ~~in the jungle.~~

When we landed, each of us
started picking up ~~tube~~ inner tubes, fishing poles
and went our seperate ways ~~off~~
into the island. The island seemed
alive with all the rats + birds ~~w~~
~~W~~atching you walk down the path,
as if they wanted to make sure you
were no threat to them.

Nobody had seen ~~anybody~~ each one all day.
As it started to get dark, One by one
the people started to come back to
the boat. You could sense there was
a change in them. they were ~~both~~ Loose, Laughing,
~~and~~ talking to^eachother. As we went
back to the harbor they seemed to
be thinking about the next week
of work that would leave them
frustrated and tense.

It was early morning. In
the boat everybody seemed to be tense, afraid
to relax, as the boat cuts through the water.
Approaching the beach, something about it reminds (1)
me of a movie of people going to a deserted
island. To die

When we landed, each of them us started picking
up our inner tubes and fishing poles and went
their seperate ways off into the island The
island seemed alive, with all the rats & birds
watching you walk down the path, as if
they wanted to make sure you were no threat (2)
to them.

[Handwritten manuscript with corrections:]

Nobody had seen any one all day. As it
started to get dark, one by one the people started
to come back to the boat. You could sense
there was a change in them. They were loose,
laughing and talking to and at each other.
As we went back to the harbor ~~they~~ we/they seemed ③
to be thinking abought the next week of
work that would leave them frustrated
and tense,

[Teacher's response, handwritten:]

Ken: This is your best writing so far — one of the best
pieces in the class. It is alive with detail and worded
so as to make the reader feel it. I hope your group enjoyed
it as much as I.

① Don't change tenses. You began with "seemed" — past tense —
so keep it with "reminded".

② Very effective sentence.

③ Are these two different groups of people? no

Beware of using capital letters in the middle of words and
in the middle of sentences (unless these are proper nouns)

By our next assignment, it became apparent to the class that we had
been engaged in a series of autobiographical pieces that ultimately would be
a portrait of the writer. A plan began to take shape in my mind to find
some way to supply each student with a book in which, near the end of
the course, he would copy all his pieces, complete with title and table of
contents. I did not tell them of this plan out of fear they would find it too
formidable a task. Once again, they later proved my fears unfounded.

As in all assignments, we began the next with varied pre-writing activities that included sharing memories orally. This process looks like a
gigantic bull session and probably appeared that way to some students but
is an invaluable part of the writing process. Below is our next assignment
and my response.

Write a paper telling about the first time you did something.*
Suggestions:

- the first time you thought you loved someone not in your family
- the first time you smoked a cigarette
- the first time you got in trouble with a teacher

---

*This assignment was suggested by a presentation by Gerry Camp in the Bay Area Writing
Project Open Program, summer, 1977.

- the first time you kissed someone who was not in your family
- the first time you drove a car or motorcycle
- the first time you got lost
- the first time you were away from home overnight
- the first time you won an argument with your mom or dad
- the first time you cut a class
- the first time you broke up with a girlfriend or boyfriend
- the first date
- the first day in a new neighborhood or city
- the first day in a new school

Your paper might include:

1. Introduction: background
2. People involved: what are they like?
3. Setting in which incident occurred, including feelings
4. The incident in detail
5. How it worked out in detail
6. Conclusion: what you learned from the experience that is still part of your life.

The First Time

Discipline. Most families are concerned with it but it is usually a one way street: whatever parents decide is the law. Thus, as a small child, it never occurred to me that it could be otherwise, at least in the early years.

Mom was hopelessly Irish in temperament and personality, a strong, determined woman with a sense of humor who, at five feet, towered over my younger sister and me. She ruled us with a firm, loving hand. She was always right. Probably because she was often away working, she appeared to trust us a great deal, particularly when we were left alone from around age ten on. Like most children, on these occasions, my kid sister and I sometimes got into squabbles and I, being my mother's son, would attempt to settle the argument as she did, firmly and with a whack across my sister's butt with whatever was near. Once it was an umbrella.

My usual punishment for some infraction was a good licking across my backside with the firm, cold, ivory hairbrush, normally displayed in a prominent position along with other acouterments of beauty, atop my mother's dresser. After the incident with the umbrella one evening when mom was away at work, I knew the inevitable scene would occur the next day after my sister, Georgia, reported me for overstepping the limits of my self-proclaimed authority. The hours of terror I experienced from that evening until the next afternoon when I returned from school were ri-

*valed only by the Inquisition. I had been wrong. I knew it. And
I also knew I would be punished in the traditional manner. Still,
it seemed unfair at age ten to be so demeaned.*

*After school the following day, the trial began. The plaintiff
stated her charges. The judge made the usual inquiries to establish their validity. The defendant pleaded "guilty." The instrument
of punishment was produced. The punishment carried out. But
in the midst of it, full of indignation and relying on the advantage
of finally towering a good inch over my mother, I swung round,
grabbed the brush from her hand and laid a hard crack right
across her ass. To this day I have never known what entered her
mind at that precise moment, but I have never been struck by
her since, nor have I ever used this form of punishment on my
young daughter.*

J. R. Friss

Ken continued his love affair with the water, using this new assignment
to focus on another aspect. Following are his three drafts. The first is his
very first attempt. He wanted me to read it before putting it on ditto. I did.
We discussed the paper, made some changes, largely in spelling, tenses
and sentence signals. Then follows his second draft with a few changes
suggested by his writing group. Last is his final draft. Here notice greater
control over language, tightness of expression, clear, vivid details, a new
sophistication with language, but always the authentic voice: his.

It was the 4th of July and
the man on the radio said it
was going to be 105°.
My Dad came in and said
we were going to go out in a
boat on the river with his brother
and his family. When we all got
to the launching dock, there
was too many of us to go to the
beach at once, we had to
go in two trips. When we
got to the beach some of us
started fishing and some of us swimming.

My Dad's Brother started to talk about water skiing so I decided to give it a try, — ~~will~~ I got into the water. they handed me the skis and the rope. they told me to put on the skis, and hang on for dear life to the rope, and ~~told me~~ to holler when I was ready. The skis ~~got~~ started to float as I got in deeper water. It seemed they had a mind of ~~their~~ their own. they were floating every where except ~~the~~ where I wanted them to. finally I half way mastered them and ~~&~~ said "go". ~~Nothing happened.~~ ~~except~~ I must have ~~so~~ swallowed 5 gallons of water and inspected the river bottom personaly. I didn't try water skiing for a long ~~to~~ time after thate

It was the 4th of July and the man on the radio said it was going to be 105°F. My Dad came in and said we ~~were~~ are going to go out in a boat on the river ~~with~~ with his brother and his family." When we all got to the launching dock, there were to many of us to go to the beach at one time, so we had to make two trips. when we got to the beach some of us started fishing and some went swimming.

                uncle

My ~~dad's brother~~ started to talk abought water skiing so I decided to give it a try. I got into the water. They handed me the skis and the rope and ^{said} to holler when I was ready.

The skis started to float as I got
in deeper water. It seemed they
had a mind of their own. They were
floating every where except where I
wanted them to. Finally I half way
mastered them and said "go". Nothing
happened. I must have swallowed 5
gallons of water and inspected the
river bottom personally. I didn't try
to water skiing for a long time
after that.

It was the 4th of July
And the man on the radio said it
was going to be 105°F. My Dad
came in and said, "we are going to
go out in a boat on the river with
his brother and his family". When we
all got to the launching dock, there
were to many of us to go to the
beach at one time, so we had to make
two trips. When we got to the beach
some of us started fishing and some
went swimming.

My uncle started to talk
abought water skiing so I decided to
give it a try. I got into the water.
They handed me the skis and the rope
and told me to holler when I was ready.
The skis started to float as I got in
deeper water. It seemed they had a ①
mind of their own. They were floating
every where except where I wanted them
to. Finally I half way mastered them
and said "go". Nothing happend ②. I must

have swallowed 5 gallons of river water
and inspected the river bottom personally (1.)
I didn't try to water skiing for a
long time after that.

This is a well written account of your first times on
water skis. Clear, vivid details make the experience come
alive for your readers.

(1.) Good detail

(2.) This short, blunt sentence, coming after "so", is very effective.

When Thanksgiving week arrived, I had much to be thankful for. My enthusiastic students had enabled me to escape the demoralizing aftermath of the teachers' strike that had begun our school year, to replace those feelings of frustration my colleagues were still laboring under with excitement and a sense of accomplishment. Our class had taken on a school-wide identity as a place of work that somehow was fun. Visitors dropped in, particularly on days when writing groups met. On this three-day Thanksgiving week, Ken embarked on his most ambitious piece of writing in terms of effort, staying power, and sensitivity. He asked if he could change the assignment slightly. I agreed. I am still moved by this piece of writing a year later. In the following pages, notice that he has a first draft, a second draft, his ditto copy shared with his group, and his final paper with my comments. The directions given students for the assignment and my paper precede Ken's work.

Assignment

Write about an incident, using the vignette form:*
a) begin with a few lines of dialogue;
b) then explain what the dialogue is about;
c) then narrate (tell the incident working in more dialogue);
d) then give any analysis of your own that seems appropriate.

When you have finished your first draft, review the above to make sure your paper includes all the necessary information. You might care to begin by reviewing your lists of memories: 0-5 years; 5-10 years; 10-the present (in your journal).

---

*This assignment was suggested by a presentation by Tim Boorda in the Bay Area Writing Project Open Program, summer, 1977.

Rainy Day Reverie

"It's coming down in buckets!"
"Beat you to the porch!"
"Last one there's a sissy!"

Racing from the street to the protection of our wooden porch, sweating from the run and wet from the mid-western summer rain, we collapsed in rapturous giggles on the inside hall stairs, safe from the sudden downpour outside.

No matter where I've gone in all the years since then, the smell of cold, sudden rain sizzling on summer sidewalks takes me back to my childhood in St. Louis. Driven indoors from play by the fickle weather, my friend Tom, my sister Georgia, and I huddled together, laughing in the energy of love. I idolized Tom, so often in recycled army fatigues or T-shirt and worn jeans and, always, the battered hat, symbol of his freedom from convention.

How I had wished I could be like that, free of the past that always enveloped me, forcing me to be more correctly dressed, always color coordinated, neat and clean, fresh after hours of play: my armour that denied the pain that had begun when dad went away and my world fell apart. My creaseless clothes proclaimed a smoothly unruffled childhood. It would be years before I could relax enough to live in the moment, like Tom. At the time, it never occurred to me that he might have had his private disaster.

As I looked at her then, convulsed by the communion of laughter, Georgia appeared not to be my younger sister at all. Pigtails, once fresh strands of perfectly braided hair, now came out like porcupine quills in disarray. Escaped ringlets framed her smiling freckled face. Her clothes of many patterns, in comfortable conflict, ignored the adult-commanded dress code, mirroring eclectic childhood games where identities changed with the latest fantasies. A loving, wren-like girl, all soft and plump, she filled my heart with love.

I no longer remember how such days ended. It seems unimportant now. But what returns with the smell of cold rain sizzling on summer sidewalks, in any part of the world I happen to be, is the memory of friendship and love and the knowledge that these are ever present in all life's circumstances if we only choose to **be.**

J. R. Friss

1

Gregg you got a hit your pole

The place - a small Boat in the middle
of the river, resting Behind a rusting away
moth balled ship. Three people fishing,
to of them talking the third is lissoning
in and watching the poles. Then the
Tip of one of the poles gose wild. gerking
down and then relaxing and then down
again. again. ~~Too one ~~ ~~one of the~~
~~people it~~ a person jumps up and
grabs the pole and starts to set
to hook. half way over his sholde
he is stoped in and ~~swing~~ swing. The
pole is bemg bent by the weight
of the fish as it run's. By ~~this~~
Time the other two people in the
boat are standing on the seats and
playing the fish in thire minds
as if they were fighting the fish. —
The ~~Drag~~ is screaming as the line
is being polled out of the open Faced
real He tightens down the Drag
to no avail as a last resourse He
puts his thump on the line and
Stops the fish and starts to real
the fish ~~in the draps out of th line~~
~~out of the water that are in The battle~~
is ~~ar~~ the fisherman is winning
Almost over

2

~~The fish wasn't ga~~ Then all of
sudden the fish breaks water in
a large splash and starts to run
again But is stoped by the a wip
of the pole, the fish and the fisharman
are exosted from the Fight. As ~~they~~ the
2 that were watching pull the fish into
the boat the a tired man sets
down with his pole ~~to the boat~~ and
with his loose hand he pries his
hand off his pole his prize a
72 inch sturgen the most ugryest andstron.
fish in the river

✱✱✱

Hey you got a hit, your pole

     A small boat in the middle
of the river, resting behind a rusting away
moth balled ship. Three people fishing, two
of them talking, the third listening in
and watching the piles. Then the tip of
one of the poles gose wild, jerking down and
then relaxing and then down again. A person
jumps up and grabs the pole and starts
to set the hook, half way over his shuider
he is stop in mid swing as the fish starts
to run. The drag is screeming as the
line is being pulled out of the open faced
real over the bent pole and into the water.
he trys to tighten down the drag to no avale
as a last resourse he puts his thumb on

line and stop the fish in its tracks. The
Battle is all most over the fisherman is
winning. As a last fighting chance the fish
breaks water in a large splash and starts to
run again but is stoped by a wip of the pole,
the fish is exhausted from the fight, by
this time the other two people in the boat are
standing on there seats and playing the fish
in thire minds as if they were fighting the
fish. As the two that were watching pull the
fish into the boat a tired man sets down
with his pole in his hand and with his
lose hand prys his fingers off the pole, His prize a
72 inch sturgen the most uglyest fish and the strong

in the river

Bite

Hey you got a ~~bite~~ strike, your pole

A small boat in the middle
of the river, resting behind a rusting away
moth balled ship. Three people fishing, two
of them talking, the third listening in
and watching the poles. Then the tip of
one of the poles gose wild, jerking down and
then relaxing and then down again. A person
jumps up and grabs the pole and starts
to set the hook. Half way over his sholder
he is stoped in mid swing as the fish starts
to run. The drag is screeming as the
line is being pulled out of the open faced
real over the bent pole and into the water.
He trys to tighten down the drag to no avale.

As a last resourse he puts his thumb on
line and stop the fish in it mid stream. The
Battle is all most over, the fisherman is
winning, As a last fighting chance the fish
breaks water in a large splash, and starts to
run again but is stoped by a wip of the poleg
The fish is exhausted from the fight. By
this time the other two people in the boat are
standing on there seats and playing the fish
in thire minds as if they were fighting the
fish. As the two that were watching pull the
fish into the boat A tired man sets down.
with his pole in his hand And with his
lose hand prys his fingers off the pole, His prize A
72 inch sturgeon, the most uglyest fish and the strongest

*= the river

"Hey, you got a hit. your pole? (1.)

A small boat in the
middle of the river, resting behind a rusling
away mothballed ship Three people are fishing,
two of them talking, the third listening in
and watching the poles. Then the tip of one
of the poles goes wild, gerking down, and
then relaxing and then down again. A person
jumps up and grabs the pole And starts
to set the hook. Half way over his sholder
he is stoped in mid swing As the fish starts
to run. The drag is screeming as the line
is being pulled out of the open faced reel
over the bent pole and into the water.
He thys to tighten down the drag to no
avale. As a last resourse he puts his thumb
on the line and stops the fish in mid stream.
The battle is allmost over, the fisherman
is winning. By this time the other two people

Great
detail.

in the boat are standing on their seats and
playing the fish in their minds, as if they
were fighting the fish. As a last fighting
chance the fish breaks water in a large
splash and starts to run ~~again~~ but is stopped
by a wip of the pole. The fish is exhausted from
the fight. As the two that were watching
pull the fish into the boat a tired man
seats down with his pole in his hand and
with his free hand prys his fingers off the
pole. His prize: A 72 inch sturgen, the ~~most~~
~~ugliest~~ and strongest fish in the river.

(over)

Each time I go fishing out at the
moth ball fleet, I remember that fishing
trip and hope maybe this time it will
be my turn to ~~dush~~ catch a monster
fish.

This is a very successful, exciting account of a particular
kind of fishing. Some of the words are new to me so I'd
like you to read it to me. I think you wrote for a fishing audience
(1.) meaning is not clear here. "I guess you've got a hit. Your pole!"
(2.) I have trouble picturing this as worded. The
limitation may be mine. Perhaps you
could explain it to me.

I really like this piece of writing. It reminds
me of a big fisherman I've known: my dad. My
daughter follows in his footsteps. My favorite picture
of her was taken at dawn on Pinecrest Lake as
she waited and waited for her first bite. She
was ten years old. So your memory led me
to two of mine. Thanks for the trip.

Heading into Christmas, we began our next major piece of writing. Because of its scope, I decided to write my paper ahead of time and present it to the class along with the directions for the assignment, a paper about someone who had influenced me. I found myself writing about an instructor in college, one of my most memorable teachers. I remember that when I finished reading the paper to the class, silence filled the room seeming to last forever. I had been so caught up in my reading and the flood of memories that tears were in my eyes. Such are the risks one takes. After a moment, someone asked, "Is that paper about you? I mean...are you the teacher? It sounds like our class." Until then I had not realized just how much Jack Sheedy *had* influenced me. Writing really *is* a process of discovery. Furthermore, when the teacher shares his writing with his students, they may lead him to discover even more than he was aware of.

Assignment

Write a short but detailed paper about one person or about a group of people who have influenced you.* Use incidents and typical conversation to make the person(s) you are writing about come alive for your readers. *Show* your readers; don't be satisfied just to tell them.

Suggestion: Intro-Background
Interaction with person
a) beginning
b) middle
c) end
Conclusion: Explain the person's influence on you.

*Remember how Angelou, in *I Know Why the Caged Bird Sings*, writes about mother, Daddy Bailey, Bailey Jr. and Uncle Willy, using incidents and typical conversation to make them come alive.

Take Sheedy

I had saved a required course called "Principles of Literary Form" until my senior year in college. From friends on the faculty and fellow students I'd heard it was the hardest: the most demanding in thought, creativity and in the number of papers to be written. Looking through the college catalogue, I saw two names. One was that of an instructor I'd had for "Psychology in Literature" the year before. He was an easy-going man whose background in his subject matter was adequate, but I felt I had learned all I could from him. Besides, if I were in his class, I could predict in advance what each day would be like. What I really wanted was a challenge. The other name listed for the course I was about to take was "Sheedy." I'd never heard of him.

The unknown might be a challenge, but still I hesitated and asked around.

"Take Fineberg. It's an easy 'A' for you."

"What's to learn from him except where the best ski slopes and bunnies are?"

"Well, if you really want to work your ass off but learn from a fantastic teacher, take Sheedy."

"Sheedy? Are you kidding?"

"That guy thinks all we've got to do is write his papers. Besides, he's weird."

*Well, I couldn't resist. I "took" Sheedy but by the end of the second-week I felt like **I'd** been taken. I was snowed under with work and bombarded from all sides with ever changing ways of examining a piece of literature. The idea of symbolic structure in a poem, play or novel was difficult to perceive, something like a hologram. You could examine a segment of a good piece of writing and in its structure see the structure of the whole. Another weird thing about this man was that he required us to submit rough drafts of major papers two weeks before the final paper was due. It seemed like extra work. I later learned he did this so he could help us, that if we were taking an unfruitful direction, he could turn us around and we'd still have time to revise or begin anew. Even when my writing was not so hot—a "C" paper—he commented endlessly regarding what was good about it and made suggestions for improvement. Often I found myself up half the night, writing and rewriting, hating the extensive invasion of my already diminished time but loving those moments when I had succeeded, had surpassed myself in intellectual analysis and writing skill. Further evidence of his "weirdness" was that in an academic system where instructors had to have a Ph.D., he had only a master's degree. How'd he get away with it and be rehired each year? He was an extensively published writer! Learning this, my admiration soared. He was actually doing what he was trying to teach us: writing and succeeding.*

*By the end of the semester, after a months work of reading, research, conferences, writing and rewriting, I handed in a typed twenty-two page paper on the symbolic structure of Ibsen's **Hedda Gabler**. This was my final piece of writing for the course. Into it I had put the best of my newly found abilities. I was satisfied that I had done my best but, more than that, I wanted it to be something Sheedy would like to read. The week that went by before the papers were returned was sheer hell. I tried to lose myself in work for other courses, but in the midst of this work I found myself wondering if Sheedy had read my paper. In class I tried to read some reaction in his face. Nothing. Then came the* *day when the papers were returned. With trepidation I opened the cover, saw a clean title page and began to read through. No comments. Then, at the bottom of the last page, in his usual precise handwriting, was one line: "an excellent job: this is, I believe, the best of the papers produced by the class."*

In that one semester with Jack Sheedy, sixteen years ago, I learned that writing is a demanding mistress. Then, as now, he serves as a model writer and teacher. By his actions, he taught me that "if you're going to be a maverick in a conventional world, you'd better be damn good; then, and only then, will you be allowed to do what you do best." In working tirelessly and patiently with me, he gave me a part of myself I'd not known before: the writer. But above all, he led me to an understanding of symbolic structure in all of life, helping me to make sense of an often senseless universe.

J. R. Friss

Before presenting Ken's final piece of writing, I want to share a few additional details about our class. We did go on to create our individual autobiographies. With a friend's help, I acquired some blank booklets into which the students copied all their major pieces of writing. It was a formidable task and one that took almost two weeks in class. It was worth it. As each entry was carefully copied, further editing took place, for this book was to be their best writing. In reviewing their work, the students saw their own growth as writers, some not believing just how much growth had taken place but being proud and eager to share. Many proverbs come to mind as I write this now—something like "Sweet are the uses of adversity," or "No growth without pain." However it is said, it was one of the best times of my teaching career.

And now Ken's final paper. Here you can see the emergence of a poetic quality that lay buried in his first "I want out of this class." Our working relationship during a few months of our lives calls to mind the motto that hung in our classroom:

If you give a man a fish,
he will have a single meal;
if you teach him how to fish,
he will eat forever.

warrour
warvrior

She

~~She~~

She is vast at the End
and small at the begining.
She can give life or take it in
an unmerseiful way. she is a
warrour. she can be white & bubbly ~~in~~
~~some others~~ and dark and ~~calm~~ calm in
others.

she first influenced me when
I was 10 years old, I was fishing. ~~I~~
I was proud of the Fish I had
caught and the skill I had coght
them with. I was relaxed when I
was with her. later in the
years she satsficd my desire to show
my skill at water skiing and driving
boats, she ~~wase~~ fun and satisfieing to
my ego, she was the river

gave
to   I am changed by these
expriences. ~~and still became the river~~
come I had something to look for at the
End of the week. On those ~~sundays~~
my family became a family, there was
no fighting, just fun and relaxed
fun. I am still changing because of
her, she is part of my life — the
river

She

She is vast at the ▓
end and small at the begining. She
can give life or take it in an unmerciful
way. She is a warrior. She can be
while and bubbly and dark and calm
in some places or neither.

She first ▓▓▓ influnced me
when I was 10 years old. I was fishing.
I was proud of the fish I had caught
and the skill I had cought them with.
I was relaxed when I was with her,
later in the years she satified my desire
to show my skill at water skiing and
driving boats. She was fun and satisfying
to my ego. She was the river

I am changed by these sure
expirences, and will be by those that are share
to come. I had something to look for at the
end of the week. On these sundays my
family became a family. There was no
fighting, just fun and relaxation. I am
still changing because of her, she is part
of my life — the river

She

She is vast at the end
and small at the begining. She can give life
or take it in an unmerciful way. She is a
warrior. She can be white and bubbly and
dark and calm in some places or neither.

She first influnced me when I
was 10 years old. I was fishing. I was proud
of the fish I had caught and the skill I
had caught them with. I was relaxed when
I was with her. Later in the years she
satisfyed my desire to show my skill at waterskiing and driving boat. She was fun to be
with and satisfyeng to my ego. She was the
river

I am changed by these experiences,
and will be by those that are sure to come.
I had something to look for at the end of the
week. On those sundays my family became
a family; there was no fighting, just fun
and relaxation. I am still changing because
of her, she is part of my life — the river.

Be definite about periods. Never confuse them with commas

*Again, this is a beautiful piece of writing,
very much like a poem. I was glad Bilich
told you this also so you didn't think it was
"just an English teacher's opinion" which often,
to students, seems worthless or weird. A
pleasure to read —*

References

Anderson, Richard C. *Schema-Directed Processes in Language Comprehension.* Center for the Study of Reading, University of Illinois, Technical Report No. 50, 1977.

Applebee, Arthur. *Writing in the Secondary School.* Urbana, IL: NCTE, 1981.

Armstrong, Michael. *Closely Observed Children: The Diary of a Primary Classroom.* London: Writers and Readers, 1980. (Available from Boynton/Cook)

Arnheim, Rudolf. *Visual Thinking.* Berkeley: University of California Press, 1969.

Barnes, Douglas. *From Communication to Curriculum.* London: Penguin Books, 1976. (Available from Boynton/Cook)

——————————, James Britton and Harold Rosen. *Language, the Learner and the School.* London: Penguin Books, 1971. (Available from Boynton/Cook)

Barr, Mary, Pat D'Arcy and Mary K. Healy. *What's Going On? Language/Learning Episodes in British and American Classrooms, Grades 4-13.* Montclair, NJ: Boynton/Cook Publishers, 1982.

Beach, Richard. *Writing about Ourselves and Others.* Urbana, IL: NCTE/ERIC, 1977.

Berger, John. *Ways of Seeing.* London: British Broadcasting Corporation, 1972.

Berthoff, Ann E. *Forming/Thinking/Writing: The Composing Imagination.* Montclair, NJ: Boynton/Cook Publishers, 1978.

——————————. *The Making of Meaning: Metaphors, Models, and Maxims for Writing Teachers.* Montclair, NJ: Boynton/Cook Publishers, 1981.

Bess, James L. "The Motivation to Teach." *Journal of Higher Education,* XLVIII (May/June, 1977), 243-258.

Booth, Wayne. "The Rhetorical Stance." *College Composition and Communication,* 14 (October, 1963), 139-145.

Bradford, Arthur. *Teaching English to Speakers of English.* New York: Harcourt Brace Jovanovich, 1973.

Brannon, Lil, Melinda Knight and Vara Neverow-Turk. *Writers Writing,* Montclair, NJ: Boynton/Cook Publishers, 1982.

Bransford, J. C. and N.S. McCarrell. "A Sketch of a Cognitive Approach to Comprehension." *Cognition and the Symbolic Processes.* Edited by Weimer and Palermo. Hillsdale, NJ: Lawrence Erlbaum Associates, 1974.

Britton, James. *Language and Learning.* London: Penguin Books, 1970. (Available from Boynton/Cook)

——————————. *Prospect and Retrospect: Selected Essays of James Britton.* Montclair, NJ: Boynton/Cook Publishers, 1982.

——————————, et al. *The Development of Writing Abilities (11-18).* London: Macmillan, 1975. (Available from NCTE)

Bruner, Jerome. *The Process of Education.* New York: Vintage Books, 1960.

Buckley, Marilyn Hanf. "A Guide for Developing an Oral Language Curriculum." *Language Arts,* 53 (September, 1976), 621-627.

Burgess, Carol, *et al. Understanding Children Writing.* London: Penguin Books, 1973. (Available from Boynton/Cook)

Buzan, Tony. *Use Both Sides of Your Brain: New Techniques to Help You Read Efficiently, Study Effectively, Solve Problems, Remember More, Think Creatively.* New York: E. P. Dutton, 1976.

Camp, Gerald. *A Success Curriculum for Remedial Writers.* Berkeley: National Writing Project, 1982.

Carkeet, David. "Understanding Syntactic Errors in Remedial Writing." *College English,* 38 (March, 1977), 682-686, 695.

Cheever, John. *The Short Stories of John Cheever.* New York: Ballantine Books, 1978.

Chickering, A. W. *Education and Identity.* San Francisco: Jossey-Bass, 1969.

Christensen, Francis. *Notes Toward a New Rhetoric: Six Essays for Teachers.* New York: Harper & Row, 1967.

_____, et al. *The Sentence and the Paragraph.* Urbana, IL: NCTE, 1966.

Clapp, Ouida H., ed. *Classroom Practices in Teaching English, 1975-76: On Righting Writing.* Urbana, IL: NCTE, 1975.

Connelly, Peter J. and Donald C. Irving. "Composition in the Liberal Arts: A Shared Responsibility." *College English,* 37 (March, 1976), 668-670.

Cooper, Charles. "Measuring Growth in Writing." *English Journal,* 64 (March, 1975), 111-120.

_____. *What College Writers Need to Know.* Presentation to the Department of Literature, University of California, San Diego, April 5, 1978 (unpublished address).

_____ and Lee Odell, eds. *Evaluating Writing: Describing, Measuring, Judging.* Urbana, IL: NCTE, 1977.

Coulthard, Malcolm. *An Introduction to Discourse Analysis.* London: Longman, 1977.

Cross, K. Patricia. *Accent on Learning.* San Francisco: Jossey-Bass, 1976.

Degnan, James "Masters of Babble: Turning Language into Stone." *Harper's Magazine,* September, 1976, p. 27; reprinted in *Speaking of Words,* edited by James MacKillop and Donna Woolfolk Cross. New York: Holt, Rinehart and Winston, 1978.

Dellinger, Dixie Gibbs. *Out of Heart: How to Design Writing Assignments for High School Courses.* Berkeley: National Writing Project, 1982.

Diederich, Paul. *Measuring Growth in English.* Urbana, IL: NCTE, 1974.

Doctorow, E. L. *The Book of Daniel.* New York: Signet Edition, Random House, 1971.

Donelson, Kenneth, ed. *Rhetoric and Composition in the English Classroom.* Tempe, AZ: NCTE, 1974.

Donovan, Timothy R. and Ben W. McClelland. *Eight Approaches to Teaching Composition.* Urbana, IL: NCTE, 1980.

Doughty, Peter, *et al. Exploring Language.* London: E. Arnold, 1972.

Eagleson, Robert D. *English in the Eighties.* Norwood, South Australia: Australian Association for the Teaching of English, 1982.

Edwards, Betty. *Drawing on the Right Side of the Brain: A Course in Enhancing Creativity and Artistic Confidence.* Los Angeles: J. P. Tarcher, 1979.

Elbow, Peter. *Writing Without Teachers.* New York: Oxford University Press, 1973.

_____. *Writing with Power.* New York: Oxford University Press, 1981.

Emig, Janet. *The Composing Processes of Twelfth Graders.* Urbana, IL: NCTE, 1971.

_____. *The Web of Meaning: Essays on Writing, Teaching, Learning, and Thinking.* Montclair, NJ: Boynton/Cook Publishers, 1983.

Fawcett, Susan and Alvin Sandberg. *Grassroots/The Writer's Workbook.* Boston: Houghton Mifflin, 1976.

Foley, Joseph. "Evaluation of Learning in Writing." *Handbook on Formative and Summative Evaluation of Student Learning.* Edited by Benjamin Bloom, *et al.* New York: McGraw-Hill, 1971.

Foster, David. *A Primer for Writing Teachers: Theories, Theorists, Issues, Problems.* Montclair, NJ: Boynton/Cook Publishers, 1983.

Gere, Anne Ruggles. "writing and WRITING." *English Journal,* 66 (November, 1977), 60-64.

Gibson, Walker. *Persona.* New York: Random House, 1968.

——————. *Tough, Sweet and Stuffy.* Bloomington, IN: Indiana University Press, 1966.

Gray, James and Robert Benson. *Sentence and Paragraph Modelling.* Berkeley: Bay Area Writing Project, 1982.

Graves, Richard L., ed. *Rhetoric and Composition: A Sourcebook for Teachers.* Montclair, NJ: Boynton/Cook Publishers, 1976.

Grossmann, Florence. *Getting from Here to There: Writing and Reading Poetry.* Montclair, NJ: Boynton/Cook Publishers, 1982.

Hailey, Jack. *Teaching Writing K-8.* Berkeley: Publications Office, School of Education, University of California, 1979.

Haley-James, Shirley. *Perspectives on Writing in Grades K-8.* Urbana, IL: NCTE, 1981.

Halliday, M. A. K. *Learning How to Mean.* London: E. Arnold, 1975.

—————— and R. Hasan. *Cohesion in English.* London: Longman, 1976.

Hanf, Marilyn Buckley. "Mapping: A Technique for Translating Reading into Thinking." *Journal of Reading,* 14 (January, 1971), 225-230+.

Harrison, Myrna. *On Our Own Terms.* Encino, CA: Dickenson, 1972.

Hawkins, Thom. *Group Inquiry Techniques for Teaching Writing.* Urbana, IL: NCTE/ERIC, 1976.

Haynes, Elizabeth. "Using Research in Preparing to Teach Writing." *English Journal,* 77 (January, 1978), 82-88.

Herman, Jerry. *A Time in Their Lives.* San Francisco: Canfield, 1974.

Hill, Ada and Beth Boone. *If Maslow Taught Writing: A Way to Look at Motivation in the Composition Classroom.* Berkeley: National Writing Project, 1982.

Hofstadter, Douglas. *Gödel, Escher, Bach.* New York: Basic Books, 1979.

Hogan, Robert. "After Sending Freshmen to Describe a Tree." *American Association of University Professors Bulletin* (Winter, 1957); reprinted in *College English: The First Year,* Edited by Alton C. Morris, *et al.* 7th ed. New York: Harcourt Brace Jovanovich, 1978.

Holbrook, David. *English for the Rejected: Training Literacy in the Lower Streams of the Secondary School.* London: Cambridge University Press, 1964.

Howgate, Lynn. *Building Self-Esteem Through the Writing Process.* Berkeley: National Writing Project, 1982.

Irmscher, William. *The Holt Guide to English.* New York: Holt, Rinehart and Winston, 1972.

Kelly, George. *The Psychology of Personal Constructs.* New York: W. W. Norton, 1955.

Kelly, Lou. *From Dialogue to Discourse: An Open Approach to Competence and Creativity.* Glenview, IL: Scott, Foresman, 1972.

Kempson, Ruth. *Semantic Theory.* Cambridge: University Press, 1977.

The Kids in Room 14. *Our Friends in the Waters.* Mill Valley, CA: Old Mill School, 1979.

Kinneavy, James E. "The Basic Aims of Discourse." *College Composition and Communication,* 20 (December, 1969), 297-304.

Kirby, Dan and Tom Liner. *Inside Out: Developmental Strategies for Teaching Writing.* Montclair, NJ: Boynton/Cook Publishers, 1981.

Koch, Kenneth. *Rose, Where Did You Get That Red?* New York: Vintage, 1973.

——————. *Wishes, Lies and Dreams.* New York: Vintage, 1970.

Labov, William. *Language of the Inner City.* Philadelphia: University of Pennsylvania Press, 1972.

——————. *The Study of Nonstandard English.* Urbana, IL: NCTE/ERIC, 1970.

Langer, Susanne K. *Philosophy in a New Key.* Cambridge: Harvard University Press, 1942.

Laque, Carol and Phyllis Sherwood. *A Laboratory Approach to Writing.* Urbana, IL: NCTE, 1977.

Lawrence, Mary S. *Writing as a Thinking Process.* Ann Arbor, MI: University of Michigan Press, 1972.

Loban, Walter. *Language Development: Kindergarten Through Grade Twelve.* Urbana, IL: NCTE, Research Report No. 18, 1976.

Macrorie, Ken. *Searching Writing.* Rochelle Park, NJ: Hayden Book Company, 1980.

_____. *Telling Writing.* 3rd ed. Rochelle Park, NJ: Hayden Book Company, 1980.

_____. *Uptaught.* Rochelle Park, NJ: Hayden Book Company, 1970.

_____. *A Vulnerable Teacher.* Rochelle Park, NJ: Hayden Book Company, 1974.

_____. *Writing to Be Read.* 2nd ed. Rochelle Park, NJ: Hayden Book Company, 1976.

Maimon, Elaine P., et al. *Writing in the Arts and Sciences.* Boston: Little, Brown, 1981.

Marashio, Nancy and Center School's Eighth Graders. *Writing: A Window to Our Minds.* Berkeley: National Writing Project, 1982.

Marik, Ray. *Special Education Students Write: Classroom Activities and Assignments.* Berkeley: National Writing Project, 1982.

Martin, Nancy. *Selected Essays.* Montclair, NJ: Boynton/Cook Publishers, 1983.

_____, ed. *Writing Across the Curriculum Pamphlets.* London: Ward Lock Educational, 1973-1977. Montclair, NJ: Boynton/Cook Publishers, 1983.

_____, et al. *Writing and Learning Across the Cirriculum 11-16.* London: Ward Lock Educational, 1976. (Available from Boynton/Cook)

_____, et al. *Understanding Children Talking.* London: Penguin Books, 1976. (Available from Boynton/Cook)

McCrimmons, James. *Writing with a Purpose.* 6th ed. Boston: Houghton Mifflin, 1976.

McCullers, Carson. *The Ballad of the Sad Cafe.* Boston: Houghton Mifflin, 1936. Bantam, 1971.

McKim, Robert H. *Experiences in Visual Thinking.* Monterey: Brooks/Cole, 1972.

Medway, Peter. *Finding a Language: Autonomy and Learning in School.* London: Writers and Readers, 1980. (Available from Boynton/Cook)

Mellon, John C. *Transformational Sentence Combining.* Urbana, IL: NCTE, 1969.

Miles, Josephine. *Working Out Ideas: Predication and Other Uses of Language.* Berkeley: Bay Area Writing Project, 1979.

Miller, George. "Information and Memory." *Scientific American.* August, 1956, 22+.

Moffett, James. *Teaching the Universe of Discourse.* Boston: Houghton Mifflin, 1968.

_____. *Active Voice: A Writing Program Across the Curriculum.* Montclair, NJ: Boynton/Cook Publishers, 1981.

_____. *Coming on Center: English Education in Evolution.* Montclair, NJ: Boynton/Cook Publishers, 1981.

_____ and Betty Jane Wagner. *Student-Centered Language Arts and Reading, K-13: A Handbook for Teachers.* 2nd ed. Boston: Houghton Mifflin, 1976.

Morrow, James. "The Pitfalls of Right Hemisphere Emphasis: A Minority Opinion." *Media and Methods,* January, 1979, 74-78.

Murray, Donald. *A Writer Teaches Writing: A Practical Method of Teaching Composition.* Boston: Houghton Mifflin, 1968.

_____. *Learning by Teaching: Selected Articles on Writing and Teaching.* Montclair, NJ: Boynton/Cook Publishers, 1982.

Myers, Miles. *A Procedure for Writing Assessment and Holistic Scoring.* Urbana, IL: NCTE, 1980.

Nystrand, Martin, ed. *Language as a Way of Knowing.* Toronto: The Ontario Institute for Studies in Education, 1977.

Odell, Lee and Joanne Cohick. "You Mean, Write It Over in Ink?" *English Journal,* 64 (December, 1975), 48-53.

O'Hare, Frank. *Sentence Combining: Improving Student Writing Without Formal Grammar Instruction.* Urbana, IL: NCTE, 1973.

Ohmann, Richard ed. *Teaching English in Two-Year Colleges.* Urbana, IL: NCTE, 1974.

Ong, Walter. *Interfaces of the Word.* Ithaca, NY: Cornell University Press, 1977.

——————. *Ramus, Method, and the Decay of Dialogue.* Cambridge: Harvard University Press, 1958.

Ornstein, Robert. *The Psychology of Consciousness.* San Francisco: W. H. Freeman, 1972.

Piaget, Jean. *The Language and Thought of the Child,* trans. by M. Gabain. London: Routledge and Kegan Paul, 1926. New York: New American Library, 1955.

Pinnell, Gay Su, ed. *Discovering Language with Children.* Urbana, IL: NCTE, 1980.

Pirsig, Robert M. *Zen and the Art of Motorcycle Maintenance: An Inquiry into Values.* New York: William Morrow, 1974.

Ponsot, Marie and Rosemary Deen. *Beat Not the Poor Desk—Writing: What to Teach, How to Teach It, and Why.* Montclair, NJ: Boynton/Cook Publishers, 1982.

Rico, Gabriele Lusser and Mary Frances Claggett. *Balancing the Hemispheres: Brain Research and the Teaching of Writing.* Berkeley: Bay Area Writing Project, 1980.

Russell, Peter. *The Brain Book.* New York: Hawthorn Books, 1979.

Schultz, John. *Writing from Start to Finish: The 'Story Workshop' Basic Forms Rhetoric-Reader.* Montclair, NJ: Boynton-Cook Publishers, 1982.

Searle, John. *Speech Acts.* Cambridge: University Press, 1969.

Shaughnessy, Mina P. *Errors and Expectations: A Guide for the Teacher of Basic Writing.* New York: Oxford University Press, 1977.

Smith, Frank. *Writing and the Writer.* New York: Holt, Rinehart and Winston, 1981.

Spolin, Viola. *Improvisation for the Theatre.* Evanston, IL: Northwestern University Press, 1963.

Squire, James R. *What Will Be Basic in the Next Quarter Century?* (Tape) Urbana, IL: NCTE, 1976.

Stibbs, Andrew. *Assessing Children's Language: Guidelines for Teachers.* London: Ward Lock Educational, 1979. (Available from Boynton/Cook)

Stock, Patricia L., ed. *fforum: Essays on Theory and Practice in the Teaching of Writing.* Montclair, NJ: Boynton/Cook Publishers, 1983.

Strong, William. *Sentence Combining: A Composing Book.* New York: Random House, 1973.

——————. "Sentence Combining: Back to Basics and Beyond." *English Journal,* 65 (February, 1976), 56, 60-64.

Tate, Gary. *Teaching Composition: Ten Bibliographic Essays.* Fort Worth: Texas Christian University Press, 1976.

Terkel, Studs. *Working.* New York: Avon, 1972.

Torbe, Mike and Robert Protherough. *Classroom Encounters: Language and English Teaching.* London: Ward Lock Educational, 1978.

——————— and Peter Medway. *The Climate for Learning.* London: Ward Lock Educational, 1981. (Available from Boynton/Cook)

Tough, Joan. *Talk for Teaching and Learning*. London: Ward Lock Educational, 1979.

Weathers, Winston. *An Alternate Style: Options in Composition*. Montclair, NJ: Boynton/Cook Publishers, 1980.

Wolfe, Tom. *The New Journalism*. New York: Harper & Row, 1973.

Woodworth, Patrick and Catharine Keech. *The Write Occasion*. Berkeley: Bay Area Writing Project, 1980.

Writing Lessons That Work. Berkeley: Bay Area Writing Project, 1980.

Yates, Frances. *The Art of Memory*. Chicago: University of Chicago Press, 1966.

Young, Richard E., Alton L. Becker and Kenneth L. Pike. *Rhetoric: Discovery and Change*. New York: Harcourt Brace and World, 1970.

Zinsser, William. *On Writing Well.*New York: Harper & Row, 1976.